von Sven Ludwig !

The Digital Journey of Banking and Insurance, Volume I

"Not everything is changing, but most of the things changing can be of a disruptive character—so I'm happy that *Disruption and DNA* is picking up exactly this intention."

—Gerhard Lahner, *COO of Vienna Insurance Group*

"In *Disruption and DNA*, finally someone is saying out loud that not everything is changing, but most of the things changing can be of a disruptive character."

—Dr. Carsten Stolz, *CFO Baloise Group*

"This first volume *Disruption and DNA* of the book series *The Digital Journey of Banking and Insurance* offers an extensive market view of digital transformation, including special insights into accounting and risk management. The book explores the often underestimated topics culture and project management."

—Bernhard Hodler, *Former CEO Julius Baer Group*

"Virtually all financial institutions have embarked on ambitious digital journeys, both to provide better products and customer experience more efficiently and in response to the threat of industry disruption by FinTech competitors. There is no doubt that there will be winners, and there will be losers. I am convinced that *The Digital Journey of Banking and Insurance* series is indispensable reading for the future winners."

—Thomas C. Wilson, *CEO, President and Country Manager at Allianz Ayudhya*

"This first volume of the incredible book series sets the stage just right for digital transformation with the interplay between change (disruption) and stable objectives (DNA)."

—Erik Podzuweit, *Founder, Co-CEO Scalable Capital*

"We do remember when we started our digital journey, but we do not know when it will be over. Therefore, we are definitely in the middle. The book series *The Digital Journey of Banking and Insurance* is a must-read for of all of us."

—Christian Peter Kromann, *CEO, SimCorp*

Volker Liermann · Claus Stegmann
Editors

The Digital Journey of Banking and Insurance, Volume I

Disruption and DNA

palgrave
macmillan

Editors
Volker Liermann
ifb SE
Grünwald, Germany

Claus Stegmann
ifb Americas, Inc.
Charlotte, NC, USA

ISBN 978-3-030-78813-1   ISBN 978-3-030-78814-8 (eBook)
https://doi.org/10.1007/978-3-030-78814-8

© The Editor(s) (if applicable) and The Author(s), under exclusive license to Springer Nature Switzerland AG 2021
This work is subject to copyright. All rights are solely and exclusively licensed by the Publisher, whether the whole or part of the material is concerned, specifically the rights of translation, reprinting, reuse of illustrations, recitation, broadcasting, reproduction on microfilms or in any other physical way, and transmission or information storage and retrieval, electronic adaptation, computer software, or by similar or dissimilar methodology now known or hereafter developed.
The use of general descriptive names, registered names, trademarks, service marks, etc. in this publication does not imply, even in the absence of a specific statement, that such names are exempt from the relevant protective laws and regulations and therefore free for general use.
The publisher, the authors and the editors are safe to assume that the advice and information in this book are believed to be true and accurate at the date of publication. Neither the publisher nor the authors or the editors give a warranty, expressed or implied, with respect to the material contained herein or for any errors or omissions that may have been made. The publisher remains neutral with regard to jurisdictional claims in published maps and institutional affiliations.

Cover credit: Stutterstock/Yevhenii Chulovskyi

This Palgrave Macmillan imprint is published by the registered company Springer Nature Switzerland AG
The registered company address is: Gewerbestrasse 11, 6330 Cham, Switzerland

Introduction to the Book Series

Disruption is a word often used when the groundbreaking changes in the financial industry are summarized and to a broad extent it is true. While singing the song "everything is changing" to the financial industry, the prophets forget that not everything is changing in a world driven by digital transformation.

The first differentiation to be made is what we do and how we do it. This is when we look at the internal departments, such as settlement, accounting and risk management. The tasks (settle transaction, make a balance sheet or predict the repayment ability) are still the same, but the way we perform these tasks changes to more automation, more analyzing of data and using the discovered patterns to optimize (make better decisions) and accelerate the tasks (make quicker decisions or provide information for decision-making quicker). In this area of inside digitalization, institutes still do—to a broad extent—the same things (DNA), but they change the way of doing them. The picture looks different in the context of external digitalization, especially the customer-oriented part. Fintech,[1] Big Tech[2] or more generally the platform operating companies have moved closer to the customer and therefore have

---

[1] Fintech is an abbreviation for financial technology and summarizes technology and the innovative delivery of financial services in competition with traditional players in the financial services market.

[2] The Big Tech, sometimes also referred to as Tech Giants or the Big Five, are the largest companies in the information technology sector. Another abbreviation is GAFA(M) for Google, Amazon, Facebook, Apple and Microsoft or BATX in China for the largest internet companies there (Baidu, Alibaba, Tencent and Xiaomi).

the opportunity to cut out the traditional providers of financial services from direct customer contact. This intermediary pattern was more established in the insurance industry than in the banking industry. The game-changer is not the existence of an intermediary, but the strength of the intermediary and the willingness to better understand the customer needs. While some institutes still try to sell products, fintech companies aim to discover and solve problems for customers.

In the past, an insurance broker connected the customer to the insurance company and to the products of the insurance company. If the broker was smart, they had a good understanding of the customer's needs, but were restricted to the product spectrum of the insurance companies they worked with. There was a possibility to trigger product innovation, but it was far from a lean, agile process.

A successful fintech or insurtech company is excellent at understanding the customer and their needs. Additionally—and this is the major point—it is able to adjust the tools provided to the customer to solve the customer's problem. It is even more successful if it has the ability to juggle and to compose existing products (maybe through a third party or a platform).[3] This intelligent composition of on-time and user-/problem-specific own products and cheap and available existing product components from third parties gives the challenger in the financial service sector the decisive competitive edge.

After this general analysis, we now look a bit closer into the two main sectors of the financial industry: banks and insurance companies.

Banking-Specific Digitalization Challenges and Structures

The banks face challenges on the revenue side, such as low interest rates (and in some countries even negative interest rates) and flat interest rate curves, making it difficult to generate additional profit from interest rate arbitrage. Regulatory requirements have risen since the financial crisis one decade ago in terms of the amount (more capital and more liquidity) and complexity of the requirements (especially in the Pillar II of Basel III (Basel Committee on Banking Supervision 2021)). In addition, new competitors (fintech companies, but also tech companies) are about to or have already entered the market, bringing additional pressure to the already historically low margins. The COVID-19 induced economic downturn will put further

---

[3] This product outsourcing is one of the important components of Open Banking.

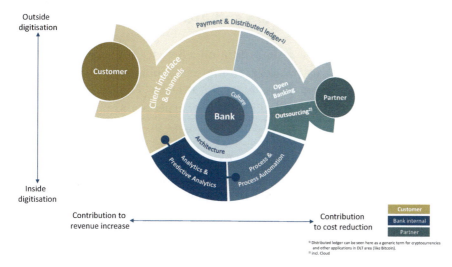

Fig. 1 Overview digitalization areas—banking © ifb SE

pressure on the P&L and balance sheet, narrowing the room to move towards a significant change in digital transformation.

Another field of disruptive change is payments: (A) Bitcoin and other distributed-ledger-based payment frameworks can carve out the banks as intermediaries, (B) competitors (PayPal, Klarna, …) offer a more convenient way to pay and again the Big Tech (here Apple and Google) bring their own offers into direct customer contact (Apple Pay and Google Pay). While the latter (PayPal, Klarna, Apple, Google) just improve the customer convenience and experience without changing the infrastructure for settlement outside[4] these companies (which in most cases traditionally involves settlement by credit or debit card), distributed-ledger-based payment has more disruptive potential because it goes beyond the companies' borders.

Figure 1 shows eight popular areas in banks where digital transformation is happening. The three main acting entities are illustrated as circles, from left to right: the customers, the bank and the partners.

The areas are positioned along the dimensions contribution (x-axis) and digitalization focus (y-axis). The contribution spans from revenue increase to cost reduction, and the digitalization focus spans from outside digitalization to inside digitalization. The location of the areas is not an exact quantitative location, instead it is a more approximate position with some blurriness.

---

[4] PayPal and Klarna offer to transfer money from one account (within PayPal/Klarna) to another (within PayPal/Klarna).

Cross-Cutting Areas (Culture and Architecture)

The corporate culture of a credit institution represents the values, norms and attitudes lived within its own organization and influences the actions and cooperation of employees across hierarchical levels. Digital transformation promises to meet current and future customer expectations more quickly and easily and to reduce costs in order to work more profitably through the use of new technologies.

A company-wide internalization of the vision and meaning of a bank's digital agenda requires consistent communication of goals and collaboration with employees to overcome reservations about the opportunities and challenges of digitalization.

Culture is the most important and most underestimated ingredient for a successful digital transformation. Fintech companies not only have the more cutting-edge infrastructure and tools. They have a culture and a way of doing things that differentiate them (FiCuTech would be a more appropriate abbreviation for the banks' challengers, emphasizing the differentiator culture).

Due to the combination of monolithic applications and individual solutions, the software architecture of credit institutions has a complexity that poses challenges for the implementation of digital transformation or regulatory measures. For the profitable integration of novel technologies, a preparation of the system architecture is necessary to adapt products and services to changing market conditions in the digital transformation ecosystem.

In order to prepare the existing system architecture for digital transformation, it is necessary to restructure the system architecture according to processing system components and presentation-oriented system components. This supplements an orchestration layer and enables participation in the service economy of digitalization and a quick reaction to changing market conditions and customer expectations by combining different system components or by adding service offerings from partners.

The cultural aspects are addressed in Part V of this first volume (especially in Chapter 12, (Merkt, Lang and Schmidt, Digi-Cultural Mindset 2021)). The project culture and framework alternatives are a major component of this part. Other cultural aspects are additionally touched on in Chapter 2 (Merkt, Thiele and Dinges, Digitalization Landscape Banking 2021), Chapter 3 (Stegmann and Ludwig 2021) and Chapter 4 (Negenman 2021).

Architecture is a more technological subject, so most of the parts in volume III address this component in one way of digital transformation or the other.

Chapter 6 (Krätz and Morawski 2021) in particular opens up new data architecture patterns incorporating streaming and its opportunities. Nonetheless, some articles in this first volume touch on the architecture subject (Chapter 2 (Merkt, Thiele and Dinges, Digitalization Landscape Banking 2021)).

Client- and Payment-Related Aspects

Banks have multiple ways to interact with their clients. The different channels (branch with human contact, phone via a call center, websites on the internet and smartphone-based apps) have improved, driven by ongoing digitalization.

Banks have continuously improved on combining these channels to contact and serve the customer in a way that is most appropriate and convenient for them. Furthermore, banks have improved on the timing of the solutions and offers presented. Data analysis focusing on the next best offer (NBO) or on the next best action (NBA) guide[5] the banks regarding when and what to offer to the customer.

Distributed ledger technology (DLT) is assigned to the decentralized databases, which do not require a central administration instance to legitimate a transaction between network participants. The data for a transaction is stored on each participating node in the network, so that there is a consensus about the truthfulness. Participants within a DLT network have unlimited read and write rights. A distinction is made between "permissioned" and "unpermissioned" distributed ledgers[6] when participating within a network. Participants in a "permissioned" DLT network are unpermissioned and authorized for the network before participating in an exam to ensure a basis of trust. An "unpermissioned" distributed ledger network is accessible without restriction. The basis of trust in this network is established through proof-of-work mechanisms. An example of an "unpermissioned" network is the blockchain used for transactions of crypto currencies. Storage of transactions in the blockchain is subject to specific rules and, after a transaction has been authorized, forms a block that is added to the historized chain of blocks. DLT opens up a variety of business opportunities for storing internal and external transaction data across company boundaries, e.g. in securities transactions. In order to use the technology to increase turnover and reduce costs in credit institutions, regulatory framework conditions must be defined in cooperation with credit institutions, use cases must be worked out and the system architecture must be adapted for implementation.

---

[5] For details on NBO and NBA see (May 2019).

[6] In the area of blockchain private and public blockchains are more common expressions.

The client-facing aspects are viewed in Chapter 4 (Negenman 2021) of this volume and in Chapter 10 (Floß and Velauthapillai 2021) of the third volume. Distributed ledger technology is appraised in the context of self-sovereignty in Chapter 12 in volume III.

Aspects of Internal Optimization

Due to the digitalization of business processes and the intensification of information technology, the volume of data within companies is constantly growing. The networked storage of business management and system data enables past-, present- and future-oriented evaluation of data in order to make well-founded business decisions.

For the instrumentalization of data analyses and the implementation of future-oriented data analyses, relevant data sources must be identified and assumptions for the creation of algorithms must be developed in cooperation with companies in order to derive recommendations for action or to uncover customer needs based on behavioral patterns, dependencies and the relationship structure. Through the targeted combination and analysis of business management and system data, optimization potential and trends in the business processes of a credit institution become visible and the persons responsible are enabled to decide on preventive or mitigating measures.

Processes are a totality of successive, influencing procedures within a company, which achieve business objectives by transporting information and materials. The process landscape of a credit institution defines the daily work routine within an organization and is mapped in the system landscape and corporate structure. In order to reduce costs, an automation of process steps that can be standardized by using technology is aimed for. The goal of automation is to handle the elements of a process using technical components with little manual effort. The manual effort results from the initiation of the process and the evaluation of the process results.

The use of novel technologies enables the visualization of the lived process landscape with the help of data analyses beyond system boundaries in order to compare these with the desired process images, to recognize optimization potential and to bring about a holistic reduction of process complexity. By reducing complexity and standardizing process activities, a targeted automation of process activities is achieved with the help of suitable technology.

Many of the use cases presented in the second volume are located in the area of analytics and predictive analytics and process and process automation. Part 2 of volume III collects many aspects of these two areas. In part 4 of volume II, the whole process subject is given some space to explore and illuminate the aspects of RPA, process mining and processes as part of digitalization in general.

Partner-Related Aspects

Open banking enables credit institutions to realize the principle of platform economy and to open up new sources of income without high implementation costs by cooperating with partners. The exchange between the credit institutions and partners takes place via technical interfaces, e.g. APIs, which are integrated into the banks' system architectures. These interfaces enable the inclusion of additional offers in the portfolio and their provision via the distribution channels of the credit institution.

By integrating APIs into the system architecture of a credit institution, the credit institution is enabled to extend and optimize internal processes through partner offers, e.g. data analysis activities and the formulation of their own function offers for external partners. A central orchestration layer is responsible for the administration and monitoring of interfaces to and from partners.

Business models consist of a variety of cross-departmental or cross-company activities that rely on different infrastructure, hardware, software and human intelligence. In order to reduce time-to-market cycles and costs, standardizable and repeatable activities can be grouped as services to enable the offering or obtaining of services via XaaS[7] and to adapt business models and processes to individual requirements by mixing the use of internal and external services.

Instrumentalizing the advantages of XaaS requires a network of internal and external services as well as an active orchestration of services in order to provide customer-oriented, cost-sensitive and value-added services to the customer in a way that is profitable for the credit institution.

The technically driven volume III partially addresses some of the outsourcing and open banking aspects as architecture is one of the important goals in this area.

---

[7] Anything-as-a-Service, (e.g. Platform-as-a-Service, Software-as-a-Service, Reporting-as-a-Service).

Other Aspects

Another aspect of distributed ledger is tokenization. In the past, distributed ledger technology was primarily associated with payment (like Bitcoin, Etherium and e-central bank money). The tokenization of real-world assets is gaining momentum. The key defining (value-defining and value-driving) data is mirrored into a distributed ledger where the constant characteristics of the asset are held immutable and only some (like owner) can be changed by a predefined process.

An early example of tokenization of real assets is Everledger, where characteristics and ownership of diamonds[8] were tokenized. Just at the beginning of 2021, the certificates for electronic art (based on DLT or, to be more precise, NFT[9]) were discussed by a wider public.[10]

Another popular example is the tokenization of real estate documenting the construction materials used, construction descriptions and other building-defining characteristics. This kind of tokenization can address some of the issues raised by ESG[11] and the information demand regarding these assets. The demand can arise from direct investments but also from the financing of real estate. The impact of ESG is so far-reaching that anything supporting the delivery of the relevant information in an approved and quality-assured way is in high demand.

The Internet of Things is traditionally rooted in the context of insurers. In recent years, a product whose nature is close to traditional asset leasing has gained relevance. The digitalization of machines produces sensor data to characterize the usage and maturity of the machines. A common approach for insurance companies (usage-based insurance (UBI), pay-as-you-drive (PAYD), pay-how-you-drive (PHYD)) is based on sensor data. This is transferred to the financing context. The idea for the solution originates from the customers' need for the usage of a machine (and not the need for product financing). This machine financing is implemented in a DLT,[12] and sensor data (oracle[13]) is used to illustrate the usage, which is processed to calculate the financing rate. The corporate has an instant usage-dependent financing product (which differs from standard asset leasing).

---

[8] Everledger is best known for diamonds and was extended to a wider set of real objects (art, general gemstones, …).
[9] Non-fungible tokens.
[10] For example, the art of Mike Winkelmann (Beeple) or Chris Torres.
[11] Environment, Social, Governance.
[12] Distributed ledger technology.
[13] An oracle (blockchain) is any device or entity that links off-chain data (sensors or price feeds) to a blockchain.

While tokenization (in the distributed ledger context) normally refers to the digitalization of ownership and rights, additional potential arises for storing data regarding the real-world asset, such as size and material,[14] including sensor data (IoT, illustrating the asset's use).

Insurance-Specific Digitalization Challenges and Structures

Insurance companies have similar—but insurance-specific—challenges, such as regulatory requirements (Solvency II) and changes in accounting standards (e.g. IFRS 17), but also different challenges and chances that come with the availability of more and more granular data and the ability to connect all data to a holistic view.

Certain areas in Fig. 2 are to some extent similar to the areas already discussed in the banking context. These areas are client interface & channels, analytics & predictive analytics and process & process automation. Naturally, the aspects are set in the context of an insurance company (analytics & predictive analytics have an impact on the actuarial aspects).

But there are some interesting areas that differ significantly from the banking setting: client interface claims, IoT[15] & tokenization, insurance contacts via partner (broker) and reinsurance.

The aim of Fig. 2 is not to display all details of digitalization in an insurance company and it does not intend to be exhaustive. Figure 2 should help to understand the building blocks on a certain level (flying altitude).

The continuous improvements in data availability open up the chance of improvements in pricing or even completely new products. Scalable infrastructures provide the ability to process this size of data on affordable hardware. Open-source frameworks can deliver new models for improving prediction quality and enabling new business opportunities.

---

[14] In the real estate context.
[15] Internet of Things (see (Veneri und Capasso 2018)).

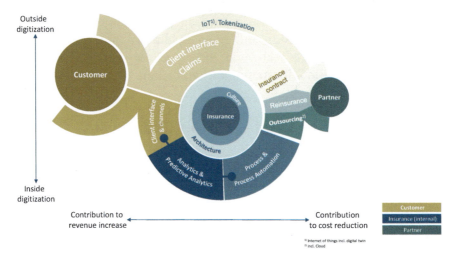

Fig. 2 Overview digitalization areas—insurance © ifb SE

Summary of the Setting

On the customer side (outside digitalization), the key components are the willingness to understand the customer's problems in combination with the ability to solve (execute) the problem by a cost optimal composition of individualized (to the problem) and common product components (leveraging the involved partners' economies of scale by using APIs[16] for a smooth integration). Therefore, cost-efficient mass-individualization is possible, serving the client's needs. The traditional institutes struggle with the culture needed to act agilely and achieve a more dynamic product cycle through this.

On the internal side, the tasks themselves have a stability (apart from the regulatory requirements or the ongoing improvements in accounting standards). The way these tasks are performed has become more automated.

Overview of Book Series "The Digital Journey of Banking and Insurance"

This book is the first volume of the three-volume book series "The Digital Journey of Banking and Insurance". The first volume "Disruption and DNA" focuses on change and the components staying stable in the banking and

---

[16] Application programming interface is more than a computing interface because it offers significant simplification by modularizing by a meaningful structure.

insurance market (outside view) as well as the effect on accounting, risk management and regulatory departments (inside view). The inside view is completed by an analysis of cultural alterations. The second volume "Digitalization and Machine Learning Applications" mainly emphasizes use cases as well as the methods and technologies applied to drive digital transformation (such as processes, leveraging computational power and machine learning models). In the last volume of the series, "Data Storage, Processing and Analysis", the shifts in the way we deal with data are addressed. The angle shifts over the volumes from a business-driven approach in the "Disruption and DNA" volume to a strong technical focus in the "Data Storage, Processing and Analysis" volume, leaving the "Digitalization and Machine Learning Applications" volume with the business and technical aspects in-between.

Literature

Basel Committee on Banking Supervision. 2021. January 22. https://www.bis.org/basel_framework/.

Floß, Johannes, and Jeyakrishna Velauthapillai. 2021. "Special Data for Insurance Companies." In *The Digital Journey of Banking and Insurance, Volume III—Data Storage, Processing, and Analysis*, edited by Volker Liermann and Claus Stegmann. New York: Palgrave Macmillan.

Krätz, Dennis, and Michael Morawski. 2021. "Architecture Patterns—Batch & Real Time Capabilities." In *The Digital Journey of Banking and Insurance, Volume III—Data Storage, Processing, and Analysis*, edited by Volker Liermann and Claus Stegmann. New York: Palgrave Macmillan.

May, Uwe. 2019. "The Concept of the Next Best Action/Offer in the Age of Customer Experience." In *The impact of Digital Transformation and Fintech on the Finance Professional*, edited by Volker Liermann and Claus Stegmann. New York: Palgrave Macmillan.

Merkt, Rainer, Markus Thiele, and Florian Dinges. 2021. "Digitalization Landscape Banking." In *The Digital Journey of Banking and Insurance, Volume I—Disruption and DNA*, edited by Volker Liermann and Claus Stegmann. New York: Palgrave Macmillan.

Merkt, Rainer, Veronika Lang, and Anna Schmidt. 2021. "Digi-Cultural Mindset." In *The Digital Journey of Banking and Insurance, Volume I—Disruption and DNA*, edited by Volker Liermann and Claus Stegmann. New York: Palgrave Macmillan.

Negenman, Ebbe. 2021. "The Knab Story: How We Turned the Bank Around." In *The Digital Journey of Banking and Insurance, Volume I—Disruption and DNA*, edited by Volker Liermann and Claus Stegmann. New York: Palgrave Macmillan.

Stegmann, Claus, and Sven Ludwig. 2021. "Digitalization Strategy." In *The Digital Journey of Banking and Insurance, Volume I—Disruption and DNA*, edited by Volker Liermann and Claus Stegmann. New York: Palgrave Macmillan.

Veneri, Giacomo, and Antonio Capasso. 2018. *Hands-On Industrial Internet of Things: Create a Powerful Industrial IoT Infrastructure Using Industry 4.0.* Birmingham: Packt Publishing.

Foreword

The banking and insurance are facing profound challenges. The world is experiencing remarkable advances in computing and communications technology even as we take these changes more and more for granted. Adapting effectively to such pervasive changes requires that we keep some basic principles in mind. One of these is encapsulated in a quote from The Leopard by Giuseppe de Lampedusa that reads:

> If things are to remain the same, things will have to change.[1]

To unpack this rather enigmatic quip we must distinguish between the two occurrences of "things." The first refers to those things that are central to an institution's mission and its value system. The second refers to secondary circumstances that serve the core mission but are not themselves fixed and immutable. Too often people become so attached to this second class of "things" that they fail to appreciate their secondary character. Clarifying this distinction is essential to coping successfully with periods of profound change.

My own experience has been focused on the banking sector where the central mission is effective allocation of savings into real investments with positive expected returns. Prior to even that basic goal, however, is the need to attract depositors' savings by providing competitive services and a reputation for competence and honorable behavior.

---

[1] I was first introduced to this quote and its analysis by Peter de Jager of Technobility.

Attracting deposits is closely tied to customer relationship management. Providing competitive tools and services that assist customers in managing their own financial resources is essential. The same can be said for insurance companies providing support to assist customers in managing their personal and corporate risks across multiple dimensions. Remaining competitive amid rapid technological change requires continuing insight into customers' priorities and preferences. This is further complicated by intergenerational differences in such preferences. How to maintain effective customer contact through multiple channels of interaction is one of the important topics of the three volume *Digital Journey* project.

For banks, meticulously accurate and timely processing of transactions is taken for granted by customers. Falling short of this expectation is the fastest way to lose business. Advancing technology provides ever better means of achieving both speed and accuracy, but it is like running on a treadmill. Success requires adopting new tools continuously as they become available to meet ever more demanding customer expectations. Staying ahead of the competition is only possible with agile software systems built with state-of-the-art twenty first Century system architecture.

Cost optimization and control is as important as ever. What has changed is the need to focus on dynamic rather than static efficiency. The cost of computer processing and data storage has fallen steadily over the past forty years. Traditional computer software architecture was designed to economize on these resources but it resulted in systems that were rigid and difficult to modify. Twenty first Century system architecture is designed to make such continuous modifications far easier and largely foolproof, as illustrated by the seamless evolution of applications on our tablets and smart phones. This enables continuous enhancement of features and functions without steadily rising maintenance costs.

Modern system architecture also enables far more effective application of predictive analytics. Data can be stored and indexed in far less structured form compared to traditional relational databases. This opens the data to meaningful access and analysis across multiple product types, organizational components and geographic areas. It also avoids constraints, inherent in relational database designs, on the types of inquiries that can be supported. Unexpected vectors of interest across enterprise data that arise suddenly can be addressed on a timely basis.

This architecture also changes the perennial buy-versus-build dilemma. Specialized proprietary components can be incorporated far more easily and seamlessly than was traditionally possible.

In summary, remaining competitive in today's environment of rapid technological change and rising customer expectations poses a daunting challenge. Meeting that challenge demands two things:

- Clear definition of an institution's core principles and standards and constant reinforcement of these to employees, customers, regulators and the general public.
- Recognition of secondary factors that an institution must be prepared to alter if it is to remain competitive in a period of rapid technological and social change.

The Digital Journey of Banking and Insurance is a guide to the many secondary factors and processes of banks and insurance companies that must be subjected to constant scrutiny and revision if an institution is to avoid falling behind the competition. Its appearance could not be timelier as we enter the third decade of the twenty first Century. It should be required reading for all senior financial executive teams.

Saddlebrooke, Arizona David M. Rowe, Ph.D.[2]

---

[2] The author is President of David M. Rowe Risk Advisory. For sixteen years Dr. Rowe wrote the Risk Analysis column in Risk and is the author of *An Insider's Guide to Risk Management—Relearning the Lessons of the Global Financial Crisis*.

Acknowledgments

The three-book series was the natural next step from the book "The Impact of Digital Transformation and FinTech on the Finance Professional" and an exciting project for us. We look back with gratitude at the many discussions with clients, partners, and colleagues at ifb. Without this vital community, such an undertaking would not be possible.

We would first like to thank all contributors (clients, partners, and colleagues), whose expertise was invaluable in exploring and formulating such a comprehensive work with a wide overview and deep insights. Their insightful feedback helped us to sharpen this work to this amazing level.

In addition, we would like to thank Tula Weis and her team from Palgrave Macmillan for advice and support in this project.

We like to thank Satzanstalt for supporting us in development and realization of the book cover idea.

We would also like to thank our colleagues Julia Horstmann, Davin Radermacher, and Jenny Klein for their support in all the small, but important things that make such an undertaking a success.

Volker Liermann
Claus Stegmann

Introduction to Volume I—Disruption and DNA

This volume "Disruption and DNA" focuses on the business aspects of digital transformation. The first part analyzes the situation banks and insurance companies face. This part also explores different strategies to implement digital transformation. The subject spans from projections of digital capabilities and digitalization strategies up to disruptive approaches such as greenfield.

The second part focuses on the accounting and controlling subject in the digital context. This part explores how to deliver the tasks for a CFO in a more efficient way. The chapter puts the spotlight on the importance and improvements of the planning process. In addition, a practical example is presented of how data collection and machine learning helped to improve accounting.

The third part looks at the possible improvements demanded in risk management. Both financial risk and non-financial risk are addressed in this part. The financial risks paradigm of a one-year horizon is relaxed and extended to a multi-period scenario-based analysis. In the area of non-financial risk management, a framework is presented to link and connect the silos in non-financial risk (the non-financial risk categories) to a risk-category-specific and risk-category-joining approach.

The last part (Culture and Projects) is dedicated to the way things are done. The topics range from the overall culture to the modern and agile project approaches. The deep dive into project management includes the solutions for remote project delivery.

Contents

Market View

Digitalization Landscape Banking 3
Rainer Merkt, Markus Thiele, and Florian Dinges

Digitalization Strategy 19
Sven Ludwig and Claus Stegmann

The Knab Story: How We Turned the Bank Around 35
Ebbe Negenman

Accounting/Controlling

The Need for Resilience and Agility in Finance 43
Jens-Peter Jensen

Value Driver-Oriented Planning—Management-Oriented Design and Value Driver Identification 53
Simon Valjanow, Philipp Enzinger, Daniel Suttner, and Maik Alexander Schmidt

AI for Impairment Accounting 67
Sören Hartung and Manuela Führer

Risk Management

Financial Navigator: A Modern Approach to Analytical Banking — 85
Markus Thiele

Actuarial Data Science — 119
Susanne Brindöpke

BSDS—Balance Sheet Dynamics Simulator (Application ABM) — 137
Volker Liermann and Harro Dittmar

Breaking New Grounds in Non-Financial Risk Management — 161
Volker Liermann, Nikolas Viets, and Davin Radermacher

Culture and Projects

Digi-Cultural Mindset — 185
Rainer Merkt, Veronika Lang, and Anna Schmidt

New Project Structure—Agile & Scrum — 213
Eljar Akhgarnush, Fabian Bruse, and Ben Hofer

Hybrid Project Management — 239
Uwe Beister and Milica Zeljkovic

Remote Projects — 263
Eljar Akhgarnush, Fabian Bruse, and Daniel Pott

Project Management and RPA — 289
Sefa Soybir and Christopher Schmidt

Summary — 307
Volker Liermann and Claus Stegmann

Index — 311

Notes on Contributors

Eljar Akhgarnush is Implementation Consultant at ifb group since April 2018. He gained knowledge in software and financial sector topics during his studies as well as the various positions he has since held. Starting out with a focus on financial supervision and regulation, he soon shifted his attention to the technical side and agile project management. After having received his B.Sc. in Business Administration from CAU Kiel, he gained his M.Sc. in International Economics and Policy Consulting at OvGU in Magdeburg. He has since remained keen on exchanging knowledge and exploring new areas.

Uwe Beister is Head of the Program and Project Management Team in the ifb group. He has almost 25 years of professional experience in managing projects on both the technical and IT side, as well as in the development of project management structures and processes in various financial institutions. He is a trained bank officer, holds a university degree in Business Administration and is, among other things, certified on the basis of PRINCE2. Based on our diverse projects, he and his team develop new project management approaches and standardization approaches for supporting projects through a PMO. Furthermore, he is responsible for training and further education in the areas of project management and PMO in the ifb group.

Susanne Brindöpke is Director at ifb group, and has been working in the financial industry for more than 13 years, ten of them as a Management Consultant. She started her career in quantitative risk management and later worked on various projects with a focus on implementing regulatory requirements related to solvency and risk. Her areas of interest include digitalization in enterprise risk management processes and actuarial data science.

Susanne has a degree in Business Mathematics from the University of Hamburg.

Fabian Bruse is Director at ifb group, and has worked here since 2011. He started his career in the regulatory reporting sector as a software tester and later moved on to SAP BW and SAP BA development with a particular focus on IRR and CRA modules for customers in Germany and Luxembourg. His more recent projects include modern ETL and reporting processes where he has the role of a—partially remote—Scrum Master (PSM2 certified). Since 2017, he has also coordinated the technical part of the ifb Blockchain Team and administrated the ifb Hyperledger system on Kubernetes. Fabian has a degree in Physics from the University of Bonn.

Florian Dinges is Senior Consultant at ifb group. He obtained his degree in Mathematics and Physics at Goethe University Frankfurt along with management studies. He has been working in the area of enterprise architecture and strategic consulting for over two years. Additionally, he is interested in financial risk management, machine learning, and innovation.

Dr. Harro Dittmar is Senior Consultant at ifb SE. He is a passionate programmer with a confident and structured approach to the modeling of complex systems. His aspiration is the thorough understanding, implementation, and troubleshooting of scenario calculations, predictions, and optimization problems from a holistic perspective. After his academic career in statistical modeling and pattern recognition of molecular systems, he started a career in the banking sector. His consulting focus includes quantitative risk modeling, strategic approaches to the optimization of data architectures, and data management.

Philipp Enzinger is Managing Consultant at ifb and responsible for insurance analytics and risk topics. At ifb, Mr. Enzinger leads the digitalization work group for insurance data science. As project manager and subject matter expert, he has been advising financial institutions on credit risk and financial transformation topics for more than five years. In recent years, Mr. Enzinger has focused on insurance companies' IFRS 17/9 implementation—in particular new risk calculations as well as impacts on planning, reporting, and financial steering. Mr. Enzinger holds an M.Sc. in Economics from the University of Cologne.

Manuela Führer has been Group Leader at Landesbank Hessen-Thüringen (Helaba) for over ten years in the Accounting division, responsible for the accounting of financial instruments under local GAAP (HGB) and IFRS. With more than 20 years of experience in the financial sector, as a consultant, in treasury and accounting, she has a deep knowledge of financial instruments, IFRS9, hedge accounting and impairment, accounting processes, and functional and technical reporting architectures. In 2019, she initiated and managed the proof of concept for the use of artificial intelligence in impairment accounting and the subsequent roll-out of the ML model in line operations.

Sören Hartung is Project and Investment Manager at Helaba. He has spent his entire career to date working on the digital transformation of financial institutions. He is interested in emerging technologies (e.g., machine learning, distributed ledger technologies) that enable new digital business models and optimize process flows. As an investment manager, he seeks investment opportunities in innovative tech start-ups to support Helaba's digitalization strategy. He has a Master of Science in Finance & Information Management from Goethe University, Frankfurt.

Ben Hofer is Senior Consultant and Manager Digital Communications at ifb group. For more than six years, he has advised insurance companies and banks in the field of digital transformation. The expert for operational excellence focuses on agile project management, change management, and process topics such as process mining, robotic process automation, and Lean Six Sigma. He holds a degree in business informatics and is certified as Professional Scrum Master (PSM), Professional Product Owner (PSPO), Lean Six Sigma Green Belt (PEEC/IASSC), and Professional for Requirements Engineering (CPRE).

Jens-Peter Jensen is Solution Manager at SAP SE. He heads the department Finance, Risk and Data Management Solutions for the financial services industry. Throughout his career, he has held various roles with a focus on solution innovation and global go-to-market in banking. He has driven solution innovations in the area of bank analyzer, risk management and regulatory reporting, financial services data platform, and financial products subledger. His current focus is on the changed role of the CFO in times of digitalization and data-driven financials. He studied Business Administration and Economics at the University of Mannheim.

Dr. Veronika Lang has a strong focus on enabling organizations during change processes with a strong user-centered approach. Her neuroscience background, systemic coaching expertise as well as experience as a consultant (ifb, 2016-2019) make her an expert regarding the development and roll-out of tailored employee development solutions. At Forever Day One, we initiate starting points for reinvention of organizations regarding the development of new digital services and transforming company culture. Forever Day One also means that learning to learn and adapt is at the core of our work. We believe that an agile learning workforce is the key to overcoming the challenges of the future.

Volker Liermann is Partner at ifb group, and has worked in the banking industry for over two decades, primarily focusing on financial risk management. Throughout his career, he has focused on developing integrated and comprehensive frameworks to help organizations correctly project risk at a strategic and tactical line of business and departmental level. He has also focused on developing frameworks to integrate stress testing and regulatory stress tests. In recent years, his focus has shifted to digitalization, machine learning, and digital processes including improvements to classical financial and non-financial risk management. He has a background in Economics and a degree in Mathematics from the University of Bonn.

Dr. Sven Ludwig is Senior Advisor, Governance, Risk and Compliance at ifb group. In addition, Sven holds the position of Regional Director at PRMIA, the international risk management association with more than 50,000 members globally.

Before joining ifb group, Sven held several management positions at FIS^{TM}. He served as global Head of Subject Matter Experts and Advisory, among other roles at FIS. During his career, Sven was also responsible for trading and risk management IT at a major German bank. He started his professional career as a financial consultant for trading and risk management.

Sven studied Economics at Friedrich Wilhelm University of Bonn in Germany. He conducted his doctoral thesis in the field of mathematical economic research and behavioral finance.

Dr. Rainer Merkt has more than 20 years of consulting experience in the banking industry and has his background in risk, regulatory, and overall bank controlling. For more than one decade, he has been working on concepts and models for enterprise architecture and strategy. Rainer is especially interested in state-of-the-art and visionary approaches for holistic enterprise models including environmental, cultural, and sociological aspects of the digi-human hybrid ecosystem.

Dr. Ebbe Negenman is the Chief Risk Officer (CRO) of Knab. As a member of the executive board of Knab, he is co-responsible for the management of the bank. He has over 30 years of experience in risk management. Until 2017, Ebbe worked as Head of Regulatory Risk at ABN Amro and was highly involved in the innovation of the sector. Up to 2010, Ebbe was employed as Managing Director Risk Management at ING Bank in Amsterdam and for several years was based in the Real Estate division and in Hong Kong, where he was responsible for the Asia-Pacific region. He started his career at the Dutch merchant bank MeesPierson in the market risk management area. Ebbe has two master's degrees (mathematics and econometrics) and a Ph.D. in operations research, and considers the ability to learn faster than your competitors the only sustainable competitive advantage. He has therefore made learning a way of living.

Daniel Pott is Partner at ifb group and Managing Director of ifb Services, has been working at ifb since 2004. He is a graduate economist and has special expertise in regulatory reporting (Basel II/III), finance and risk architectures. Daniel is an IPMA-certified project manager with a focus on SAP products, such as SAP Bank Analyzer, Business Warehouse, FPSL, etc. He moved into project management more than ten years ago and has worked with outsourcers and outsourcing in remote projects in these fields. He is Head of Project Management, Remote Consulting, and Application Managed Services at ifb group.

Davin Radermacher is a Consultant in ifb group's Treasury & Portfolio Management unit specializing in risk management and risk reporting. He is part of the team that has developed ifb's new Non-Financial Risk Management framework and is involved in several topics related to non-financial risks and digitalization. Davin holds a degree in Economics.

Anna Schmidt is a Consultant, and has worked at ifb SE since the beginning of 2020. She joined the company after graduating in Psychology. In her studies, she focused on clinical client consulting and on initiating organizational development. Anna is deeply interested in topics affecting communication, employee satisfaction, and work atmosphere and thus engages in all activity related to cultural change.

Christopher Schmidt is Senior Consultant with a strong record of managing complex projects in international environments as well as a proven skillset in developing automated processes with RPA technology. He joined ifb group in April of 2019. The certified RPA Advanced Developer focuses on the development of software robots as well as the design of target operating models and overall RPA strategy. Before joining ifb, he already gathered experience as a consultant in projects within the financial sector, at both insurance companies and banks.

Maik Alexander Schmidt is a Consultant at ifb and supports the Controlling and Management Accounting practice for banks. He has an academic background in Mathematics and holds an M.Sc. degree in Mathematics from the University of Paderborn with a focus on analysis. Now he leads the development of the topic "predictive analytics" for financial controlling/accounting. His focus is on the optimization of planning processes and currently on the open-source software R and its applications for predictive analytics, especially on regressions in R.

Sefa Soybir is a Senior Consultant in the ifb group since April 2020. The certified Six Sigma Green Belt has a strong record in core process advice to the banking sector. Before he joined ifb group, he worked at a major German bank, where he successfully managed to implement a variety of automated processes leveraging RPA technology. His focus lies on the strategic establishment of excellence centers as well as project management and process evaluation with regard to their automation potential.

Claus Stegmann is Co-CEO of ifb group—an international consulting firm—and has acquired extensive know-how over the last three decades in the financial industry regarding finance transformation, risk management, and regulatory compliance. He is intensively engaged with the current challenges of the financial industry, which result from strong changes to customer behavior, a changing competitive environment, and new technologies due to digitalization. He has also co-authored books on Stress Tests in Banks, Basel III as well as Digitalization in the Finance Industry, and graduated from Business School at the University of Passau, Germany.

Daniel Suttner is Managing Consultant at ifb group with a focus on controlling and management accounting since 2018. His current thematic priority consists of integrated strategic and operating revenue and cost budgeting (value-driver oriented). Mr. Suttner is also skilled in the area of optimizing controlling processes as well as business analysis. He started his career at Baader Bank AG and earned several years of experience in financial controlling with a focus on planning and reporting. After having received his B.A. in Banking and Finance, he obtained an M.Sc. in Risk Management and Treasury at the Hochschule für Oekonomie und Management (FOM).

Dr. Markus Thiele is a Consultant in the financial industry for almost two decades. He advises clients on various topics, including risk management, regulatory supervision, enterprise architecture, software selection processes, data quality management, and test management. His advisory activities cover both the business and the implementation side, and he considers a thorough understanding of both sides key in many projects. His particular interests are credit risk modeling and architecture-based approaches for integrative analytical banking.

Simon Valjanow is Director at ifb and leads the Controlling and Management Accounting practice for banks. In the role of project manager and subject matter expert, he has been advising financial institutions on financial controlling topics for more than 13 years. In recent times, he has been developing solutions for the optimization of planning processes and integrated reporting. In addition, Mr. Valjanow has advised on transformation projects as well as change processes regarding the implementation of business cases and user stories. His academic background consists of a certified diploma in Business and Law.

Nikolas Viets is CFA, and heads ifb group's Treasury & Portfolio Management unit. He has been working as a Consultant for the CRO/CFO agenda for 15 years. His work experience includes a wide variety of industries, from large utilities and e-commerce companies to investment managers, with a primary focus on financial institutions. Nikolas holds degrees both in business administration and political economics and is a Certified Corporate Treasurer VDT®.

Milica Zeljkovic is Consultant, who started her career with ifb in April 2020. She is in the Program and Project Management Team. During her studies in International Business Administration, she focused on change management, innovation management, and languages. She spent two semesters and an internship of six months in French-speaking countries. Her master's thesis deals with the topic of Heterogeneity in Innovation Teams and its influence on the project outcome.

List of Figures

Digitalization Landscape Banking

Fig. 1	Architecture House (© ifb SE)	5
Fig. 2	Example of a hierarchical functional structure (the cluster and business capability level are not displayed) (© ifb SE)	7

Digitalization Strategy

Fig. 1	Investment in IT for transformation per year of traditional banks versus all-time money raised by challenger banks (*Sources* HSBC, Barclays, Lloyds, RBS, N26, Revolut, Monzo, Monese and authors' research, following illustration of Bó © ifb SE)	20
Fig. 2	Illustration of the need for digitalization to counter margin pressure (© ifb SE)	22
Fig. 3	Illustration of the 90° transformation of the financial ecosystem (© ifb SE)	25
Fig. 4	Digitalization and innovation in the context of customer frontend (© ifb SE)	28
Fig. 5	Illustration of areas of digitalization that typically have potential beyond like-for-like and offer disruptions (© ifb SE)	31

The Need for Resilience and Agility in Finance

Fig. 1	The changing mandate of the CFO (© SAP SE)	45

Fig. 2	From daily routine to supporting new business models (© SAP SE)	45
Fig. 3	Business processes in finance (© SAP SE)	46
Fig. 4	Bringing business processes and data in sync (© SAP SE)	48

Value Driver-Oriented Planning—Management-Oriented Design and Value Driver Identification

Fig. 1	Illustration (Relationship: Planning on the level of result vs. planning on the value driver level) (© ifb SE)	54
Fig. 2	Illustration of integrated planning model by value driver areas—business view, group functions and associated sub-plans (© ifb SE)	55
Fig. 3	Value driver map framework (© ifb SE)	57
Fig. 4	General procedure of predictive analytics (© ifb SE)	60
Fig. 5	Unscheduled repayments and merging to P&L (© ifb SE)	61
Fig. 6	Process of driver identification and integration (© ifb SE)	63

AI for Impairment Accounting

Fig. 1	Data analytics (© Helaba)	69
Fig. 2	Overall identification process (© Helaba)	69
Fig. 3	Challenges in data quality management (© Helaba)	71
Fig. 4	Goals of the POC (© Helaba)	72
Fig. 5	Systems involved and data flow (© Helaba)	73
Fig. 6	Tool data and analysis (© Helaba)	73
Fig. 7	Overview artificial intelligence (© Helaba)	74
Fig. 8	Project steps (© Helaba)	76
Fig. 9	Modeling results (© Helaba)	77

Financial Navigator: A Modern Approach to Analytical Banking

Fig. 1	Depiction of the basic model situation (© ifb SE)	91
Fig. 2	Functional modules and their input–output relationships (black arrows) (© ifb SE)	95
Fig. 3	Macroeconomic indicator determination (© ifb SE)	96
Fig. 4	Probability-of-Default determination (© ifb SE)	98
Fig. 5	Loss-Given-Default (© ifb SE)	99
Fig. 6	Exposure-at-Default determination (© ifb SE)	100
Fig. 7	Sketch of the determination of the temporal evolution of the portfolios (red circle: own bank) (© ifb SE)	104
Fig. 8	Property value determination (© ifb SE)	105
Fig. 9	Economic Capital determination (© ifb SE)	106
Fig. 10	Risk reporting (© ifb SE)	107

Fig. 11	Example interactive dashboard (© ifb SE)	107
Fig. 12	Sketch of the example IT architecture scenario (© ifb SE)	111

BSDS—Balance Sheet Dynamics Simulator (Application ABM)

Fig. 1	Overview financial navigator (© ifb SE)	141
Fig. 2	Balance sheet dynamics simulator—overview (© ifb SE)	142
Fig. 3	Preliminary considerations for the modeling of complex systems (© ifb SE)	145
Fig. 4	ABM—essential elements (© ifb SE)	147
Fig. 5	Development of the macroeconomic indicators. Historical data is shaded in grey (© ifb SE)	150
Fig. 6	BSDS—Agents—Simple setting (© ifb SE)	152
Fig. 7	BSDS—Agents—Elaborate setting (© ifb SE)	153
Fig. 8	Aggregation supply and demand and client matching (© ifb SE)	155
Fig. 9	Supply and demand matching with prices (© ifb SE)	156

Breaking New Grounds in Non-Financial Risk Management

Fig. 1	Initial situation and motivation (© ifb SE)	163
Fig. 2	NFR approach/structure (© ifb SE)	164
Fig. 3	Overview of example risk categories (© ifb SE)	165
Fig. 4	NFR taxonomy (© ifb SE)	166
Fig. 5	Example impact graph (in Neo4J) (© ifb SE)	167
Fig. 6	Impact graphs—nodes and edges (© ifb SE)	168
Fig. 7	Negative effects (© ifb SE)	169
Fig. 8	Vulnerabilities—definitions (© ifb SE)	170
Fig. 9	Example impact graph—ESG—stylized design (© ifb S)	171
Fig. 10	Impact graph—collapse (© ifb SE)	171
Fig. 11	Coexistence of integrative and detailed analyses (© ifb S)	172
Fig. 12	Other dimensions in assessing indicators and risk indicators (© ifb SE)	173
Fig. 13	Threshold values—transition from indicators to risk indicators (© ifb SE)	175
Fig. 14	Key risk indicator tree for person risk (© ifb SE)	176
Fig. 15	Duality between key figure trees and impact graphs (© ifb SE)	177
Fig. 16	Reporting approach – design sketch (© ifb SE)	179
Fig. 17	Example system landscape (© ifb SE)	180

Digi-Cultural Mindset

Fig. 1	Successful digitalization is where culture, business strategy and technology are aligned (© ifb SE)	187

Fig. 2	Digi-cultural mindset spreads through all organizational contexts (© ifb SE)	190
Fig. 3	A mindset is constituted of the interdependence of thoughts, feelings and behavior (© ifb SE)	191
Fig. 4	SORC model (Kanfer and Saslow 1969) (© ifb SE)	196
Fig. 5	Definition of a digi-cultural mindset (© ifb SE)	202
Fig. 6	Digi-cultural mindset Maturity Model (© ifb SE)	203
Fig. 7	Digi-cultural mindset mapped to Competing Values Framework (© ifb SE)	205
Fig. 8	Cycle of learning and developing a growth mindset (© ifb SE)	208

New Project Structure—Agile & Scrum

Fig. 1	The Agile Manifesto (© ifb SE)	215
Fig. 2	The five Core Scrum Values (© ifb SE)	215
Fig. 3	The interplay between the Scrum layers (© ifb SE)	217
Fig. 4	A visualization of the Scrum process (© ifb SE)	221
Fig. 5	The adapted Stacey matrix (© ifb SE)	224
Fig. 6	Burnup Chart (© ifb SE)	228
Fig. 7	Simple Scrum Board variation (© ifb SE)	230
Fig. 8	Retrospective—five phases (© ifb SE)	232

Hybrid Project Management

Fig. 1	The evolution of project management (© ifb SE)	242
Fig. 2	Criteria to be considered for hybrid management methods (© ifb SE)	246
Fig. 3	Hybrid variants (© ifb SE)	250
Fig. 4	Onion model of agile planning (© ifb SE)	253
Fig. 5	Kanban board (© ifb SE)	256
Fig. 6	Hybrid model: Water-ScrumBan-Fall (© ifb SE)	258
Fig. 7	Summary of advantages for traditional, agile and best practices (© ifb SE)	258

Remote Projects

Fig. 1	Two distinct teams with one connection (© ifb SE)	264
Fig. 2	Connections between remote project team members (© ifb SE)	266
Fig. 3	Illustration of synchronous groupware and some of its characteristics (© ifb SE)	278
Fig. 4	Illustration of asynchronous groupware and some of its characteristics (© ifb SE)	278
Fig. 5	Illustration of Paul Zak's key management behaviors leveraging trust (© ifb SE)	283

| Fig. 6 | Illustration of PMI's five-point communication model (© ifb SE) | 285 |

Project Management and RPA

Fig. 1	The four phases of an RPA project (© ifb SE)	290
Fig. 2	Five sub-phases of RPA process identification (© ifb SE)	291
Fig. 3	Parameters for assessing RPA suitability (© ifb SE)	292
Fig. 4	Advantages and disadvantages of application and process-driven development approaches (© ifb SE)	296
Fig. 5	Illustration ramp-up phase (© ifb SE)	297
Fig. 6	Documented vs. actual process (© ifb SE)	299
Fig. 7	Seven phases of emotional response to change (Streich 1997)	301
Fig. 8	Functional integration of RPA (© ifb SE)	303
Fig. 9	Centralized center of excellence (© ifb SE)	304
Fig. 10	Federated center of excellence (© ifb SE)	305

List of Tables

Financial Navigator: A Modern Approach to Analytical Banking

Table 1	Symbols and their explanations © ifb SE	94
Table 2	Determination of the Loss-Given-Default © ifb SE	99

BSDS—Balance Sheet Dynamics Simulator (Application ABM)

Table 1	Example target credit rating structure by client type for the distribution of exposures (© ifb SE)	150

New Project Structure—Agile & Scrum

Table 1	Scrum Artefacts explained (© ifb SE)	220
Table 2	Common mistakes with prevention and improvement options (© ifb SE)	227

Remote Projects

Table 1	Communication tool allocation to purposes (© ifb SE)	280

List of Equations

Financial Navigator: A Modern Approach to Analytical Banking

Equation 1	Future values of the macroeconomic indicators (general)	97
Equation 2	Future values of the macroeconomic indicators (actually used for the example)	98
Equation 3	Future values of the Rating and the Probability-of-Default	99
Equation 4	Future values of the Loss-Given-Default	100
Equation 5	Future values of the Exposure-at-Default	104
Equation 6	Future values of the property value	105
Equation 7	Future values of the expected loss and the unexpected loss	106

Market View

The part "Market View" mirrors the trends and activities observed in banks and insurance companies. The companies in the financial service sector face numerous challenges on the revenue and cost side of the business model. The causes are partially macroeconomic (lower interest rate, impairments driven by the COVID-19 pandemic), but primarily sector-specific challenges triggered by competitors (fintech and Big Tech).

Given the challenges, this part offers a view of the capabilities and tools needed to overcome them. The chapters in this part offer structures to analyze and group the upcoming requirements for digitalization. An open discussion regarding the strategies to drive a successful digital transformation is carried out.

Even extreme approaches like the greenfield approach (start a new company with a differentiating culture and a state-of-the-art infrastructure and architecture) are explored.

The first chapter of this part (Merkt, Thiele and Dinges 2021) discusses the projected needs and capabilities of banks in a five-year horizon. The authors start with an Enterprise-Architecture-based approach and give an overview of the business capabilities for a digitally capable bank. A structure to group the diverse topics of digitalization is also offered in this chapter.

Chapter 3 (Stegmann and Ludwig 2021) discusses the paths to implement a digitalization strategy. Furthermore, the challenges and the underestimated catalysts of digital transformation are presented. The analysis runs along a structure given by main aeras of digitalization. The chapter emphasizes the importance of the underlying business model. In addition, the chapter enables the reader to determine the degree of an institute's digital maturity.

The last chapter in the part (Negenman 2021) gives insights into a practical greenfield implementation driven by Knab (a Dutch challenger bank arising from the Aegon bank). The chapter assembles the critical topics for such an undertaking. The chapter underlines the importance of compliance, culture and a client-first[1] approach.

Literature

Ludwig, Sven, and Claus Stegmann. 2021. "Digitalization Strategy." In *The Digital Journey of Banking and Insurance, Volume I—Disruption and DNA*, edited by Volker Liermann and Claus Stegmann. New York: Palgrave Macmillan.

Merkt, Rainer, Markus Thiele, and Florian Dinges. 2021. "Digitalization Landscape Banking." In *The Digital Journey of Banking and Insurance, Volume I—Disruption and DNA*, edited by Volker Liermann and Claus Stegmann. New York: Palgrave Macmillan.

Negenman, Ebbe. 2021. "The Knab Story: How We Turned the Bank Around." In *The Digital Journey of Banking and Insurance, Volume I—Disruption and DNA*, edited by Volker Liermann and Claus Stegmann. New York: Palgrave Macmillan.

---

[1] Customer-centric.

Digitalization Landscape Banking

Rainer Merkt, Markus Thiele, and Florian Dinges

1 Introduction

1.1 Scope

The term "digitalization" encompasses a variety of individual digitalization topics where each of these topics stands for a completely new or significantly improved technology in the wider sense. The different digitalization topics have the potential to change existing business services considerably and permanently. One can argue that considering the new digitalization topics will become a matter of economic survival. On the one hand, the digitalization topics represent a great chance for lasting improvements, on the other their application poses major challenges for banks. The first major challenge is to achieve a solid understanding of what the different digitalization topics actually are and mean. This is because there is no agreement on the naming

---

R. Merkt (✉) · M. Thiele · F. Dinges
ifb SE, Grünwald, Germany
e-mail: Rainer.Merkt@ifb-group.com

M. Thiele
e-mail: Markus.Thiele@ifb-group.com

F. Dinges
e-mail: Florian.Dinges@ifb-group.com

and the meaning of the different digitalization topics and how to differentiate between them. The second major challenge is to appropriately classify the different digital topics according to a clear pattern of order. Such a classification is the prerequisite for a structured assessment of which of the existing capabilities and disciplines have to become involved for the establishment of a particular digital topic. The third major challenge is to get a clear view of which of the digitalization topics can serve which of the existing capabilities and disciplines. To phrase it differently, it is crucial to understand which of the different digital services can indeed support specific tasks. Against this background, the scope of this article is twofold:

1. In the article we have compiled a list of digitalization topics with well-known and frequently used suggestive names and compact definitions. This structured list is a basis for the further classifications.
2. The digitalization topics are mapped onto the existing banking business capabilities, where the mapping is performed from two different viewpoints and the business capabilities themselves are structured appropriately.

As a result, one has a clear, high-level view of the digitalization topics. Apart from being of major importance for a clear view of digitalization, this also serves the purpose of the book, since it provides a pattern for the categorization of the digitalization topics addressed in the book.

For the whole structuring and mapping tasks of this article, the methodology of the Enterprise Architecture is applied, since it can be seen as the best-suited means for conducting an analysis and a structuring of topics and banking capabilities.

1.2 Structure of the Article

The article is structured as follows: The second section provides a brief overview of the relevant aspects of Enterprise Architecture, since it represents the methodological framework for the task of this article. Without a basic understanding of the methodological framework, one probably cannot fully appreciate the approach and its results. The third section contains the structuring of the digitalization topics and the (twofold) mappings. The fourth section gives a short summary of the results obtained and provides hints of how to use the results, also in the context of this book.

2 Architecture-Based Approach

On the one hand, Enterprise Architecture is in itself quite a large topic with many different elements and facets, but on the other just some core elements are required for the purpose of this article. Against this background, a brief explanation is provided of primarily those elements of the Enterprise Architecture that are key for the purpose of this article, leaving other aspects less relevant in this context completely aside or giving just a very short description. Enterprise Architecture in its most general sense is a methodological discipline for the general modeling of a system (the enterprise) and its interrelations in order to describe the elements of the business in a structured and efficient manner. The modeling refers both to the information and to the tasks characteristic of the business. The architecture objects for the modeling are business capabilities, business objects and attributes, which are explained in the following subsections.

The Enterprise Architecture refers to almost all aspects of an enterprise. It can be represented by the so-called Architecture House, which is built from the following elements (also see Fig. 1): "Organization & Governance" comprises above all the business strategy, the organizational structure and the overall management of the enterprise. "Business Capabilities" stands for the totality of the capabilities of an enterprise required to run the specific business of the enterprise. "Information & Data" stands for the totality of the information and of the data as its technical counterpart necessary to perform

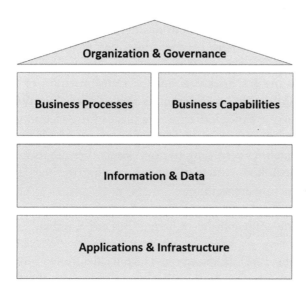

Fig. 1 Architecture House (© ifb SE)

the business tasks. "Application & Infrastructure" refers to the technical tools and means for carrying out tasks in an automated manner. In the context of this book and in particular for the purpose of this article, the business capabilities are the most important architectural objects. This is because digitalization is primarily about new or significantly enhanced digital services. For this reason, business capabilities are described in greater detail in the next subsection. Since business capabilities use and transform information, thereby producing new pieces of information, business objects and attributes are also generally relevant for an architectural description, but not for the purpose of the article. For this reason, they are briefly described in the subsection about other architectural artifacts for the sake of providing an idea of the extent of the architectural approach.

2.1 Business Capabilities

A business capability is an encapsulated, atomic abstraction of a capability necessary to perform a corresponding activity as part of a business process (manually or automated). A business capability transforms a well-defined input into a well-defined output according to a well-defined methodology. The property of being atomic refers to the fact that the extent of the transformation that makes a specific business capability should be such that, firstly, from a business point of view, it can be considered a minimal functional unit and, secondly, that it allows the unambiguous definition of responsibilities for it. Of course, there is usually no unique specification of the content and of the size of a business capability from the outset, instead its content and its size are usually an agreement between the different views of different people combined with best practices. With respect to the financial industry, where a larger part of the activities is about the transformation of information, a business capability could be, for example a calculational portion of the determination of a performance indicator or a piece of the accounting calculation. There is further structuring in the form of a multi-level hierarchical grouping of business capabilities according to how closely they are related with respect to an overall goal. The structural units according to their level within the hierarchical structure are as follows:

Area – Domain – Sub-domain – Cluster – Business Capability

For example, the EAD (Exposure-at-Default) determination as a function can be grouped together with other functions e.g., PD (Probability-of-Default) determination into Credit Risk parameter determination as their

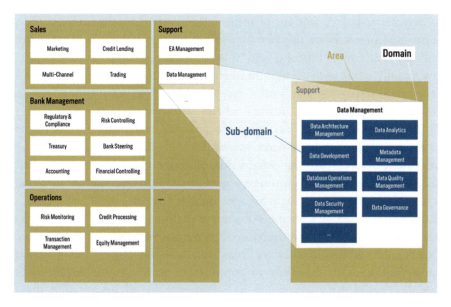

Fig. 2 Example of a hierarchical functional structure (the cluster and business capability level are not displayed) (© ifb SE)

cluster. The Credit Risk parameter determination can be grouped together with other clusters (e.g., Credit Economic capital determination) into Credit Risk Controlling as their sub-domain. Credit Risk Controlling, Market Risk Controlling, Liquidity Risk Controlling, etc. can be grouped together into Risk Controlling as their domain. Risk Controlling in turn is one large part among several other large parts, which altogether can be grouped into Bank Management as their area, which is a grouping on the same level as other areas such as "Sales" or "Operations." There are now industry standards for this kind of hierarchical structuring of functions, most notably the BIAN Service Landscape (Banking Industry Architecture Network 2020). A pictorial representation of the hierarchical structure (in this case for the area "Support") can be seen in the figure below (Fig. 2).

2.2 Other Artifacts

Other important architecture artifacts are business objects and attributes as a means for a strict and transparent structuring and definition of information. They are closely linked to business capabilities, since business capabilities use input information and transform it into output information. A business object is an abstract representation of real-world objects from the perspective of one's own business. It carries certain information, by which it can be characterized. The amount of information carried by the business object is restricted precisely by the fact that some information is completely irrelevant for one's own business and thus can be neglected. For example, a bank usually deals with a large number of business partners in the form of clients, counterparties, guarantors, etc. All these different business partners could be represented by a business object "business partner." The conception and use of business objects are quite a natural undertaking, since human beings in their everyday life perceive and think about the world as consisting of different objects, carrying certain properties by which they can be distinguished from each other. A business object carries information that is relevant for one's own business, such as age, industry sector, etc. The pieces of information carried by a business object are attributes. An attribute is a representation of a property and therefore represents a well-defined, encapsulated piece of information. It is always linked to a business object, and its semantical definition is unique only in conjunction with a business object. For example, the industry sector is a well-defined piece of information that is linked to and characterizes a business partner. The industry sector "Mining" could be the specific property of a specific business partner.

3 Digitalization Landscape

The digitalization landscape is an attempt to structure, to relate (to each other) and to categorize digitalization topics twofold by means of Enterprise Architecture, which will be described in the following subsections.

3.1 Digitalization Topics

There is a fairly large number of terms standing for various digitalization aspects. A closer inspection of these terms shows that often two different terms actually define pretty much the same thing, or that the same term, used by different people, defines two significantly different things. In the former case the terms are synonymous, in the latter case the terms are homonymous. One also finds that a term is mistaken for its superordinate term. For example, "blockchain" is often used to mean the same as "distributed ledger technology," but the former is actually just a special occurrence of the latter. Against this background and for the sake of identifying individual digitalization topics, the following approach was used:

- To achieve a rough list of digitalization topics, a market analysis in the wider sense has been conducted. The market analysis combined our own project experience with targeted interviews with clients, scanning of the academic literature and discussions with universities and research institutions. Also, an assessment of the relevance of the different topics was part of the analysis, so that only those topics with a high potential impact were considered.
- The rough list of digitalization topics was then consolidated in the sense that both synonymy and homonymy and the consideration of both a term and its superordinate term are avoided (see above).

The result of this approach is the following list of the digitalization topics most frequently referred to, where each of the digitalization topics within the list can be seen, for good reason, as addressing something specific and separate from the other topics. The list with suggestive names and explanations represents the targeted structuring of the digitalization topics:

- **Distributed Ledger Technology (DLT)**: Consensus of replicated, shared and synchronized digital data geographically spread across multiple sites, countries or institutions; a specific type of this technology is blockchain (Government Office for Science [UK] 2016).
- **Artificial Intelligence (AI)**: A broad term meaning the methods and technology for an automation of intellectual tasks, which are usually performed by humans; comprises both the automation of complex tasks based on prescribed rules (e.g., chess computer) and machine learning, where the functional dependency between a set of input information on the one hand and output information on the other is determined in an automated manner (Chollet 2017).
- **Robotic Process Automation (RPA)**: Robotic process automation is a productivity tool that allows a user to configure one or more scripts (which some vendors refer to as "bots") to activate specific keystrokes in an automated fashion. The result is that the bots can be used to mimic or emulate selected tasks (transaction steps) within an overall business or IT process. These may include manipulating data, passing data to and from different applications, triggering responses or executing transactions. RPA uses a combination of user interface interaction and descriptor technologies. The scripts can overlay on one or more software applications (Gartner 2020).
- **Hyperautomation**: Integrative combination of technologies such as robotics and process automation, artificial intelligence and process mining for the sake of a more advanced level of automation that the single contributing technology alone cannot achieve (Gartner 2019); for a

detailed description see separate article of this book (Liermann et al., Hyperautomation [Automated Decision-Making as Part of RPA] 2021).
- **In-Memory Database (IMDB)**: Database management system that primarily relies on main memory for computer data storage; faster than disk-optimized databases because disk access is slower than memory access, the internal optimization algorithms are simpler and execute fewer CPU instructions; accessing data in-memory eliminates seek time when querying the data, which provides faster and more predictable performance than disk (Plattner 2015).
- **Graph Database**: Specific type of database that uses graph structures for semantic queries with nodes, edges and properties to represent and store data (Bourbakis 1998).
- **Distributed Computing**: Computing that happens on different networked computers, which communicate and coordinate their actions by passing messages to one another; problems to be solved are divided into different tasks, where each of the tasks is solved by a different computer of the network (Tanenbaum and van Steen 2017).
- **Internet of Things (IoT)**: Network of physical objects that are embedded with sensors, software and other technologies for the purpose of connecting and exchanging data with other devices and systems over the internet (Mattern and Floerkemeier 2010).
- **Mobile Computing**: Mobile computing is human/computer interaction in which a computer is expected to be transported during normal usage, which allows for the transmission of data, voice and video. Mobile computing involves mobile communication, mobile hardware and mobile software. Communication issues include ad hoc networks and infrastructure networks as well as communication properties, protocols, data formats and concrete technologies. Hardware includes mobile devices or device components (Wikipedia 2020).
- **Quantum Computing**: A computation that is based on the explicit use of quantum phenomena, most notably superposition and entanglement; the computation happens on quantum computers, which are computers specifically designed for quantum computing (Consensus Study Report 2019).
- **Natural Language Processing (NLP)**: Natural language is processed by machines with the help of artificial methods. The goal is to have a distinct language between humans and machines (Vajjala and Majumder 2020).
- **Process Mining**: Set of techniques for the analysis of business processes for the sake of a better understanding and potential improvement of the

processes; the analysis refers to process meta-data in the form of event logs and identifies patterns and details (van der Aalst 2016).

3.2 Classification Matrix

The classification matrix is a mapping of the digitalization topics (see subsection "Digitalization Topics") onto business capability sub-domains. The mapping refers to the sub-domain level because it has a good informative value without being too complex for an overview (in the form of the digitalization landscape). The type of relationship on which the mapping is based is that of support, where a sub-domain is the subject and a digitalization topic is the object. Thus, the mapping expresses which of the sub-domains is required (supports) in a wide sense for the establishment of a specific digitalization topic. For this reason, only the business capability area "Support" is explicitly considered for the classification matrix. For the sake of compactness, the mapping only comprises those sub-domains that support at least one digitalization topic. The mapping corresponds to a classification of the digitalization topics against the background of a given Enterprise Architecture in the form of the sub-domain landscape. For this reason, the totality of these mappings is called the "classification matrix." Note that in the classification matrix a sub-domain is represented as a row and a digitalization topic as a column. In this context, the convention is applied that the subject within a subject/object relation is represented by a row and the object by a column. The classification matrix is available on our website.

3.3 Impact Matrix

The impact matrix is a mapping of the digitalization topics (see subsection "Digitalization Topics") onto the banking business capability domains. It contains the information as to which of the digitalization topics has a potential use for business capabilities within a domain. The corresponding type of relationship is that of a use where a digitalization topic is the subject and a domain is the object. To phrase it differently, the mappings express which digitalization topic can be used for or has a potential impact on a certain domain. In this case, the mapping refers to the domain level because it has a good informative value without being too complex for an overview. In contrast to the classification matrix, not just the area of "Support" is considered, since the business capability domains for banking business in a narrower sense are of particular interest here. For this reason, the totality of these mappings is called "impact matrix." Note that in the classification matrix a digitalization topic is represented by a column and a sub-domain by a row, whereas in the impact matrix the digitalization topics are represented by the different rows and the banking business capability domains by a column.

In the impact matrix, we distinguish between three levels of impact: If there are well-known, established or strong business cases for the application of a specific digitalization topic in the context of a specific business capability domain, the impact is referred to as level 1: "high potential impact." If there are business cases or reasonable ideas for use cases, the impact is referred to as level 2: "medium potential impact." If there are far-fetched or even no ideas for use cases, the impact is referred to as level 3: "low potential or no impact."

The following selected examples of entries in the impact matrix are given for illustrative purposes (high impact cases):

Distributed Ledger Technology (DLT) has a potentially high impact on

- **Operations**: Distributed Ledger Technology is of great relevance for the whole Operations area, e.g., due to the integral use of smart contracts, which can greatly increase the efficiency of the process (Bettio et al. 2019) or the credit processing for syndicated loans.
- **Payment Transactions**: DLT is considered to have a high and arguably even disruptive impact on the Payment Transactions domain, since, as the key component of Bitcoin and Litecoin, it will change payment processes and the payment infrastructure.
- **IT Management**: In the IT Management domain, DLT can greatly affect identity and access management.

Artificial Intelligence has a potentially high impact on

- **Sales**: Artificial Intelligence has a high potential to increase the sales of banks, e.g., by offering tailor-made products to their clients. It is therefore one of the key technologies for online sales companies (e.g., Amazon) to analyze their existing clients and to find new clients for the purpose of increasing sales.

- **Credit Processing**: AI can also significantly enhance the Credit Processing domain by facilitating the credit decision-making process with a sophisticated and at the same time automated analysis of a (potential) client. A similar argument holds for the ongoing Risk Monitoring of clients, where early indications for a deterioration of the creditworthiness of the clients can be obtained based on a complex analysis of behavioral data.
- **Data Management**: In the sub-topic of data quality management, a novel approach has been established by ifb (see [Liermann et al. 2019] and [Führer and Hartung 2021]). Filling a data lake with the content of the daily data flows serves as a data basis for training a machine learning model. After some training, the system appears to be an excellent benchmark for the correctness of subsequent datasets. Thus, insufficient data quality can be detected quite early in the daily data flow chain.
- **Human Capital Management**: Of course, Artificial Intelligence can also be of great value for the Human Capital Management domain, since it allows an analysis of applicants using sophisticated methods (including the analysis of data available on the internet).

Robotic Process Automation (RPA) has a potentially high impact on

- **Credit Processing & Transaction Management**: Robotic Process Automation can greatly facilitate Credit Processing and Transaction Management, which usually comprise many manual processes. Empirically, one finds that many of these processes do not have to be manual and therefore can become automated.
- **Business Process Management**: The same argument as in the case above holds for Business Process Management, since also in this case there are usually many processes that are not necessarily manual.

Hyperautomation has a potentially high impact on

- **Credit Processing, Transaction Management & Business Process Management**: The same arguments largely hold for Hyperautomation as for Robotics Process Automation and therefore it is of great potential value for both Credit Processing, Transaction Management and Business Process Management. But Hyperautomation can further strengthen automation within these domains by incorporating such elements as the identification and analysis of documents in the automation (the analysis of documents is a typical "manual" task for people busy in these domains). A detailed example of the application in the context of Credit Processing is discussed in another article of this book (Liermann et al. 2021).

In-Memory Database (IMDB) has a potentially high impact on

- **Bank Management**: An In-Memory Database is a modern technology to significantly reduce computing time, which is of particular importance for those domains where large amounts of data (e.g., whole portfolios) are to be processed. This typically refers to all domains within the area of Bank Management, where complex calculations involving large amounts of data are typical. A striking example of the impact of increasing performance by using In-Memory Databases in the Risk Management domain can be found in another article of this book (Thiele 2021).
- **Payment Transactions**: Payment Transactions is another domain where computational speed is of enormous importance, since large numbers of transactions are to be processed within very short time intervals.

Graph Databases have a potentially high impact on

- **Sales**: Graph Databases can be beneficial for sales due to the fact that within this area one usually has to deal with strongly networked (sales-related) information of very different kinds.
- **Bank Management**: Graph Databases can also be of great value for the Bank Management area for analyzing events and scenarios according to assumed complex cause-and-effect chains (a cause-and-effect chain is a specific kind of network). For non-financial risk, this is described in another article of this book (Liermann und Tieben 2021).
- **Data Management**: In addition, Graph Databases are of great value in the Data Management domain, e.g., for the storage of business and technical data-lineage-related information.

Distributed Computing has a potentially high impact on

- **Bank Management** and **Payment Transactions**: Distributed computing is (like In-Memory Databases) a modern technology by which computing time can be greatly reduced. Correspondingly, the same arguments hold as for In-Memory Databases, and it can be argued that the biggest impact is on the Bank Management and the Payment Transactions domain. Its relevance for risk management (which is a part of Bank Management) is described in another article of this book (Thiele 2021).

Internet of Things (IoT) has a potentially high impact on

- **Sales**: The Internet of Things can be very helpful in the whole Sales area. There are manifold possible use cases in this emerging field, which is sometimes called "Banking of Things." One example is gaining information about customers via user-specific data collected from real-world objects like cars or smart home objects. The information can be used to place product offerings in a more specific way or can sharpen the risk profile of potential borrowers. Beyond that, new hybrid products are becoming more and more important. For example, in the field of e-mobility, not only booking and usage of e-cars but also the payment of the corresponding fees can be connected with the user scenario.
- **Payments**: The aforementioned use case can also be regarded from a Payments point of view. In addition, a whole variety of use cases arises from interactive and internet-based loudspeakers/microphones. The acoustical placement of an order could trigger a process for the corresponding payments. Of course, banking transactions themselves could also be prompted by voice, starting from money transfers up to ordering securities (Albayrak 2017).

Mobile Computing has a potentially high impact on

- **Sales**: Mobile Computing is of particular importance in the sales area, since, for example, the offering of a new loan product, attractive conditions, etc. very often gain the attention of potential clients while using their smartphones.
- **Transaction Management**: The Transaction Management domain can be significantly affected by the significant increase in flexibility of trading.
- **Payment Transactions**: The use of Mobile Computing is also very attractive for the Payment Transactions domain, since many clients already use their smart phone to initiate payments, to check their balances, etc.
- **Data Management**: For the Data Management domain, Mobile Computing can be of great use in data quality management, e.g., for instant reporting of severe data quality issues.
- **IT Operations**: A similar argument applies to the IT Operations domain for monitoring of the correct hardware functioning.
- **Human Capital Management**: In the Human Capital Management domain, Mobile Computing can greatly facilitate recruiting, e.g., through the use of recruiting apps.

Quantum Computing has a potentially high impact on

- **Risk Management**: Quantum Computing is considered particularly beneficial for specific classes of tasks, above all mathematical optimization, solving linear equations and cryptography. Mathematical optimization and solving linear equations in turn are particularly important for the Risk Management domain in the modeling context.
- **IT Management**: Quantum Computing is of well-known and particular importance for IT Management due to its impact on identity and access management.

Natural Language Processing (NLP) has a potentially high impact on

- **Sales & Credit Processing**: Natural Language Processing is of particular importance where oral or written natural language has to be analyzed, which is key for the whole Sales area and the Credit Processing domain. Typical use cases include the automated analysis of telephone calls with clients, or the automated extraction of information from original electronic or scanned documents.
- **IT Operations**: Within the IT Operations domain, NLP can be of great value for IT security management, e.g., intrusion detection.
- **Human Capital Management**: For the Human Capital Management domain, NLP can strongly support the task of applicant (and employee) profiling.

Process Mining has a potentially high impact on

- **Sales**: The processes using business capabilities of the capability domain Sales are very much characterized by a bi-directional communication between the bank and its potential customers. Activities from the customer side are particularly worth analyzing. These can deliver insights that allow an optimization of the sales activities.
- **Credit Processing**: The business capabilities within the domain Credit Processing are the constituents of one of the largest process domains in operative banking. Process Mining provides the chance for a holistic understanding, documentation, analysis and enhancement of this variety of process components.
- **Risk Monitoring**: Risk Monitoring also requires a differentiated set of activities, depending on the industry sector, the risk classification, the underlying products, the amount at risk, etc. Therefore, potential for

harmonization and the enhancement of efficiency or even clear documentation can be expected.
- **Business Process Management**: This business capability is the natural objective of Process Mining. Business processes that are difficult to analyze can be digitally reengineered in particular. After that, documentation can be enhanced and efficiency can be optimized.

The impact matrix is available on our website.

4 Summary

This article provides an Enterprise-Architecture-based approach for a structured consideration of the various digitalization topics. The key elements of the approach are a consolidated list of the digitalization topics with compact descriptions, and two different types of mappings. These mappings are intended to mirror different views: The classification matrix expresses which of the functional sub-domains have to become involved for the establishment of a specific digitalization topic. The impact matrix describes which of the functional domains of a bank can potentially benefit from the use of a particular digitalization topic. Altogether this can serve as a solid basis for an assessment of the suitability of a particular digitalization topic for one's own business.

Literature

Albayrak, Sahin. 2017. *Der Bank Blog*. 05 08. https://www.der-bank-blog.de/banking-of-things/technologie/26763.
Banking Industry Architecture Network. 2020. https://bian.org/servicelandscape-8-0/.

Bettio, Bruse, Franke, Jakoby, and Schaerf. 2019. "Hyperledger Fabric as a Blockchain Framework in the Financial Indstry." In *The Impact of Digital Transformation and FinTech on the Finance Professional*, edited by Liermann und Stegmann. Palgrave Macmillan.

Bourbakis. 1998. "Artificial Intelligence and Automation."

Chollet. 2017. *Deep Learning with Python*. Manning Publications.

Consensus Study Report. 2019. "Quantum Computing—Progress and Prospects."

Führer, Manuela, and Sören Hartung. 2021. "AI for Impairment Accounting." In *The Digital Journey of Banking and Insurance, Volume I—Disruption and DNA*, edited by Volker Liermann and Claus Stegmann. New York: Palgrave Macmillan.

Gartner. 2019. *Gartner Top 10 Strategic Technology Trends for 2020*. https://www.gartner.com/smarterwithgartner/gartner-top-10-strategic-technology-trends-for-2020/.

———. 2020. *Robotic Process Automation (RPA)*. https://www.gartner.com/en/information-technology/glossary/robotic-process-automation-rpa.

Government Office for Science (UK). 2016.

Liermann, Volker, and Marian Tieben. 2021. "Use Case—NFR—Using Graph DB for Impact Graphs." Edited by Volker Liermann and Claus Stegmann. Palgrave Macmillan.

Liermann, Volker, Sangmeng Li, and Johannes Waizner. 2021. "Hyperautomation (Automated Decision-Making as Part of RPA)." In *The Digital Journey of Banking and Insurance, Volume I—Disruption and DNA*, edited by Volker Liermann and Claus Stegmann. Palgrave Macmillan.

Liermann, Volker, Sangmeng Li and Norbert Schaudinnus. 2019. "Batch Processing—Pattern Recognition." In *The Impact of Digital Transformation and Fintech on the Finance Professional*, edited by Volker Liermann and Claus Stegmann. New York: Palgrave Macmillan.

Mattern and Floerkemeier. 2010. "From the Internet of Computers to the Internet of Things." *Informatik-Spektrum* 33 (2): 107–121. http://www.vs.inf.ethz.ch/publ/papers/Internet-of-things.pdf.

Plattner. 2015. *A Course in In-Memory Data Management: The Inner Mechanics of In-Memory*. Springer.

Tanenbaum and van Steen. 2017. *Distributed Systems*. Pearson Prentice Hall.

Thiele. 2021. "Financial Navigator—A Modern Approach to Analytical Banking." In *The Digital Journey of Banking and Insurance, Volume I—Disruption and DNA*, edited by Volker Liermann and Claus Stegmann. Palgrave Macmillan.

Vajjala and Majumder. 2020. *Practical Natural Language Processing: A Comprehensive Guide to Building Real-World NLP Systems*. O'Reilly Media.

van der Aalst. 2016. *Process Mining: Data Science in Action*. Springer.

Wikipedia. 2020. *Mobile Computing*. https://en.wikipedia.org/wiki/Mobile_computing.

Digitalization Strategy

Sven Ludwig and Claus Stegmann

1 Introduction

Asset managers, banks, exchanges, and insurers are technology and software companies with a special financial license. This is no secret anymore. As early as 2015, the chairman of one of the largest European banks predicted: "BBVA will be a software company in the future." That fact illustrates: digitalization is possibly more important for financial organizations than for almost all other types of organization. With advanced technologies like AI, cloud, Big Data or distributed ledger, a high percentage of today's workforce can be at least partially digitalized. It is impossible to identify a department not impacted by further and substantial digitalization. However, digital transformation should not only be a means to optimize labor expenses through automation and decrease technology and IT operating spend, but also to accelerate the customer experience. The focus on customer experience is the key to improving the competitive positioning sustainably. As a consequence of the pandemic, this improvement is becoming even more important.

S. Ludwig (✉)
ifb SE, Grünwald, Germany
e-mail: Sven.Ludwig@ifb-group.com

C. Stegmann
ifb Americas, Inc., Charlotte, NC, USA
e-mail: Claus.Stegmann@ifb-group.com

The promise of total digitalization in the financial ecosystem is quickly becoming a reality thanks to advanced technology-based solutions designed to better serve clients while accelerating growth. With more such solutions unfolding, is the day coming that a full-service IT/AI bank requiring little to no human interaction could exist merely on IT servers within the cloud? In the UK, the so-called challenger banks are close to these. There, these challenger banks are said to be gaining around 50,000 customers per week. The multidimensional opportunities and challenges spanned by digitalization, business model, IT investment and customer experience allow disruptive changes. This disruptive character becomes eye-opening when comparing the IT investment of digital challenger banks in the UK (like Monzo, Revolut) with the traditional venerable institutions (like Lloyds, HSBC, Barclays). The per year investments into new technologies by a traditional bank tend to be 10 or more times higher than the all-time funding of a modern technology-based challenger bank (Fig. 1).

Several studies across all types of financial organization have proven that leaders in IT strategy and adoption of advanced technologies perform better

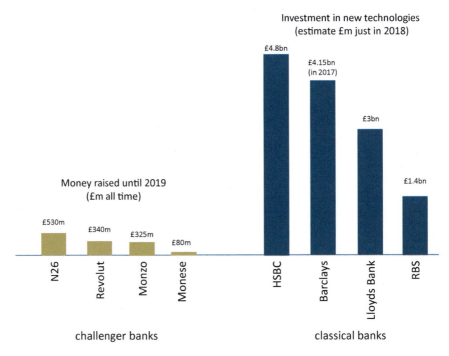

Fig. 1 Investment in IT for transformation per year of traditional banks versus all-time money raised by challenger banks (*Sources* HSBC, Barclays, Lloyds, RBS, N26, Revolut, Monzo, Monese and authors' research, following illustration of Bó © ifb SE)

than the rest. One example is the FIS Readiness Report 2019 (FIS Global 2019). This global research shows the average revenue growth over the last 12 months was more than double for industry leaders (3.3%) compared to the rest of the industry (1.5%). Assessing the differences of the groups reveals that leaders have a higher adoption of advanced technologies. Leaders have 6.5 times more AI-driven solutions implemented than the rest of the industry. 48% of industry leaders are in the process of or have already migrated to the cloud versus 25% of the rest of the industry.

In addition to the availability of new technological options, financial service providers are facing external factors that are already putting pressure on traditional business models or will do so in the coming years.

The low and flat interest rate environment, which has existed for years, is putting pressure on margins, and there is no prospect of rising interest rates. The pressure of regulatory requirements, which has been increasing steadily since the 1990s and was exacerbated by the financial crisis in 2008, has become the new norm in recent years. However, regulatory scrutiny continues to tie up a great deal of capacity, especially at institutions whose business models have evolved historically over time. New market participants, who are increasingly putting the established institutions under pressure with lean and perfectly scalable processes, serve customers at close to zero costs (compared to established banks). The dissection of the value chain also has the advantage on the regulatory requirements side that the data models can be set up efficiently from the outset when implementing the systems that manage the portfolio. This topic also includes the effect of the "sharing economy," in which the financing function is increasingly integrated into the services themselves, e.g., full-service offerings in car sharing.

But there are other factors that are forcing the finance industry to act: banks' business models are under strain due to the current COVID-19 pandemic, which also exposes weaknesses existing in customer access and communication. Furthermore, customer needs and demands themselves will change: Generations Y and Z have grown up with smartphones and social media and expect sustainability thinking to be embedded in the service offering and in the actions of the financial service provider itself. This results in changing needs in the financial institutions' interface with the customer.

To cope with these extensive and sometimes complex problems, it is necessary to derive an individually suitable strategy. The core of its implementation then lies in the sensible use of the new instruments available in the context of digitalization from a cost–benefit perspective.

No doubt, digitalization is a must-do. Figure 2 shows a simple example of traditional banks versus challenger banks. It indicates that digitalization of a

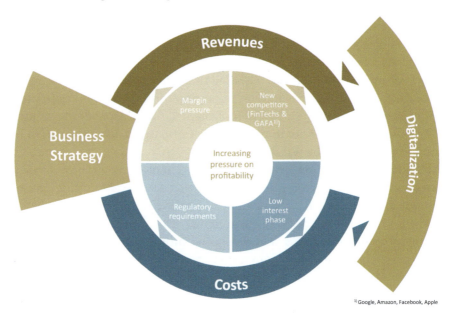

Fig. 2 Illustration of the need for digitalization to counter margin pressure (© ifb SE)

financial organization is far from straightforward. However, this needs to be at the top of the agenda of any organization.

In the following section, we provide a guideline on how to derive a digital transformation strategy. As a starting point, we analyze the evolution of the financial institutions' ecosystem.

For the remainder of this article, we use the term banks for simplification, but the outline covers asset managers, insurers, etc.

2   Digitalization of Banking is Comparable to the Industrial Age but Different

Today's transformation in banking reminds us of the innovation in the automobile production process, namely Ford's Model T, during the industrial revolution. Ford's rethinking and simplification of the production process made it possible for nearly all parts of the car to be manufactured in sequence and churned out at less expense—so much so that automobiles became mainstream (Ludwig 2018).

The key difference between the transformation taking place in banking and the initial industrialization of automobile production is that, in banking, it is not only streamlining the value chain, it is a "de-componentization" of the bank. The transformation leapfrogs the Ford approach and gets closer to the "Just-In-Sequence" method invented some decades ago and applied by car manufacturers these days. Forward-looking banks will orchestrate the manifold of their suppliers and the production line. However, the difference between the physical and the digital goods production is that the assembly belt does not need to stay within the bank. Instead, it leaves the bank and runs through the suppliers' production plants. Then it returns to the bank as a subsequent element of the value chain, the next component of the production process. This de-componentization enables the individual production stations to serve multiple banks. These production stations can become highly efficient since they are simplified to very small components. The smaller they get, the more usable in the mainstream they become. More importantly, such micro-components become infinitely scalable as they can be fully digitalized within the bank and outside the bank.

On the "orchestrating" production line, we transfer data only, nothing else. We transform data, merge it and assess it. Banks can specify a core business model for some components. These components can be offered across many banks making them infinitely scalable.

Taking this into account, it becomes obvious that a digitalization strategy requires a definition of the future business model first.

3 Digitalization Follows Strategy—Business Model Decision Comes First

The bank can transform its business model and essentially become an IT company with a banking license, but it needs to decide whether it intends to be a distributor, orchestrator, or manufacturer.

When developing the business model, the following key dimensions must be considered and put in relation to each other:

- In many cases, the efficiency of Fintech companies, for example, results from the green field approach (Negenman 2021) combining creation from scratch, technology and culture. This approach is known for certain elements of the value chain or specialization in a specific product offering, such as robo-advisors. Here, in contrast to traditional asset management which usually requires high minimum revenues, AI algorithms are applied, enabling high-quality investment decisions at favorable conditions to a broad customer base. When formulating the strategy, a fundamental decision must be made as to whether the customer benefit is achieved through a high degree of specialization of the product portfolio or whether, in contrast, a broad product portfolio offered in a "one-stop-shop" approach is the goal.

- Another objective in defining the business model can be to achieve value creation in the continuous expansion of the customer relationship through a high degree of digitalization in the external customer interface and a superb customer experience. In this case, the strategy is aimed at customer leadership. Alternatively, the strategic goal can also be to strive for cost leadership through efficient processes. Here, a high degree of digitalization in the organization's internal processes creates value that can also be made available, for example, via white labeling to other financial service providers such as Insurtech and Fintech companies that are more interested in customer leadership.
- Adjustments in the business model and also culture are usually associated with significant investments in advanced technologies. In this context, it is necessary to determine the amount and structure of these investments over time. To this end, it must be weighed up to what extent there is a willingness to accept burdens in the current income statement in favor of future earnings. This is also referred to as balancing value and vision. Resulting changes of the status quo must be coordinated with the relevant stakeholders. And even if agreement is reached in this balancing process, there is usually resistance to future technologies that are not fully developed yet. In this context, it must be considered that holding on to proven technologies, processes and methods is riskier, especially in these dynamic times. A fundamental change in our proven paradigm!
- In all decisions regarding customer champion or manufacturer, full-service provider or specialist, and in the value versus vision question, it is necessary to continually examine the (re)orientation of the business model. This is only possible within the framework of agile organizational approaches, since continuous adaptation to permanently changing framework conditions has proven too sluggish in the past with traditional waterfall methods.

Once the future business model or at least the vision is defined, we recommend validating this decisive step for the transformation process under an "entire ecosystem" perspective.

Changing the perspective from the individual organization to the big picture of the financial ecosystem, the impact of digitalization and de-componentization leads to a 90° transformation. This transformation is not a big bang event, it is merely an evolution over the next decade or potentially decades (Fig. 3).

Consequently, the individual bank's strategy needs to be agile, as the new business model is dependent on the evolution of the ecosystem as a whole—some business models may not be possible as key components are not offered at all or not offered in some regions. Thus, the business model requires an ongoing iterative review and alignment under both perspectives—the individual bank's as well as the ecosystem's.

At this point, we want to highlight that the smaller or simpler a component becomes, the higher its value (creation) typically is and hence the achievable revenue and profit. Scalability and addressable market size become the key determinants. The revenue expectation of a regionally acting minimally viable bank is limited. A large global bank can therefore most often not be transferred into a single minimally viable bank or a micro-component. A digital native and digital only bank is likely not the result of a transformation of a large global organization. It is more likely that those banks are a result of a green field approach—new and stand-alone or financed by an

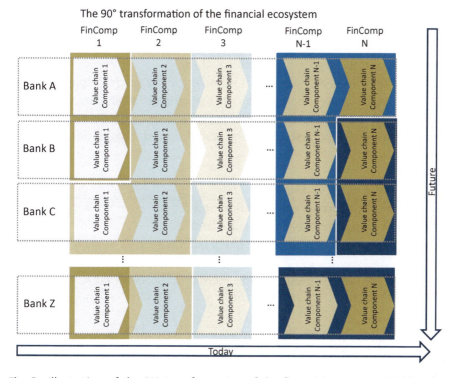

Fig. 3 Illustration of the 90° transformation of the financial ecosystem (© ifb SE)

existing banking group. Today, there are both. However, digital native does not imply success in both cases. N26, a prominent start-up bank, has withdrawn from the UK despite being successful in other countries. RBS decided to build its new digital Bank Bó from scratch. Launched at the end of 2019, Bó was closed just six months later in May 2020 having gained just 11,000 customers—including "friends and family" of the bank. This indicates that digital only banks will eventually only differentiate via their brands, not so much by the services offered. We also predict that only three to five per region will survive the competition in the medium term. The next chapter of this book will analyze and describe this green field approach in detail.

Having illustrated that, for the evolution of the financial ecosystem, it is helpful to look at components rather than a full-service bank, we will derive the possible digitalization strategy in the next step.

4 Path Toward the Digitalization Strategy—Degree of Digitalization

Total digitalization in banking could result in a full IT/AI bank—the so-called "digital native." As argued above, it is not unrealistic for a bank to exist on a server with limited human involvement. For a micro-component, this "digital native" stage is surely more realistic.

A dramatic wind-down over night is not a viable strategy of most substantial banks and thus not the outcome of the business model exercise above. To define and implement their digitalization strategy, such substantial organizations must cluster their processes and business capabilities into four groups:

- Group I: Customer-facing frontends
- Group II: Capsulate now to digitalize now
- Group III Capsulate now to digitalize later
- Group IV: Capsulate now to outsource later/as soon as possible.

We add an additional group in the section "The New Fifth Group and Strategy Dimension" below. This fifth group should be ignored for the moment.

The grouping needs to be in line with the strategic business model. It is derived from the defined business model on the one hand and the bundle of current business processes and capabilities plus IT architecture components on the other.

The grouping exercise is an iterative process. We provide further insights and guidance on this within the chapter "Digitalization Strategy" in this book. In the iterative process, each previously defined object is revisited and broken up into more granular objects in the next iteration. This allows to start with an Area, then breaking it down into Domain, Subdomain, Cluster, and finally into a Business Capability.

A micro-component in this definition is the smallest possible object, ideally a Cluster or Business Capability. Once the most granular stage is reached, the components can be analyzed one by one for the best applicable digitalization strategy. The chapter "Digitalization Strategy" summarizes important technologies and an impact matrix of these for business functions according to the structure of the BIAN Service Landscape (Banking Industry Architecure Network 2020).

Capsulating and embedding all workflows into an Application Programming Interface (API) framework allows an asynchronous transformation of micro-components and integration of the valuable asset data across the entire organization.[1] Automation, increased performance or improved capabilities in one component are directly leveraged by all upstream and downstream processes. Over time, with many decision hooks for agile adjustments, the organization is moving towards an optimal stage in the current ecosystem evolution.

Banks that have decided to remain service organizations for their customers need to demonstrate their advanced digitalization stage and modernize their frontend for customer interaction. Fully digital, mainly physical or a hybrid approach are possible. The more digital, the greater the cultural and process change for staff and clients.

4.1 Customer-Facing Frontend

As already stated, we regard a modernization of the customer access point a must-do.

A credit institution has a variety of opportunities to interact with the end customer. The end customer expects a combination of self-determined interaction possibilities via online portals or mobile applications as well as individual support for his or her concerns. The appearance, the ease of use and the functionalities of the digital customer interfaces provided in combination with the support provided by the traditional customer interfaces (e.g., the branch) influence the user experience of the end customer and his or her

---

[1] Value created from this data belongs to the fifth group.

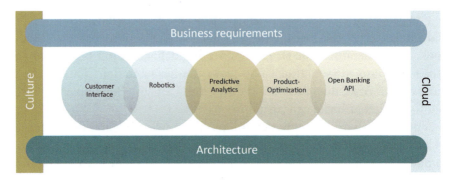

Fig. 4 Digitalization and innovation in the context of customer frontend (© ifb SE)

perception of a financial institution. The end customer expects a consistent user experience across all customer channels.

In order to provide the end customer digital customer channelson the one hand and to ensure a consistent customer experience on the other, customer-oriented processes must be viewed in their entirety and internal company structures must be aligned with them. In addition to the consideration of the end customer, the customer interface requires an analysis of the bank employees' options for action to create concepts for the simplified visualization and instrumentalization of customer data to ensure this uniform customer experience. These measures enable banks to optimize individual customer service in the branch and to enable further support via digital communication channels.

In summary, the customer-facing frontend itself already combines culture and several advanced technologies which need to be orchestrated in an adaptable and scalable architecture (Fig. 4).

4.2 Capsulate Now to Digitalize Now

For each micro-component, a cost–benefit analysis for digitalization is required. It is crucial to identify whether a micro-component can be digitalized or not. Past experience is a suboptimal advisor as technology progresses too rapidly. It is essential that each decision is made with an open mind. Advanced technologies are already used successfully in banking, far more than we tend to assume. Consider where machine learning and AI are already being used in banking—documentation analysis, customer profiling for marketing purposes, virtual assistants, fraud detection, and managing customer data, for example. AI technology replaces agents in call centers for standard issues. Credit analysts receive downgrade warnings from processing neuronal networks processing news in natural language. But what about tasks requiring a high level of expertise, such as the identification of potential sources of risks? True risks are often overlain by data issues. It is critical to identify risks caused simply by data issues but identifying them is a complex task. Petabytes of data need to be screened, put into context and often compared with history. For market risk, there is typically an interaction of market data, valuations, changes of positions and incorrectly captured information that needs to be considered when explaining changes or sources of risks. Machine learning can provide a faster, more complete and more robust but lean automated process with little use of valuable experts' time.

4.3 Capsulate Now to Digitalize Later

If a component cannot be digitalized today, the likelihood of its future digitalization or even necessity needs to be evaluated. This can impact the business case for outsourcing substantially. OTC transaction processing is a complex task today. Transferring OTC derivatives from contract to computer program code is possible. So-called smart contracts based on blockchain technologies could make entire tasks obsolete at some point. The second largest German banking group DZ BANK successfully tested the "processing" of digital OTC interest rate swaps with another major bank, BayernLB. For details see (Christian Fries 2019).

Unconstrained imagination could be helpful for this task as well as for developing stress test scenarios.

4.4 Capsulate Now to Outsource Later

For a specific bank, it may not be possible or economically viable to digitalize a component. At the same time, this component may not contribute to a specific unique selling point or improve the competitive positioning. For such situations, the bank should prepare to outsource these tasks. The iterative process above guarantees that the decision is made at the least granular level to avoid any sunk costs.

Often organizations do not take the necessary steps and outsource as they are bound to the assumption that there is no Business Process as a Service (BPaaS) offering available. Today's unavailability of offers does not imply that there is no potential service. Recent research by Reportlinker.com estimated that the BPaaS business will grow from USD 9bn today to USD 68.7bn by 2027 (Reportlinker.com 2020). The accounting and finance segment across industries will grow to USD 19.8bn on its own. A number of technology and advisory organizations are ready to onboard components and drive the 90° transformation of the ecosystem and make outsourcing possible much earlier than often expected.

BPaaS is scalable by definition and can ensure that the bank's operations are scalable end-to-end. The pandemic has shown that banks can reduce operation risks and achieve operational resilience with BPaaS providers. However, a rigorous third-party risk assessment and monitoring framework is absolutely required.

5   The New Fifth Group and Strategy Dimension

The groups mentioned above (except the customer-facing frontend itself) assume a de-componentization and digitalization in a "like-for-like" context. The transformation of the financial ecosystem does not happen on a whiteboard without the consumers.

The new financial reality with internal and external digitalization also creates new "components." A new dimension of digitalization is opened when there is an overlap of internal and external digitalization. The second new dimension and hence area of disruption is created by approaches which generate a link between internal and external digitalization. We call this second field "Analytical Customer Approach." The following Fig. 5 illustrates this distinguishing character. End customers obtain services via digital distribution channels and in real time, exchange knowledge and experience via social networks and only open initial contact with the provider after extensive research of the market offering. For the future business models of financial service providers, this means providing attractive interfaces and functionalities that ensure a simple and user-friendly experience for the customer. This is important because, in the future, competitive and market success will be determined on the one hand by positive customer experience. On the other hand, it is important to target customers with individually relevant product offers. For this purpose, the methods developed in the context of so-called predictive analytics, which apply, for instance, the tools of AI and machine learning, are important.

For the description and illustration of the distributed ledger and payments area we would like to refer to the specific chapters on distributed ledger technologies of this book.

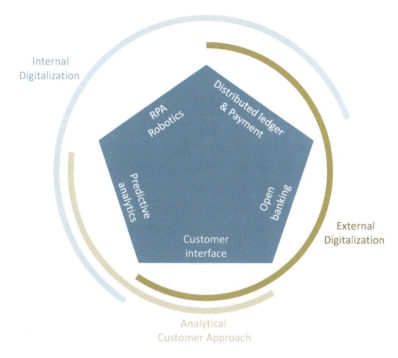

Fig. 5 Illustration of areas of digitalization that typically have potential beyond like-for-like and offer disruptions (© ifb SE)

6 Conclusion and Outlook

The more transformational the target (business) strategy, the more an agile transformation is required. As the most important core principle and priority for a successful transformation, the world's best bank DBS highlighted as a reason "[…] ensure we adopt a start-up culture […]" (Henderson 2019; Merkt et al. 2021).

Overall, the velocity of change is increasing. The speed at which a financial organization can adapt is therefore crucial for sustainable success. Much as we would like to know a strategic business model for the next two decades, external forces and events show that transformation is an ongoing aspect of uncertainty.

6.1 Technology and Financial Innovation

Innovations in technology impact financial organizations directly and indirectly. Self-driving cars are an example of a significant indirect impact. With self-driving cars, the insurance premium market will drop significantly.

Premiums from motor insurance accounted for more than 40% of the overall non-life insurance premiums in 2018 (see also [Motorintelligence 2021]). Therefore, the damage insurance market depends heavily on cars. What will happen therefore if there are close to zero car accidents?

It is well known that innovations are being adopted faster than ever. Look at the speed of penetration of innovations over time: cars, telephone, TV, email, and finally Facebook and "alikes." Some of those innovations, like PayPal, are specifically disruptions to the financial industry. Others, like machine learning and artificial intelligence, have only just started to indicate their disruptive power in this market.

6.2 Political and Government Initiatives

Political initiatives can be a trigger for innovations and change. In the European Union, there are a few examples, e.g., Open Banking, Single European Payment Area. Open Banking creates new business models and new competition. The ability to allow a layer on top of multiple financial organizations is one dimension. The ability to electronically source customer-specific data from a bank (with the approval of the customer) allows new analytics. A real-time credit approval from third-party platforms is now possible. With instant payment, the clients receive the "cash" frictionless on their bank accounts—even if the bank account is with a different credit institution.

A more global catalyst for change is the transition to a carbon–neutral economy. This has a substantial impact on the business models of financial organizations.

6.3 Regulatory and Other External Catalysts of Digitalization

Though the COVID-19 pandemic is unprecedented when it comes to disruptive character for the financial industry, it is just one example. In Europe, the European Commissions FinTech Action Plan or some elements of the CRRII Quick Fix are explicitly designed to speed up digitalization. In Singapore, the regulatory bodies push the use of Regtech, Fintech and Subtech explicitly.

If we now combine the pieces of the puzzle, it becomes obvious that the financial markets will change from the bottom up. What happens if we enable real-time features in some key areas? Instant payment, digital treasury drives us to a true 24/7 financial ecosystem. This forces banks to operate continuously without any cut-offs or end of day. This will lead to intra-day interest payments and eventually the OTC derivatives world will move to the automated smart contracts mentioned above.

Predicting the path of evolution in the financial markets is therefore becoming more challenging. However, it is clear that a de-componentized structure of a financial organization enables a continuous, cost-efficient and fast adjustment of the organization's business model. The journey of transformation is not about to start. It has begun and adoption is not optional.

Literature

Banking Industry Architecure Network. 2020. https://bian.org/servicelandscape-8-0/.

Christian Fries, et al. 2019. *Implementing a Financial Derivativeas Smart Contrac.* https://www.researchgate.net/publication/331485558_Implementing_a_financial_derivative_as_smart_contract.

FIS Global. 2019. *Readiness Report 2019.* https://thefintechtimes.com/fis-research/.

Henderson, James. 2019. *How DBS Became the 'World's Best Bank' Through Digital Transformation.* https://www.cio.com/article/3433948/how-dbs-became-the-worlds-best-bank-through-digital-transformation.html: CIO.

Ludwig, Sven. 2018. *Could a Full-Service It/Ai Bank Devoid of Human Interaction Be in Our Future?* Website. FIS Global. https://www.fisglobal.com/en/insights/what-we-think/2018/october/could-a-full-service-it-ai-bank-devoid-of-human-interaction-be-in-our-future.

Merkt, Rainer, Veronika Lang, and Anna Schmidt. 2021. "Digi-Cultural Mindset." In *The Digital Journey of Banking and Insurance, Volume I—Disruption and DNA*, edited by Volker Liermann and Claus Stegmann. New York: Palgrave Macmillan.

Motorintelligence. 2021. "GLOBAL MOTOR INSURANCE MARKET." https://www.mordorintelligence.com/industry-reports/global-motor-insurance-market.

Negenman, Ebbe. 2021. "The Knab Story: How We Turned the Bank Around." In *The Digital Journey of Banking and Insurance, Volume I—Disruption and DNA*, edited by Volker Liermann and Claus Stegmann. New York: Palgrave Macmillan.

Reportlinker.com. 2020. *Global Business Process as a Service (BPaaS) Industry.* https://www.reportlinker.com/p03283202/Global-Business-Process-as-a-Service-BPaaS-Industry.html?utm_source=GNW.

The Knab Story: How We Turned the Bank Around

Ebbe Negenman

1 Introduction

Knab Bank was introduced in 2012. It was a new star in the Dutch banking firmament. Set up in the aftermath of the global financial crisis in 2008, Knab aimed to be a fully digital bank with a human touch to put client interests first. As of today in the Netherlands, Knab is still unique in this positioning. Still among the banks with one of the highest Net Promoter Scores in the Dutch market, we are one of the clients' favorite. A steady growth in client savings resulted in a balance sheet of €16 billion, which is a sizeable amount in the Dutch market. And with a unique proposition for entrepreneurs and small businesses, Knab is still growing. After eight years, it is safe to conclude that the combination of being digital with a human touch was ahead of its time and resulted in Knab making a firm footprint on the future of the Dutch market.

But banking is adapting to change, and the balancing game never stops. In this section, we would like to share the lessons learned from our history. This is basically well summarized by the well-known quote by Churchill: "Success is not final, failure is not final. It is the courage to continue that counts."

E. Negenman (✉)
knab, The Hague, Netherlands
e-mail: ebbe.negenman@knab.nl

2 Compliance

In banking, more than one stakeholder has to be satisfied: clients, shareholders, and regulators. With the growing business also came increasing regulation and compliance responsibilities. The 2018 fine imposed on ING Bank due to KYC/AML issues reminded everyone in the sector that risking non-compliance is extremely foolhardy.

Being a far smaller bank than ING, but having to comply with similar regulations, compliance is incredibly demanding for Knab, as well. We have to be compliant without creating a business risk for the bank, i.e., a risk that the costs of being in control seriously affect shareholder return. We solved this puzzle by staying close to what we are good at: being digital. So instead of hiring dozens of KYC specialists and entering manual file checking as the others did, we chose to invest in a digital client acceptance process first and next used that to enhance our total client base. It was not an easy journey, but it also showed that to achieve great things we needed only two things: a plan and not enough budget to fulfill it. These two ingredients are the perfect base for innovation. And so we did.

3 Culture

Competition in the digital landscape has grown since Knab was launched. Also fueled by the recent Covid-19 crisis, the digital inertia seems to have faded at other banks, and more banks are pursuing a technology-driven transformation.

The Knab core, nourishing customer engagement by deploying a mix of digital and human interactions, and intelligent use of novel partnerships, is becoming the standard.

Copying is of course nothing new in retail banking. For sure, savings and current accounts do not differ in terms of product specs across banks, neither do annuity mortgages. But what cannot be easily copied is the perception clients have of the bank. Which is for the large part driven by the company culture. Therefore, we foster our company culture, of being open and honest to our clients and to ourselves. But also being entrepreneurial just like our clients and willing to take the intelligent risk for our clients. And, last but not least, the ability to learn is pivotal in our selection procedures. Because ultimately we believe, that the ability to learn faster than your competitors is the only sustainable competitive advantage.

4 The Client Really is No. 1

At Knab, we strive to put the interest of the client first in all we do. The timing of the birth of Knab, just after the global financial crisis of 2008, was not unplanned. We filled the emotional gap of the clients not feeling at ease with their old banks. As is standard in innovation, the spark for Knab was lit by this dissatisfaction of the founders with their banks.

More importantly, we held onto this vision. Although we changed offices, the slogan from one of the founders is still on the wall: "Let's do banking differently by putting the interests of the client first." It is passion for the client that is the ultimate driver: human, open, positive, and entrepreneurial. And we put our money where our mouth is: this implies no bonuses for the board members.

From the start, Knab excelled in communication with clients. Knab is and was aware that communication with the client is not about speaking, but mostly about listening to the client. At the start, Knab clients were called members. Truly putting the wording in line with the desired culture.

5 Market Segmentation

Being entrepreneurial also attracted entrepreneurial clients. Although not foreseen at the start, Knab became a market leader in this niche segment. Knab was and is very attractive to small businesses and business starters due to the ease of use, fully digital client acceptance (entrepreneurs love to do business, in contrast to spending time at the bank opening an account), and the low costs of holding an account. It was not a fully worked out plan, and we were also helped by the incumbent banks not seeing this segment as attractive, but we managed to grow the bank to almost 160,000 clients in the first five years. Relabeling products and combining the label with Aegon Bank resulted in a base of 600,000 clients today.

And we are still growing: even in the current Covid-19 situation, we are seeing strong growth and a high Net Promoter Score. Almost always in the top of the list comparing the Dutch banks. We still believe the growth is founded in being fully digital, combined with a direct and human touch unlike any other bank. Knab built up an excellent customer service desk that is readily available with knowledgeable employees (we invest large amounts in training and education).

6 Learning from Mistakes

At Knab, we make and made mistakes. At the launch in 2012, the current account product was priced at 7.50 euros per month. Completely fair and transparent pricing, which was not common at that time. But it also resulted in headlines that the new bank in town was the most expensive one. And, yes, we won the first prize in that. But Dutch clients are known for being penny wise. To get traction on our client base, we had to lower the price to 5 euros and basically accept six months delay in seeing some growth. Not so smart, if you think about it afterward.

Cost management was something we made mistakes in as well. It is said that only half of the costs of marketing are useful, but you do not know which half. It is likely that we overspent substantially. But since we have no branches in the street, how would a customer know us if we did not bring attention to ourselves? As a result, marketing budgets some years exceeded that of our shareholder Aegon. Although some of these costs might have been unavoidable, in hindsight we could probably have targeted our customer segments more efficiently. At the start we were still aiming for any client. And still, compared to other banks with a similar balance sheet volume, we are still quite costly with a high cost/income ratio. So there is work to do.

Another mistake was the prioritization o the control, Risk control was actually not as central as it is now. I only joined the board as Chief Risk Officer in 2017. And my assignment on the first years was to do some restoration on risk and compliance. Of course in hindsight, compliance in design would have reduced the costs of reparation. But this is to a large part wisdom that we gained, it is also fair to say that if you overthink the risks beforehand, you might not have started at all.

The big takeaway from all the mistakes for us is that you cannot be successful without a learning culture. Being actually open to your mistakes and see the obstacles as learning points. So, as of today, this taking of intelligent risks mentality is what we cherish most in our corporate values.

7 The Future

Although the Covid-19 shock is not a banking crisis by itself, we think it will reshape the technological transformation of banks. We have noticed an accelerated shift to digital and reconfiguration of the branch network in retail banking at other banks. And there are cost reasons for this as well: the digital-only bank can operate at very low cost, up to 70% lower compared to traditional operations. We therefore expect that tech banks will be the future.

Although we should be careful with predictions, low interest rates might be here to stay for a while and will reduce net interest margins, pushing banks to rethink their spread business models. With our lending platforms, we are already making a move from risk intermediation toward intermediation of services. We are also exploring monetizing our business in ways other than banking. To innovate with service-related income and new products that move away from the dependence on interest rates. Adding an accounting tool for our customers to the current account is a good example. Here, too, we are not alone: growing competition from tech players with embedded finance functions is expected.

The way we work will change and maintaining the company culture while working more remotely is something we are struggling with. We now often organize ourselves in groups of up to ten without formal meetings. We have found that this produces efficient output, because the teams can interact productively without having a large number of meetings to coordinate across functions.

Important decisions that banks will face when investing in new digital initiatives will be more relevant than ever. If, for example, the competitors invest in quantum computing and we do not, our market share will likely fall along with our reputation.

In any case, we think we have something in our hands that can be promising. Not because we see what has never been seen before, but because we think about what has never been thought about before—what the client needs every day.

Accounting/Controlling

This part visits the accounting and controlling department of a financial institution and tries to differentiate between the things that are about to change significantly (disruption) and those that remain more or less stable (DNA). Selected subjects range from the context of the CFO[1] to the future tasks he or she should focus on.

Naturally, most improvements driven by digital transformation in the departments of accounting and controlling are located in inside digitalization (aiming to speed up processes, reduce costs, or improve prediction using [mainly historical] data).

Given the potential of machine learning to better predict the future, the role of controlling is changing continuously. Controllers used to analyze the profits and costs of the company and support the planning process. The role has been enlarged to deliver the impact of strategic options. Controllers not only analyze and report the past but also offer (scenario-based) insights into the insecure future.

The future is dynamic in many ways, as expressed in the acronym VUCA.[2] The planning process is key in the ability to predict the future movement of the company. Value-driver-oriented planning is a concept that dynamizes planning and widens the analysis capabilities.

The role of a CFO must be redefined. The purpose and orientation of the CFO can range from giving up own goals because the CFO is reduced to a pure data provider, to master of robotics orchestrating automated processes

---

[1] Chief Financial Officer.
[2] Volatility, uncertainty, complexity, ambiguity.

and implementing automated decisions where possible,[3] to a powerful master of data having the best crystal ball (data and models) to predict the future.

The first chapter in this part seeks possible new roles for the CFO and the accounting department (see Jensen 2021). The chapter unites resilience and agility in finance. It offers—among other insights—a setup for how to keep business processes and data synchronized. The chapter summarizes the benefits of the steps proposed and delivers a roadmap to implement them. The second chapter (see Valjanow et al. 2021) revisits the concept of value-driver-oriented planning.[4] It shows the integration of machine learning to dynamize the planning process by external (and internal) value drivers. A spotlight is put on the insurance industry with a whole section dedicated to this industry. In addition, the practical challenge of integrating unscheduled repayment into the planning process is explored. The third and final chapter (Führer and Hartung 2021) delivers a project summary of a real-life example of machine learning in the context of impairment accounting. It shows the optimization potential by an automated identification and resolving mechanism of faulty postings.

Literature

Hartung, Sören, and Manuela Führer. 2021. "AI for Impairment Accounting." In *The Digital Journey of Banking and Insurance, Volume I—Disruption and DNA*, edited by Volker Liermann and Claus Stegmann. New York: Palgrave Macmillan.

Jensen, Jens-Peter. 2021. "The Need for Resilience and Agility in Finance ." In *Palgrave Macmillan*, edited by Volker Liermann and Claus Stegmann. New York: Palgrave Macmillan.

Valjanow, Simon, Philipp Enzinger, and Florian Dinges. 2019. "Digital Planning—Driver-Based Planning Levaraged by Predictive Analytics." In *The Impact of Digital Transformation and Fintech on the Finance Professional*, edited by Volker Liermann and Claus Stegmann. New York: Palgrave Macmillan.

Valjanow, Simon, Philipp Enzinger, Daniel Suttner, and Maik Alexander Schmidt. 2021. "Value-Driver-Oriented Planning—Management-Oriented Design and Value Driver Identification." In *The Digital Journey of Banking and Insurance, Volume I—Disruption and DNA*, edited by Volker Liermann and Claus Stegmann. New York: Palgrave Macmillan.

---

[3] Where the frequency and complexity of the decisions is low enough to apply machine learning.

[4] See (Valjanow, Enzinger and Dinges, Digital planning—driver-based planning levaraged by predictive analytics 2019).

The Need for Resilience and Agility in Finance

Jens-Peter Jensen

1 Industry Challenges

Banks are facing tremendous disruption and opportunity at the same time.

- The current challenges in the context of Covid-19 have clearly shown the benefits of and the need for more digitalization in financial services. As a consequence, banks will only accelerate their digital transformation efforts to compete successfully in a fast-changing environment with fintech companies and non-banks offering more and more financial services.
- Banking provides vital services to our society and its impact is poised to grow. But to fulfill this potential, banks need to become intelligent enterprises to respond to increased customer expectations, leverage data and take a hard look at their own processes.
- Banks will have open platforms to easily collaborate with third parties, providing banking and related non-banking services. They will create and become part of intelligent digital ecosystems. Data-driven insight and the ability to provide a superior customer experience will separate the successful from the less successful financial services providers.

J.-P. Jensen (✉)
Walldorf, Germany
e-mail: jens-peter.jensen@sap.com

To succeed in this new environment, many banks are focusing on a few strategic priorities:

- Seamless connectivity: Firstly, they are offering personalized products and services in real time, orchestrated across channels—from inquiry to application to fulfillment—and enabled in the cloud.
- Data-driven intelligence: In parallel, banks stream multiple data sources from various systems into a single customer view to allow deep analytics for personalized offers, risk assessment and fraud mitigation.
- Operational effectiveness: They are also standardizing technology to reduce the total cost of ownership (TCO) and optimize processes by embedding machine learning and other innovative technologies.
- Financial insight and risk control: Lastly, they are focusing on proactive financial and risk management to make faster and better decisions based on real-time data leveraging advanced analytics.

2   The Need for Resilience and Agility in Finance

In times of uncertainty and disruption, the weaknesses resulting from underinvestment in the systems and processes of financial services institutions are exposed. The lack of ability to understand, adapt and react swiftly to unexpected changes limits the ability to stay competitive. This is nothing new: financial services institutions face regulatory changes, cost pressure and new competitors all the time. What is new this time is the acceleration of change driven by opportunities arising from digital technologies in a time of global crisis.

The reaction of a CFO may be structured by three strategic perspectives: short-term survival, mid-term recovery and long-term growth. The first imperative is simply navigating the immediate challenges. Cost containment, liquidity management and running remote finance processes will be at the center of considerations. The second goal will be to evaluate and plan for the recovery that will inevitably come. This includes critically reviewing the product portfolio, operations and optimizing capital and risk. Finally, CFOs must ensure that they put their companies in a position of competitive advantage to maximize growth opportunities, increase market share and get ahead of the competition. The subsequent section will focus on this phase 3, to elaborate on the approach a CFO may take to best support the bank's strategic priorities.

3 The Changing Mandate for Finance

Many banks are approaching the strategic priorities by embracing automation, new virtual working arrangements, hiring temporary contract workers and upskilling the existing workforce in preparation for higher level analysis work. Nowhere is this change more evident than in finance, which has been experiencing dramatic changes over the last two decades, evolving from running periodical highly manual processes to influencing and shaping how the bank creates and preserves value (Fig. 1).

It is an opportunity as well as a necessity that the finance role shifts in emphasis toward management rather than limiting itself to accounting. The CFO is assumed to have the business understanding to work alongside the COO and steer the business as a co-pilot. The finance department experiences a refocus of its capabilities toward revenue and value creation. The COO demands this close collaboration as it is the CFO who is in a position to provide trusted information.

Technology is a key enabler to improve the efficiency of the finance function and build new capabilities for it. The automation of the finance function will free up capacity to focus on value-oriented insights. These insights

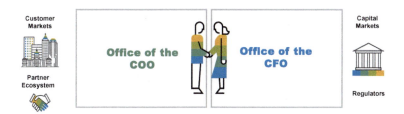

Fig. 1 The changing mandate of the CFO (© SAP SE)

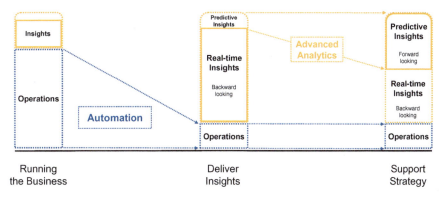

Fig. 2 From daily routine to supporting new business models (© SAP SE)

happen at the speed of business in real time. The step to include a forward-looking perspective and to utilize technologies for predictive analytics will enable the CFO to move into the role of strategic advisor (Fig. 2).

4 Business Processes

It is vital to have an aligned view of the business processes as a prerequisite to fulfilling business expectations. The targeted outcome of the Record-to-Report process is to deliver the financial reports as required by the regulators, the capital markets and internal stakeholders. In parallel, the bank runs a Financial Planning and Analysis process, which aims to steer the company internally and help the business to run better (Fig. 3).

The information needs of both processes overlap significantly. For example:

- The financial performance as determined within financial accounting will be the basis, broken down by organizational structure to allocate costs.
- Reports from the financial statement undergo a simulation and optimization process to support the planning and steering process.

5 Data Architecture

Most financial institutions are not ready to live up to the target picture as described above. To put it simply: the data is just not available at the speed, granularity, quality and completeness required. The symptoms are manifold:

- Long prep times for consistent data
- High data management efforts
- High reconciliation efforts
- Concurring data silos

Fig. 3 Business processes in finance (© SAP SE)

- Concurring "truths"
- Missing data foundation for new tech.

These issues have grown over many years. Sometimes we may even perceive them as a given and the norm, as we have never experienced a different world. However, if we want to develop into the new role of the CFO, we will need to systematically identify and address the underlying issues. First of all, we need to work out the root causes.

Probably the main cause is that the *transactional systems* banks run *do not have a commonly defined interface* when integrating with the analytical world, especially accounting. Typical banks run various systems from various vendors as well as homegrown systems originating from different technology generations and running on all types of technology. This first results in unclear and/or overlapping allocation of functionality along the downstream process. Given the resulting complexity, operations is used to working with *manual hand-overs* and *process interruptions*. Over time, *parallel data streams* have emerged fulfilling more or less disjointed capabilities and resulting in *data replication* along these various processes. As a consequence, the existing applications and processes within finance are good enough to run a periodical reporting process on aggregates of data. But they are unable to help the business run better based on mass detailed data.

6 Bringing Business Processes and Data in Sync

The solution is to transform the current data architecture by working toward an integrated accounting flow, establishing a consolidated data store for all organizational units that require finance and risk data for company steering (Fig. 4).

- Centralize common information in one information base
- Have information updated synchronously for all consumers
- Have the same information available for all consumers.

A cornerstone is established by the concept of a Universal Journal. This journal overcomes traditional data borders when thinking in subledgers, general ledgers, and group ledgers. The concept of a Universal Journal proposes to establish one common framework which ensures consistency

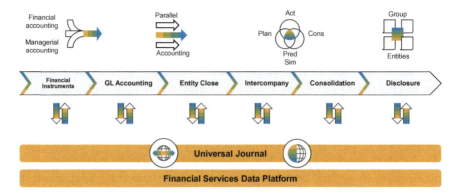

Fig. 4 Bringing business processes and data in sync (© SAP SE)

of master data and elimination of data redundancy by still allowing clear responsibility for the processes on the different levels of the organization.

This starts with establishing a transaction-level accounting capability for financial instruments. This is the handover point between operations and the finance department and requires the most consideration to succeed in simplifying the information flow in finance. Having a single transaction store as a starting point will allow a substantial simplification of the financial and managerial accounting processes.

- To fulfill the needs of multiple GAAPs in parallel, one may define a leading GAAP and generate transaction-level postings only for those areas where the accounting standards have deviating requirements
- One may allocate costs on a transaction level and thus support managerial accounting needs
- One may apply market data scenarios and generate simulation results to support risk management processes
- One may apply scenario-based market data as well as simulated transactions to provide a consistent input for the planning process.

Having established this transaction-level posting hub for all financial instruments, it will now be possible to run simplified and accelerated accounting processes. The general ledger accounting processes bring together the posting documents from additional subledgers, especially all business support areas, and run suspense accounting and multi-currency accounting. With this, we are ready for the period-end closing process at entity level. Having the posting documents from all legal entities available in a consistent quality is the prerequisite to now run your intercompany costing, matching and elimination processes, to finally have the group closing process running and be ready for disclosure.

For all these processes, the Universal Journal is the information foundation as it captures the documents by design in a granular and reconciled manner. However, business needs may even go beyond this. A CFO needs to be prepared to provide a consistent set of information for internal risk and external regulatory reporting. The key figures required for reporting on, for example, interest rate risk, credit risk, and market risk clearly go beyond the information prepared for financial accounting. However, there is still the natural demand and requirement to have the information reconciled by design with the financial accounting information. To cater for these additional information needs, the Universal Journal should be supplemented with an information platform which provides the information of the operational world in a multi-purpose format to any analytical engine and consumer. Such a platform—serving specifically the needs of the financial services industry—may be called the Financial Services Data Platform. All financial instrument master data and transaction data is made available from any source system for any consumer. Such a data integration layer in conjunction with the Universal Journal will allow the CFO of a bank to have all financial-instrument-related information available

- at any speed up to real time
- in a semantic that can support any consumer, be it internal or external, finance or risk
- at a level of granularity relevant to the business and allowing insights instead of just reporting on the past
- in a quality reconciled by design.

7   The Value

Realizing the described future state of finance will require a holistic effort by the financial services institution beyond the CFO. This makes it all the more important for the benefits aimed for to be aligned. There are multiple institutions who have started to work toward the described vision. And there are a few who are already in a position to report back on realized achievements.

- **Simplified operations.** Multinational companies frequently look to simplify operations by harmonizing the finance setup across various entities and jurisdictions. This may lead to a single finance instance for more

than 100 legal entities (SAP, Standardizing Financial Processes Across the Group to Accelerate Central Closing 2020).
- **Accelerated closing process**. Internal and external stakeholders expect to receive information earlier than in the past. This goes hand-in-hand with an accelerated decision-making process and the demand to support business at its accelerating speed of change. Harmonized and automated processes may accelerate period-end closing by up to four weeks (SAP, Standardizing Financial Processes Across the Group to Accelerate Central Closing 2020).
- **Prepared for growth**. The companies who successfully complete their digital journey may experience extraordinary success. The proposed business architecture is prepared to support strong business growth. This makes it relevant for both the incumbent service provider as well as newly established businesses (SAP, How Does Intelligent, Integrated Accounting Support Growth for Financial Services Companies? 2020).
- **Cost savings**. The foundation of a finance transformation business case will be an improvement of the current cost profile. A reduction in manual workload and less reconciliation effort will be important contributors to this ambition (SAP, How Does a Unified Financial Management System Help Local Banks Expand Internationally? 2020).
- **Value-adding services**. As described at the very beginning of this chapter, it is one of the main ambitions of the CFO to act in alignment with the business and provide services to support business critical decisions. Success could be measured by the ratio of accounting staff freed up to focus on value-adding tasks (SAP, How Does Intelligent, Integrated Accounting Support Growth for Financial Services Companies? 2020).

8 The Roadmap

The values achieved make it very convincing to strive for the illustrated target view. It is even more impressive as most of these successes have been achieved by well-established businesses with a long history of investments into legacy technology as well as business processes not ready for the future described.

Having said that, every roadmap will need to be individual, taking into account the technology starting point, perceived pain points and business priorities. However, there are some similarities and learnings which can be laid out as a starting point.

- A leading-edge finance process can be established in no more than six months—if we put legacy technology aside (SAP, How Does Intelligent, Integrated Accounting Support Growth for Financial Services Companies? 2020).
- The most critical capability is the transaction-level posting hub for financial instruments as the starting point of the end-to-end finance process. Finding the right balance between quality (business transaction information) and speed (interface readiness of source systems) will be key.
- The end-to-end design will need to be well understood from the very beginning. One may choose a demanding deliverable like FinRep (European Banking Authority 2020) to prove the consistency and completeness of the overall concept.

Literature

European Banking Authority. 2020. "EBA Reporting Frameworks." *EBA*. Accessed December 15, 2020. https://eba.europa.eu/risk-analysis-and-data/reporting-frameworks.

SAP. 2020. "How Does a Unified Financial Management System Help Local Banks Expand Internationally?" *SAP*. Accessed December 15, 2020. https://www.sap.com/documents/2020/12/46a54faa-bf7d-0010-87a3-c30de2ffd8ff.html.

———. 2020. "How Does Intelligent, Integrated Accounting Support Growth for Financial Services Companies?" *SAP*. Accessed December 15, 2020. https://www.sap.com/documents/2020/12/88762283-bf7d-0010-87a3-c30de2ffd8ff.html.

———. 2020. "Standardizing Financial Processes Across the Group to Accelerate Central Closing." *SAP*. Accessed December 15, 2020. https://www.sap.com/documents/2020/12/1e6c927f-c27d-0010-87a3-c30de2ffd8ff.html.

Value Driver-Oriented Planning—Management-Oriented Design and Value Driver Identification

Simon Valjanow, Philipp Enzinger, Daniel Suttner, and Maik Alexander Schmidt

1 Introduction

Planning, like thinking about future conditions or results today (Argenti 2018), is an omnipresent activity of everyday life. Planning a birthday event or the next vacation are practical examples. Should an event take place outside or inside? With continuative questions, like what the weather on the day of the celebrations will be and how rain or sun will affect the event, the core of the topic value driver-oriented planning is already reached.

Formally described, value-based planning is all about identifying relevant influencing factors for a future result and taking them into account in the planning process (Zwicker 2009). In the operational enterprise planning and therefore in the context of midterm financial planning, the value drivers of the P&L, balance sheet and key performance indicators must be identified

---

S. Valjanow (✉) · P. Enzinger · D. Suttner · M. A. Schmidt
ifb SE, Grünwald, Germany
e-mail: Simon.Valjanow@ifb-group.com

P. Enzinger
e-mail: Philipp.Enzinger@ifb-group.com

D. Suttner
e-mail: Daniel.Suttner@ifb-group.com

M. A. Schmidt
e-mail: Maik-Alexander.Schmidt@ifb-group.com

and integrated with the existing planning model (Lossin and Martin 2004). In view of the wide range of internal and external dependencies and thus also the factors influencing the operations of banks and insurance companies, achieving a high level of planning quality is far more complex. However, a high quality of planning, i.e., an ambitious, realistic and integrated prediction of the income, net worth and risk situation, is a prerequisite for achieving consistency regarding short- and midterm targets, long-term investments and compliance with regulatory requirements in the operational implementation of the plan.

It is therefore questionable by which means an optimization of the planning quality can be achieved. Value driver-based planning can make a contribution to increasing quality. With the basic concept of planning not the result itself (e.g., P&L), but the influencing factors (e.g., existing and new business of loans and insurance contracts), the planning level is aligned with the operational business (Albrecht Deyhle et al. 2016). A value driver thus offers a higher connectivity to business activities and transparency than a more condensed planning value, which aggregates the result of business activities (see Fig. 1). Thus, the traceability and the consideration of the dimensions is ambitiously and realistically supported.

Similarly, value driver planning supports integrity and planning consistency, since individual value drivers in a planning model are designed or set in relation to each other and to different results. Planned portfolio changes thus act as drivers in the income statement (net interest income/insurance results), but are also linked to the impact on the balance sheet and can be used as a basis for deriving Risk Weight Assets and risk provision estimation (see Fig. 2). As a result, redundant and inefficient planning data is avoided,

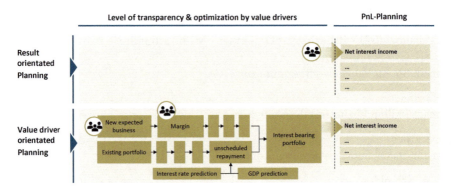

Fig. 1 Illustration (Relationship: Planning on the level of result vs. planning on the value driver level) (© ifb SE)

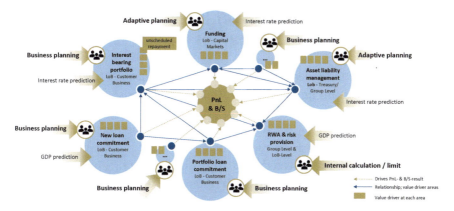

Fig. 2 Illustration of integrated planning model by value driver areas—business view, group functions and associated sub-plans (© ifb SE)

the data quality increases, and this eliminates manual reconciliations and validations.

Even if the optimization potential of value driver-based planning is obvious and an advised best practice (Grabel and Anne 2016), the disruptive change in planning process, methods and the technical implementation poses challenges for the business and IT departments involved. Further skills and new approaches for the planning process are necessary and must be built (Barrett 2007).

In addition to the skills for business design and analysis as well as for technical implementation, the use of predictive analytics and the handling of Big Data are critical factors for success. Predictive analytics can be used to analyze individual value drivers and identify significant ones. The goal is to integrate the relevant drivers into the planning model and exclude unnecessary complexity drivers or non-material drivers (Barkalov 2015). Big Data in the planning context provides the necessary data basis for the applied predictive analytics methods and use cases to ensure valid results and the planning quality.

1.1 Structure of the Article

The following two chapters address the issues of a value driver framework as the starting point and the analysis, identification and integration of individual value drivers. The chapters cover, on the one hand, the derivation of a strategic basic framework of value drivers to cover the business model using the example of an insurance company and, on the other hand, the procedures for the use of predictive analytics in a use case from the banking sector.

2 Design of Value Driver Planning for Insurance Companies

Many insurance companies are using the implementation of the requirements of IFRS 17/9 to set up financial transformation programs, which can include new data platforms, new subledger and general ledger solutions, new finance architecture setups, and much more. As IFRS 17/9 significantly affects the structure of the balance sheet and profit recognition, the financial planning process (FP&A) is also affected. This provides an opportunity for insurers to redesign the FP&A process to make it more efficient and effective. This chapter shall provide a basis for how to use value driver-oriented planning as a framework to redesign the FP&A process toward these goals.

2.1 Definition

Value-based management (VBM) was established in the 1980s and describes the management approach of tailoring management actions to the goal of maximizing shareholder value instead of revenue or profits (Gabler Wirtschaftslexikon 2020). This necessarily leads to the question of what is driving value? At the beginning of the twentieth century, this framework was extended to include financial planning. Although profit and revenue are not the primary drivers of VBM, shareholder value is driven by the potential of insurance companies to produce cash flows in the future. As these are the expected outcome of the financial planning process, the two concepts naturally intertwine. One often-cited benefit of using VBM and value driver-oriented planning (VDoP) is that it allows for the **operationalization** of top management strategy. It also allows the use of planning assumptions to **incentivize management** to reach the planned financial results. Furthermore, in more sophisticated implementations VDoP allows for the **ad-hoc analysis** of management actions through continuous planning.

> *Value-based management can best be understood as a marriage between a value creation mindset and the management processes and systems that are necessary to translate that mindset into action.* (Koller 1994)

2.2 Framework

The most essential prerequisite for a VDoP process is the value driver map (VDM). The VDM provides the company's view of how top management's steering measures can be broken down into operational value drivers down the corporate value chain. VDMs are usually broken down according to the organizational complexity. The number of levels in VDMs should be selected such that it allows for accurate measurement but does not introduce unnecessary complexity into the planning process. Simplicity should be key in setting up VDoP programs. Most insurance companies suffer from very complex planning processes that produce far too granular results for top management which are not used for steering—therefore, the relevance of planning outcomes should always be considered as well. A successful implementation of a VDM allows for translation of top management specifications into explicit requirements for every organizational unit, e.g., in terms of pricing, all the way down to operational management, thereby aligning the company strategically. Whether strategies create value is up to the quality of the management but whether the strategy is executed consistently with top management's intent depends on the proper implementation of the value driver framework. The next benefit of VDoP is incentivizing according to planned financial results. Incentives can be aligned with operational value drivers. Also, value drivers should be selected in a manner that allows an inclusion of the most important factors that can be controlled by the insurance company. Therefore, it is crucial to build up the value driver map from top-level KPIs to bottom external drivers. One of the most difficult tasks is disaggregating the value drivers of top management into operational value drivers that can be used for management and forecasting. A high-level value driver map only focusing on ratios of balance sheet items usually fails to capture the true dynamics of the insurance company's financial performance. A development that may be used to support the process of identifying value drivers and modeling the relationship with management KPIs is the evolution of predictive analytics tools which allow more data-driven approaches in value driver selection (Fig. 3).

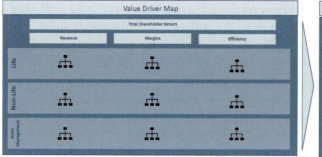

Fig. 3 Value driver map framework (© ifb SE)

So why have so many insurers not yet adopted a value driver-oriented framework? Insurance companies are inherently different from other industries as they receive cash but do not provide any product or service in a traditional sense. They buy risk from policyholders by assuming the obligation to settle uncertain future claims and gain certain cash flows in premiums. This affects the way key performance indicators (KPIs) for FP&A and management reporting are designed. KPIs and value drivers need to be structured along with management. This typically means setting up different KPIs for Life and Non-life business and for asset management. VDoP frameworks should also take into account whether KPIs will also be published publicly via financial statements and disclosures like return on equity, or whether the KPIs are used for management and financial steering. The level of detail of the planning outcome should decrease with increasing forecasting horizons, e.g., in the first five years it might still be possible to forecast line items. After that, only the main steering KPIs should be forecast.

2.3 Challenges in Setting Up and Implementing VDoP at Insurance Companies

The planning methodology is impacted in particular by the introduction of IFRS 17, but the long period left for implementation by the standard-setter also offers a lot of potential to get a feeling for the new numbers. A value driver framework can be valuable in understanding the dynamics of the new balance sheet and P&L structure. IFRS 17 affects profits, revenue, expenses and other KPIs. Therefore, it is crucial to start with analyzing the current KPI landscape for the effects of IFRS 17/9 and whether KPIs are still usable after adoption of the new accounting framework. Only after this is done can KPIs be integrated and mapped to the VDM. Another important point that should be taken into account is that in the insurance industry almost 90% of the variance in a company's P/B multiple relative to its peers can be explained by fundamentals: profitability metrics (ROE and dividend payout), balance sheet health (credit rating, liabilities and debt), forward growth expectations and size (BCG 2017). This means that a lot of the volatility introduced by IFRS 17/9 on market valuations can be predicted by integrating VDoP methodology into the projects. Nevertheless, many insurance companies will struggle with setting up a consistent value driver map including all data feeds and system integration until the first application of IFRS 17. Therefore, interim solutions may have to be considered to understand the dynamics.

When implementing a VDoP concept, software choice is obviously a key success factor. Several components have to be taken into account. Many insurers are now transforming their finance architecture for reasons such as IFRS 17/9 implementation, digitalization or integration. This means that a new BI or predictive analytics tool has to integrate well with the new architecture. In particular, accounting data needs a high integrability, preferably a native interface to the general ledger and the business warehouse. A state-of-the-art BI tool should be able to deliver suitable AI functionalities like suggesting clustering or data points or using natural language processing for automated commenting on reports. When using AI functionality in particular, data security is an issue due to the highly confidential nature of management reporting. Finally, the Covid-19 pandemic once again shows how important ad-hoc reporting is and it should not be neglected in the software choice as well as having dynamic dashboards and drilldowns to analyze the data on the spot.

All in all, the most important lesson in implementing a VDoP system in times of IFRS 17/9 is to start early and to start at the top.

3 Approach to Identify Value Drivers in Regard to Unscheduled Repayments with Predictive Analytics

This section will deal with predictive analytics and its exemplary application in value driver modeling. In times of "Big Data" and "data is the new oil," the processing and analysis of data becomes more and more important. A subarea of data processing is business analytics, which consists of five subareas. There are descriptive analytics and diagnostic analytics, which deal with the processing and analysis of the past, as well as real-time analytics, which includes traditional monitoring and deals with current events. The last areas are the future-oriented predictive analytics and prescriptive analytics, where the former deals with the prediction of the future and the latter deals with possible measures (Mentel 2015). Therefore is the planning process, which focused on a time period in advance, naturally predestined as a predictive analytics use case.

3.1 Predictive Analytics, What is That?

Before possible fields of application, methods and procedures can be discussed, it must first be shown what predictive analytics is all about in detail. This is first done by a general definition:

Predictive analytics is used to predict the probability of future results from existing historical data. The goal is to use an analysis of past events to best predict the future.

Predictive analytics is always based on historical data, which is why data quality and data volume are of high relevance here. The core of each process is the analysis, where historical data is processed with the help of different methods, which mostly come from the statistics. The analysis tries to identify patterns, relationships, trends and other findings that allow conclusions to be drawn about the future. It should be noted that these are usually predictions with a certain probability (McCarthy et al. 2019) (Fig. 4).

3.2 Fields of Application and Added Value of Predictive Analytics

The major added value of predictive analytics is that it allows conclusions to be drawn about the future based on internal and external history. This makes it possible to better prepare for crises, improve the quality of planning and better comply with regulations predictive analytics offers a broad field of applications from risk to balance sheet to profit and loss statement. The added value is particularly high for financial controlling. In financial controlling, many business capabilities offer possible fields of application, starting with pricing calculation to improve the quality of cost and risk determination (Hsu 2014), through scenario calculation and performance calculation to improve parameterization and parameter estimation, up to the planning process.

The planning process offers the highest benefit, as the planning quality can be improved enormously through more accurate predictions, patterns and relationships for the future. One special feature is value driver planning, where the individual relationships can be identified and quantified

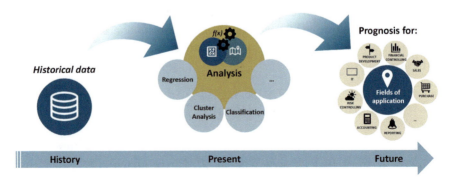

Fig. 4 General procedure of predictive analytics (© ifb SE)

more accurately using predictive analytics. A major driver here is unscheduled repayment and thus the prediction of unscheduled repayment rates.

3.3 Definition of Unscheduled Repayment and its Impact

The driver unscheduled repayment is now used as an example to show what a possible application of predictive analytics could look like and what opportunities it offers. However, before this can be discussed, it is necessary to define what unscheduled repayments or unscheduled repayment rates are:

> *Unscheduled repayments are payments made by a business partner that differ from the contractually agreed and expected payments. It is therefore the drawing of a contractual option by the business partner. One form are unscheduled loan repayments, in particular early repayments by debtors in banks' customer business. Similarly, an unscheduled termination or repayment of an investment amount by the issuer of a (fixed-) interest-bearing bond is to be regarded as an unscheduled repayment.*

Unscheduled repayments are a significant volume driver and thus also a driver for the profit and loss account. If the unscheduled repayment increases, the interest-bearing portfolio decreases and thus also the interest income. If there are fewer extraordinary repayments than usual, the interest income is higher. Further essential effects of unscheduled repayments are also found in risk planning and in the volume dependent RWA approximation of future periods. From the point of view of planning for a bank, the challenge now is to approximate future customer behavior with regard to unscheduled repayments. This is mainly done by predicting the future unscheduled repayment rates. This rate can be used within a planning model (Fig. 5).

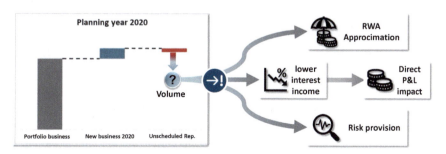

Fig. 5 Unscheduled repayments and merging to P&L (© ifb SE)

3.4 The Challenge with Unscheduled Repayments

For this reason, determining the level of this volume driver or the unscheduled repayment rate is an important success factor for predictive functions in financial controlling. Based on our market observation and project experience, the determination of the amount is mainly carried out as an expert estimate or in the best case as a rudimentary analysis of the past years. In the worst case, the value from last year's plan is simply reused for new "determinations." A serious methodical and thus transparent and objective analysis or prediction is not available. Furthermore, it is often even unclear what influence internal and external factors can have on unscheduled repayment rates.

The problem is therefore the absence of a transparent and neutral or objective method for predicting the volume driver unscheduled repayments or unscheduled repayment rates. Predictive analytics can close this lack of methodology by using historical data to determine the patterns, relationships, and levels of unscheduled repayment rates, and then building a model for determining unscheduled repayment rates that can be used to determine future unscheduled repayment rates based on the planning assumptions.

3.5 Approach to Unscheduled Repayment Rates with Predictive Analytics

Before the analysis can start and such a model can be set up, it must be determined from a professional point of view which factors have an influence on unscheduled repayments or unscheduled repayment rates. A distinction is made between internal and external factors. The external factors include the environment, such as macroeconomic facts (e.g., GDP and interest rate level), and the internal factors refer to the customer characteristics, such as age and salary level and events such as a salary increase or similar financial bonuses, and the product characteristics that the contract contains, such as volume, effective interest rate, or the repayment amount.

The historical data of these factors can then be analyzed and processed in the further development, whereby a distinction must be made between numerical data (e.g., age) and non-numerical data (e.g., loan type). Non-numerical data is more difficult to process. In this case, analysis methods must be chosen that can recognize correlations and patterns without the need for numbers. Cluster methods are the most suitable for this purpose, so that groups with similar behavior can be identified. In this way, the data can be divided into different clusters and then analyzed in detail. It should be noted

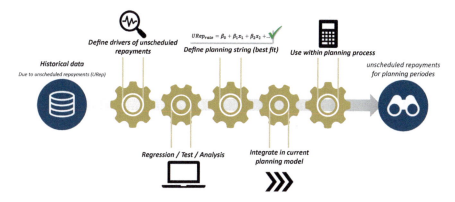

Fig. 6 Process of driver identification and integration (© ifb SE)

that numerical data can also be used for this step, for example to identify age groups with similar behavior.

If the previous step has been performed, the further steps are performed in the respective clusters, otherwise with the entire dataset. Next, the dataset can be reduced to the numerical factors, which are now to be analyzed for correlation and quantitative relationships. Regression analysis is used for this purpose and, because there are several factors involved, multilinear regression has to be chosen. The regression analysis is executed for all possible combinations, which means 2^n regressions for n factors. The results are then classified and sorted according to an established evaluation model, which contains the maximum number of factors and model quality with different measures. From this list, the most suitable model can be selected.

The desired result is thus one or more functions for each cluster, which can then be integrated into the planning process. The concept of regression analysis has been integrated into a program in R, so that the process can be automated. This then allows a transparent, valid and objective determination of the volume of unscheduled repayments and thus an improvement of the planning quality (Fig. 6).

4 Summary

Looking back, why should financial institutions choose to invest in a VDoP framework? First of all, most planning processes are still far too granular in contrast to what top management needs for steering purposes. This produces costs, lacks value orientation and demotivates employees. Additionally, lean planning processes allow for more flexibility. Secondly, many financial institutions are still unable to consistently include external and internal information in their planning assumption. This also holds true for ad-hoc and scenario capabilities. Thirdly, the evolution of new BI tools with AI capabilities, the current wave of financial transformation and/or digitalization projects and the implementation of IFRS 17/9 for insurance companies are a great chance to set up VDoP projects now in an efficient manner and avoid the risk of transferring outdated processes into new architectural setups. Finally, being able to get fast insights into the effects of external events (e.g., Covid-19) and internal actions (acquisitions) on short- and midterm financial performance while including relevant market data will be the key to dominating the challenging financial industry in the next decade.

Literature

Argenti, John. 2018. *Pracitcal Corporate Planning*. London: Routledge.
Barkalov, Igor. 2015. *Effiziente Unternehmensplanung*. Wiesbaden: Springer Gabler.
Barrett, Richard. 2007. *Planning and Budgeting for the Agile Enterprise*. Burlington: Elsevier Ltd.
BCG. 2017. *A CEOs Guide to Building Value*. https://www.bcg.com/de-de/public ations/2017/corporate-development-finance-commercial-reinsurance-ceo-guide-building-value-2017-insurance-value-creators-report, July 14.
Deyhle, Albrecht, Klaus Eiselmayer, and Guido Kleinhietpaß. 2016. *Controller Praxis*. Freiburg: Verlag für ControllingWissen AG.
Gabler Wirtschaftslexikon. 2020. *Wertorientiertes Management*. https://wirtschaftsl exikon.gabler.de/definition/wertorientiertes-management-53889, December 6.
Grabel, Elaine Stattler and Joyce Anne. 2016. *Controllers Best Practices*. Montvale: ima.
Hsu, William H. 2014. *Emerging Methods in Predictive Analytics: Risk Management and Decision-Making*. IGI Global: Kansas State University.
Koller, Timothy. 1994. *Valuation: Measuring and Managing the Value of Companies, 2nd Edition*.
Lossin, Daniel Knüsel and Martin. 2004. "Besonderheiten der Bewertung von Banken nach dem Ertragswertverfahren." In *Bankenrating—Kreditinstitute auf dem Prüfustand*, edited by Oliver Everling and Karl-Heinz Goedeckemeyer, 100ff. Wiesbaden: Gabler.
McCarthy, Richard V., Mary M. McCarthy, Wendy Ceccucci, and Leila Halawi. 2019. *Applying Predictive Analytics*. Springer.
Mentel, Susanne. 2015. *Predictive Analytic und die Haftung für fehlerhafte Ergebnisse gegenüber betroffenen Einzelpersonen*. Berlin: Fachmedien Recht und Wirtschaft.

Zwicker, Eckart. 2009. "Zur Verknüpfung von operativer und strategischer Planung." In *Perspektiven des strategischen Controllings*, edited by Marko Reimer and Stefanie Fiege, 33ff. Wiesbaden: Gabler.

AI for Impairment Accounting

Sören Hartung and Manuela Führer

1 Introduction

1.1 Initial Situation

In the euro zone, the interest rates are still at a historically low level. Regulation, driven by the last financial crisis, puts additional cost pressure on the banks. The traditional banks must face agile competitors (Fintech companies) and technologically strong and well capitalized companies (BigTech[1]) in the retail banking segment.

With serious threats to the revenue potential of certain segments, the traditional banks seek to improve their offerings and evaluate where to save costs by using automation (like RPA) and artificial intelligence to optimize processes.

---

[1] GAFAM (Google, Amazon, Facebook, Apple and Microsoft) and BATX (Baidu, Alibaba, Tencent and Xiaomi).

S. Hartung · M. Führer (✉)
Helaba, Frankfurt, Germany
e-mail: Manuela.Fuehrer@helaba.de

The imperative of efficient improvement is there; the banks recognize that cost cutting needs to be applied in an intelligent manner: by optimizing processes and keeping the functionality required.[2]

1.2 Bank-Wide Setup

For Helaba, data analytics is one facet of digitalization. In Fig. 1, this facet is broken down into six sub-areas. These areas are sorted by topics. There are sections with a strong client focus, such as text mining or segmentation, and units with a more internal concentration, such as anomaly detection and forecasting. Classification and frequent patterns are applied in both (client-related and internal) areas.

Helaba identifies use cases for digitalization with a well-orchestrated process. The use cases are always driven by the business units, solving a problem formulated by the business department.

Figure 2 shows the three main steps in use case selection and the timeframe given for the different steps. The data innovation workshop took place in March 2019 and 13 departments participated in the workshop. After selecting three use cases, the feasibility was tested within the framework of POCs and evaluated. The use cases with a positive evaluation were then implemented in a productive environment.

The basic concept for the underlying process has been to generate and discuss multiple ideas with a diverse and cross-functional group of internal experts, test these ideas in the shortest possible time and with as few resources as possible and to bring only the ideas that are worth the effort into the operationalization phase.

The second phase took around eight months.[3] The two success factors in this phase were getting open-minded colleagues on board who are eager to work on innovative solutions for day-to-day problems, and getting the commitment of senior management to try new solutions even if there is a high probability that the immediate results are not good. One of the POCs that actually delivered very good results is described in detail in the following sections.

---

[2] The dysfunctional cost cutting would be to brute force reduction of needed functionality.
[3] The Proof of Concept (POC) only took eight weeks.

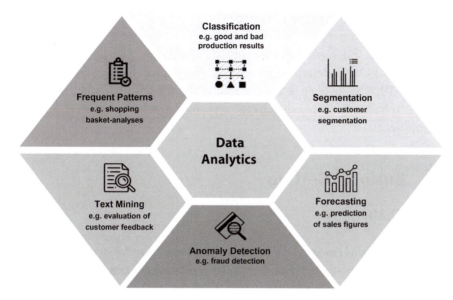

Fig. 1 Data analytics (© Helaba)

Fig. 2 Overall identification process (© Helaba)

1.3 Situation—Accounting Department

Generating financial statements in the accounting department means collecting huge amounts of data from several sources, and unavoidably some of the data is incorrect. The textbook approach would be: identify the errors, adjust the data delivery, customize the calculation software itself. The reality looks different. Identification of errors is not that simple and means manual workload. Certain errors only occur in one month and are gone the next. Some errors can only be solved through very high investments in technical and organizational process flows. However, this would not always be efficient from a cost/benefit perspective. Sometimes, adjusting the error after the process is more efficient than adjusting the process that produces good results for 99.9% of the cases.

1.4 Structure of the Chapter

In Sect. 2, the business requirements are discussed. The chosen technical setup of the POC is described in Sect. 3. The approach taken in the project (POC) is delivered in Sect. 4 and the results and the lessons learned are shown in Sect. 5. Section 6 sums the chapter up and provides an outlook of future developments.

2 Business Setting

2.1 Challenges

The bank has implemented decentralized responsibility for accounting material and data quality. This means that the recording of data to ensure correct posting processes and business transactions as well as the monitoring of accounts is carried out locally in the product areas, because knowledge of the economic facts is concentrated there. Nevertheless, the accounting department has a control function through its overall responsibility for the financial statements and the internal control system. For impairment accounting, approximately 80,000 transactions per month are performed and processed for posting risk provisions using >15 systems. The process for preparing the financial statements is subject to tight time restrictions.

Every month, approximately 5000 anomalies occur in the processing chain, about 50 of which must be corrected manually every month due to their criticality. The various causes of errors include data inconsistency, time lags in the provision of data, technical restrictions in the system landscape and the generally sensitive and complex processing chain (Fig. 3).

2.2 Correction Process

Today's error correction process is structured as follows: two employees in the accounting department identify and analyze error constellations every month after the last day of business. In this largely manual process, three Microsoft Excel-based applications are currently still in use. Errors are either forwarded to product areas or to IT operations for correction or corrected by the accounting department independently. Since errors often only become apparent late in the processing, they can sometimes only be corrected in

AI for Impairment Accounting 71

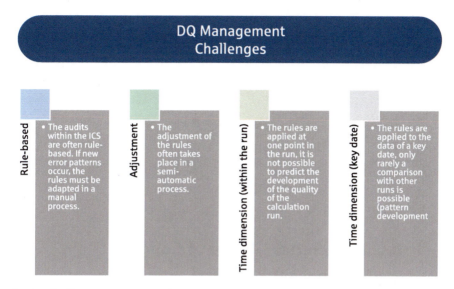

Fig. 3 Challenges in data quality management (© Helaba)

subsequent systems. Other departments do not benefit from these correction entries and rely on an incorrect database. The total expenditure for the outlined process is about 20 person days/month.

2.3 POC Target

In general, POCs aim to validate a technology or show the feasibility of an approach. This specific POC aims—in addition—to generate practical experience with data analysis and machine learning. This experience should enable the department to validate other subjects in terms of their automation potential.

The main goals of the POC are shown in Fig. 4. The major objective is to identify error patterns and improve the data quality. The identification of anomalies by using machine learning can improve the time to correct the errors. This verification with machine learning models can be established as an alternative to the existing rule-based approach.

A second objective is to review the appropriate machine learning models and their performance in terms of the challenge.

Furthermore, the POC also targets the knowledge build-up and the important practical experience with the models and tools.

Fig. 4 Goals of the POC (© Helaba)

3 Technical Setup—Proof of Concept

3.1 Data Flow

The POC analyzes the data flows in the context of processing the impairments in the accounting department. For this purpose, the data from the upstream systems and the systems used to determine the amount of the impairment are compared with the values in reporting or consolidation. If there are deviations, an error has occurred (ICS rule).[4]

In Fig. 5, the landscape of the systems involved is presented. The data flow is from bottom to top. The data is extracted from the impairment system[5] and the operative systems (core systems). In a data warehouse, the data is harmonized and can then be transferred to the accounting subledger systems (SAP AFI). Afterward, the data is passed on to the reporting system and further to the consolidation system.

One rule (among many other rules) checks if the sum of the key figures used for the impairment value compilation (in the reporting system) is still equal to the original values in the impairment system. In terms of machine learning, we call the result of the comparison a label (the values the model should predict). In the POC flow, we decided to differentiate based on the severity of the deviation (impact sensitivity).

Data scientists call the data used to predict these labels "features." The most valuable fields (features) identified by the model come from the master data. Therefore, trained algorithms can predict the deviations very early in the

---

[4] It was a big advantage that the POC could use the ICS rules as labels.
[5] The impairment system calculates the impairment value by using credit risk methods like life-time expected loss for stage 2 and 3 transactions.

AI for Impairment Accounting

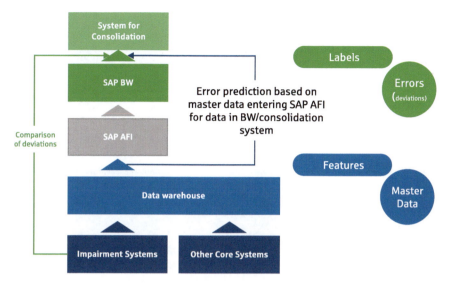

Fig. 5 Systems involved and data flow (© Helaba)

process (based on the core-system data/master data). The algorithm recognizes patterns in the source system data that lead to incorrect changes in the impairment key figures during processing in SAP AFI.

3.2 Data Architecture—Modeling

Given the nature of the POC, the technology sophistication used was pragmatic. As Helaba did not heavily invest in data lake technology at the start of the POC and the POC also restricted the data period to a statistical minimum, the task could be carried out with standard technology.

In the first steps of the POC, the raw data was only provided by text files. During the POC, the raw data was stored in a traditional SQL database (Microsoft SQL server 2014). The raw data was connected by standard SQL statements in the server and some links were carried out as preprocessing to the model in R using the famous package dplyr (Fig. 6).[6]

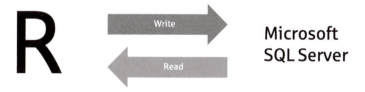

Fig. 6 Tool data and analysis (© Helaba)

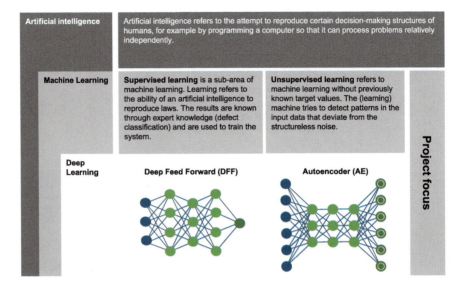

Fig. 7 Overview artificial intelligence (© Helaba)

The data to train the model is provided by the SQL views and some data transformation in R so that the common models (FFN[7] random forest,[8] etc.) can be used. In addition, H2O[9] was used for some of the more advanced models. After the cross validation of the model,[10] the model parameters (and hyperparameters) are stored in a text file so the application (error pattern recognition) can be performed using the information in the text file.[11]

3.3 Modeling

In the machine learning environment, there is a wide range of different models available (by academia and by frameworks see Liermann, Overview Machine Learning and Deep Learning Frameworks [2021]). A common structure to differentiate the model is shown on the left side of Fig. 7. Artificial intelligence is the umbrella term, followed by machine learning

---

[6] See information about the R package (Wickham et al. 2020) and, for an introduction, see Institute for Statistics and Mathematics of WU (2020).

[7] Deep Feed Forward network—see Section 3.1 in Liermann et al., Deep Learning—An Introduction (2019a).

[8] See Section 3.7.1 in Liermann et al., Introduction in Machine Learning (2019b).

[9] H2o.ai is a machine learning framework (see H2O.ai 2019).

[10] See Section 4.1 in Liermann et al., Introduction in Machine Learning (2019b).

[11] It was beyond the scope of the POC to establish a proper infrastructure to organize the parameter and hyperparameter storage and reading.

as a sub-category and further broken down into deep learning (for more details see Section 1.1 in Liermann et al., Introduction in Machine Learning [2019b]).

Both machine learning and deep learning can be separated into supervised learning (e.g., for classification problems a label is given for the classes) and unsupervised learning (e.g., for classification problems no label is defined but the model groups the different elements).

In the POC, supervised learning (classification models) is used to identify the severity of an error in the impairment reporting. In addition, some unsupervised learning methods (classification models, like autoencoder) are applied. Although anomaly detection is a traditional field for autoencoders[12] the performance of the supervised models was far better.

In the outlook (Sect. 6), we will discuss some reasonable applications for unsupervised learning in the context of the impairment process.

4 Project Approach

The journey of the digital transformation of a bank is not easy and not always entirely successful. We see the best efficiency when the journey starts with the business divisions because the value needs to be created there and not only in the IT department. We find it helpful to support the business departments with a staff division focusing on digitalization and helping the business divisions to understand the technology and the contexts in which the tools work best.[13]

The Proof of Concept was embedded within a larger initiative in which the bank sought relevant and fitting use cases to explore new technologies in a practical environment.

The project setup was not purely agile (Scrum, see Akhgarnush et al. [2021]), but we used agile components, such as daily standups and an iterative and Sprint-oriented temporal structure for data discovery, data cleansing and model development.

Figure 8 shows the five steps of a classic machine learning project.

---

[12] See Section 3.3 in Liermann et al., Deep Learning—An Introduction (2019a).

[13] The opposite approach would be to start with the technology and incorporate the business divisions once the infrastructure is up and running.

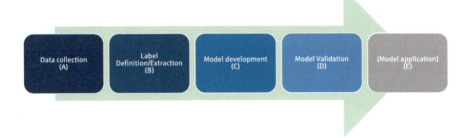

Fig. 8 Project steps (© Helaba)

5 Results and Project Experience

The result of the POC has many dimensions. The major result is that there is potential to discover patterns in data flows. The potential can be realized and leads to a reduction in process time[14] and in manual effort.[15] In addition, the quality of an error prediction[16] has improved. This quality improvement even offers the option to predict the key figure[17] causing the error.

5.1 Modeling Results

The data scientist expresses the quality of a model[18] by the rate of incorrectly predicted values. These incorrectly predicted values are differentiated into (A) if the value should be true (in our case, the transaction has a deviation) but is predicted as false (the model overlooked the error) and (B) the value should be false (the transaction is correct) but the model predicts a true one (the model saw an error but there was none). (A) is called false positive (FP) and (B) is called false negative (FN).

To transfer the absolute figures of the false positive and the false negative into relative figures, the data scientist uses precision (for expressing the false positive) and recall (for expressing the false negative). On the right side of Fig. 9, the model accuracy is shown for two of the observed labels.[19] On the left side of Fig. 9, the key model accuracy figures are displayed.

---

[14] Errors are discovered earlier in the process.

[15] More steps in the reconciliation are automated.

[16] A distinction can be made between a minor error (not relevant) and significant deviation.

[17] The total impairment value is composed of up to fifteen different key figures. The deviation is usually connected to one key figure that has not been processed properly.

[18] Especially in classification models we applied in the POC.

[19] Even if sixteen transactions were predicted falsely, one should bear in mind that over 80,000 were properly identified.

AI for Impairment Accounting

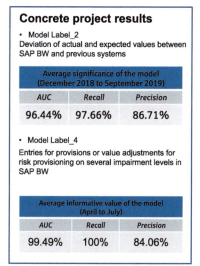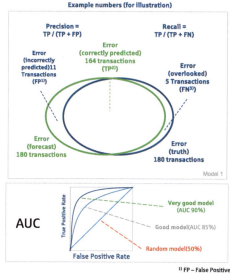

Fig. 9 Modeling results (© Helaba)

The accuracy of the trained models is high. The high accuracy is to keep in balance while decreasing overfitting.[20] It was another modeling challenge to deal with the low quantity of errors (80,000 transactions and approximately 170 significant deviations, corresponding with a rate of 0.2%). However, the data scientist found model types to handle this challenge. This is the art of the data scientist. This aspect will be given more attention in the productive implementation.

5.2 Lessons Learned

As the POC was a complete success,[21] we feel encouraged by the path we took. Starting with the business requirements and pain points is the key to success. Technology is an important component overall, but it has less importance without a business context to show the possibilities of the new technologies.

Given the relatively small data size (especially in the context of a POC), the technology was handled perfectly with standard data storage and open source

---

[20] Overfitting can occur when the historical data is too similar over time and the model can only predict these patterns but is unable to follow changing patterns.

[21] In 2020, the project started to place the results and processes in a productive environment.

components. It was key to have colleagues with technological skill sets[22] to understand the components used (SQL database and R within Microsoft visual studio). In the long-term outlook, the setup could be improved efficiently by data lake technology and extended infrastructure for data scientists (like Cloudera or other providers of data scientist-related infrastructure).

Open source offers a wide variety of models and tools to get the data processing and model development in place.

If we analyze where we spent most of our time and human resources during the project, it was definitely data and data infrastructure, and we expect this to remain the precondition for good models. However, the models offer sufficient leverage to achieve the business requirements.

6 Summary and Outlook

There are different roads to a successful digital transformation. We are quite happy with the track we took by starting in the business domains. Naturally, a technology-focused approach has advantages too,[23] but we achieved our business needs with minimum technological overheads by using standard technology that is available at the bank as well as open source technology that is approved by the IT department.

The reasonable investment gave us the opportunity to evaluate the right processes and the right technology to improve these processes.

Literature

Akhgarnush, Eljar, Fabian Bruse, and Ben Hofer. 2021. "New Project Structure." In *The Digital Journey of Banking and Insurance, Volume I—Disruption and DNA*, edited by Volker Liermann and Claus Stegmann. New York: Palgrave Macmillan.

H2O.ai. 2019. *h2o.ai Overview,* January 29. Accessed January 29, 2019. http://docs.h2o.ai/h2o/latest-stable/h2o-docs/index.html.

Institute for Statistics and Mathematics of WU. 2020. "The Comprehensive R Archive Network." *dplyr: A Grammar of Data Manipulation.* Accessed October 15, 2020. https://CRAN.R-project.org/package=dplyr.

Liermann, Volker. 2021. "Overview Machine Learning and Deep Learning Frameworks." In *The Digital Journey of Banking and Insurance, Volume III—Data*

---

[22] The employees involved came from a physics and mathematical background.
[23] Better up and running infrastructure.

Storage, Processing, and Analysis, edited by Volker Liermann and Claus Stegmann. New York: Palgrave Macmillan.

Liermann, Volker, Sangmeng Li, and Norbert Schaudinnus. 2019a. "Deep Learning—An Introduction." In *The impact of Digital Transformation and Fintech on the Finance Professional*, edited by Volker Liermann and Claus Stegmann. New York: Palgrave Macmillan.

———. 2019b. "Introduction in Machine Learning." In *The Impact of Digital Transformation and Fintech on the Finance Professional*, edited by Volker Liermann and Claus Stegmann. New York: Palgrave Macmillan.

Wickham, Hadley, Romain François, Lionel Henry, and Kirill Müller. 2020. "Tidyverse." *dplyr*. Accessed October 15, 2020. https://dplyr.tidyverse.org/articles/dplyr.html.

Risk Management

The third part is dedicated to the aspects of risk management and the improvements digitalization can bring to the risk management department. This part shows several new concepts to enhance risk management in dynamic times.

A new trend in risk management is to move from the traditional one-year view to a multi-period projection. This trend was initiated by regulators and the setters of accounting standards. The stress testing frameworks in the European Union (EBA stress test[1]) and the United States (DFAST[2] and CCAR/CLAR[3]) arose after the financial crisis in 2008/2009 and are now a well-established tool in the risk management setup. Even after being performed several times over the years, stress testing still challenges the organization in terms of speed in execution (and number of scenarios[4]) and flexibility in adapting to changing requirements (the COVID-19 pandemic unceremoniously revealed the lack of computational scalability and the insufficient adjustability of most of the existing setups).

The part's first chapter (Thiele 2021) introduces a framework to cover the multi-period view in a flexible, technologically advanced way with a state-of-the art user interface. The chapter spans from the conceptional view to the subject of a multi-period scenario framework, down to infrastructure

---

[1] European Banking Authority stress test (see European Central Bank 2020), for the methodology in 2021 see (European Banking Authority 2020).
[2] DFAST—Dodd–Frank Act Stress Test, part of the Dodd–Frank Act (see (US Congress 2010)).
[3] Comprehensive Capital Analysis and Review (see BOARD OF GOVERNORS of the FEDERAL RESERVE SYSTEM 2015) and the unpublished Comprehensive Liquidity Analysis and Review.
[4] That can be performed in a suitable time.

and architecture to implement the various conceptional building blocks. It finishes with practical guidelines for an implementation and a conceptual evolution. The second article (Brindöpke 2021) switches to the requirements of insurance companies in liability-oriented actuarial management, focusing on the new models possible thanks to rising data availability. The chapter lines up various machine learning applications in life as well as non-life insurance. It closes by summarizing the challenges of such model implementations. The third chapter of this part (Liermann and Dittmar, BSDS—Balance Sheet Dynamics Simulator [Application ABM] 2021) offers a new concept to deal with the dynamics coming from the market and market share impacting the banks' balance sheet. The chapter gives an introduction into the new model paradigm of agent-based modeling and offers a schema to map the requirements of a dynamic balance sheet to an agent-based model approach. The final article in this part (Liermann, Viets and Radermacher, Breaking New Grounds in Non-Financial Risk Management 2021) summarizes the urgent demands in non-financial risk management and how to cover the challenges of integration. The chapter shows the importance in a transparent visualization of the connection and the interconnectedness of the task. It touches on the importance of Big Data in the context of managing the threat level by non-financial risk category and how to resolve it using key risk indicators. The chapter closes with an approach to integrate impact graphs (showing the connectedness) and key risk indicators (illustrating the threat level) into a homogeneous reporting framework. The chapter underlines the importance of both integrated non-financial risk models as well as non-financial risk-category-specific models.

Literature

BOARD OF GOVERNORS of the FEDERAL RESERVE SYSTEM. 2015. "Comprehensive Capital Analysis and Review 2015." *BOARD OF GOVERNORS of the FEDERAL RESERVE SYSTEM*, March 18. https://www.federalreserve.gov/bankinforeg/stress-tests/CCAR/201503-comprehensive-capital-analysis-review-preface.htm.

Brindöpke, Susanne. 2021. "Actuarial Data Science." In *The Digital Journey of Banking and Insurance, Volume I—Disruption and DNA*, edited by Volker Liermann and Claus Stegmann. New York: Palgrave Macmillan.

European Banking Authority. 2020. "European Banking Authority." *European Central Bank—Banking Supervision*, November 13. https://www.eba.europa.eu/eba-publishes-methodology-2021-eu-wide-stress-test.

European Central Bank. 2020. "Stress tests." *European Central Bank—Banking Supervision*, December 15. https://www.bankingsupervision.europa.eu/banking/tasks/stresstests/html/index.en.html.

Liermann, Volker, and Harro Dittmar. 2021. "BSDS—Balance Sheet Dynamics Simulator (Application ABM)." In *The Digital Journey of Banking and Insurance, Volume I—Disruption and DNA*, edited by Volker Liermann and Claus Stegmann. New York: Palgrave Macmillan.

Liermann, Volker, Nikolas Viets, and Davin Radermacher. 2021. "Breaking New Grounds in Non-Financial Risk Management." In *The Digital Journey of Banking and Insurance, Volume I—Disruption and DNA*, edited by Volker Liermann and Claus Stegmann. New York: Palgrave Macmillan.

Thiele, Markus. 2021. "Financial Navigator—A Modern Approach to Analytical Banking." In *The Digital Journey of Banking and Insurance, Volume I—Disruption and DNA*, edited by Volker Liermann and Claus Stegmann. New York: Palgrave Macmillan.

US Congress. 2010. *Dodd–Frank Wall Street Reform and Consumer Protection Act*. Washington, DC: US Congress.

Financial Navigator: A Modern Approach to Analytical Banking

Markus Thiele

1 Introduction

1.1 Scope

For overall bank management (e.g., risk controlling, financial controlling), comprehensive and complex calculations of key performance indicators and their subsequent detailed analysis for large portfolios of financial instruments of various types and complexity are absolutely crucial, since they are the basis for decision-making. Of particular importance is the study and analysis of the dependency of the calculational results on the change of the values of the input parameters and/or on the change of the methodology—for the sake of getting a much better insight into the complex (usually non-linear) interdependencies, the functioning of various cause-effect chains and the impact of new methodologies on the quality of the results. Due to the complexity and the variety of the models involved and in addition to the large amount and variety of data required, the calculations and the subsequent provisioning of the result data for reporting are usually very time-consuming, often cumbersome processes. Thus, in practice, large computing times severely limit the number of calculations (scenarios) that can be performed and analyzed each

M. Thiele (✉)
ifb SE, Grünwald, Germany
e-mail: Markus.Thiele@ifb-group.com

time, and for this reason alone the choice of modifications must be made with great care. The scenarios refer to performing essentially the same calculation several times, but each time with different values for certain input parameters and/or (usually an only slightly) changed methodology. The consequence of the limitation of the number of scenarios is a limitation of the possible insight into one's own portfolio with respect to getting a better understanding of the sensitivity of the results regarding the values of the input parameters and the methodology used. In other words, large computing times due to the amount of data required in conjunction with the comprehensiveness and complexity of the methodology involved is a permanent challenge and severely limits the extent of the analysis of a bank's own portfolio. In the past, these limitations were simply taken for granted, since—leaving enterprise-specific aspects aside—they simply reflected the capacity of the technological means of the time and the associated IT architectures.

For a fairly long time, technological improvements tended to happen in the form of gradual enhancements of computer power or data storage capacities. But it can be argued that the current (wave of) digitalization is different and will have a significant impact on banks and on the financial industry as a whole due to the combination of the following facts:

I. The recent improvements of technological means, above all in-memory databases (Kopic et al. 2019) and distributed computing (e.g., Hadoop cluster [Liermann et al. 2021]) represent not just a gradual improvement but can be considered a quantum leap in computing power. It is a leap in the sense that huge progress has been made in a fairly short timeframe. This alone must have an impact on how activities are exercised in the business departments since types of calculation have become available that just a few years ago seemed practically impossible.
II. The drastic improvements of technological means were also key for the recent boost in new methodologies, most notably machine learning and agent-based modeling,[1] which on the one hand represent powerful new approaches, but on the other require considerable computing power. For example, the theoretical basis of artificial neural networks has been well known for a fairly long time, but the extent of its use in the industry was rather modest. The networks simply turned out to be too small to reach or even outperform established, conventional methods. But now, where much larger artificial networks can be built and used on much faster

---

[1] Introduction into ABM (Wikipedia 2021).

technological devices, they often outperform conventional (non-machine-learning) methods (Goodfellow et al. 2016). There are now numerous examples available in the literature (Thiele and Dittmar 2019).

In the remaining part of this article, the Financial Navigator is introduced as a conceptual framework for how overall bank management can and arguably should be carried out against the background of the quantum leap of technological means. "Navigator" refers to the necessity of a bank to consider and assess (a broad range of) future scenarios for the portfolio and based on this make the best decisions ("navigating") for a profitable development of the portfolio and at the same time an acceptable risk.

In the first main part of the article, an explanation of the impetus and of the principal functioning of the conceptual framework is given from a purely business point of view. In the second main part, a description of illustrative IT architecture scenarios is given as possible technical realizations of the conceptual framework.

Note in this context that for specific parts of the conceptual framework there are separate articles within this book. This has been carried out against the background that these parts in themselves are both comprehensive and new, which means that they deserve a separate description. This refers in particular to the agent-based modeling part (Liermann and Dittmar 2021).

1.2 Article Structure

The remaining (main) part of the chapter is organized as follows: Chapter "Conceptual Framework" describes the conceptual framework of the Financial Navigator. In Chapter "Framework Application" the conceptual framework is exemplified for Credit Risk. Chapter "Implementation" describes implementation scenarios for the technical realization of the conceptual framework. Chapter "Practical Guidelines" contains some guidelines and recommendations of how to respond to typical practical challenges one encounters, when planning a realization of the conceptual framework. In Chapter "Summary" a brief summary is given.

2 Conceptual Framework

The Financial Navigator as the conceptual framework for how overall bank management (primarily in risk management and financial controlling) can be carried out against the background of the recent technological advances will be described on the basis of an illustrative example in the form of the portfolio credit risk. This means, the example is not intended to show and discuss results of a particular calculation, but instead it aims to illustrate how to put the different technological means together to serve the goal of significantly different, modernized overall bank management. Against this background, it should be fairly easy to imagine a similar realization in another context, e.g., financial controlling. First, the key ideas of the conceptual framework are described, followed by a description of the illustrative example. The main (interdependent) characteristics of the conceptual framework are, firstly, real-time capability, secondly, interactivity, thirdly, methodological and infrastructure flexibility, and fourthly, architecture-based modularization. Note that architecture-based modularization is a specific aspect of an enterprise-architecture-based approach (Merkt et al. 2021), which enters the conceptual framework in a number of places in the article. The key characteristics will be explained in greater detail in the following four subsections.

2.1 Real-Time Capability

Real-time capability means that complex calculations and their subsequent analysis of large portfolios can be carried out in real time or at least near real time. This possibility is a direct and quite obvious consequence of the drastically enhanced computing power now available due to in-memory and/or distributed computing (e.g., Hadoop cluster). Since the time for calculations of a whole portfolio can potentially be reduced by several orders of magnitude, this must have a profound impact on the way calculations of portfolios are carried out.

In the past, the large amount of data required in practice alone severely limited the possible number of calculations that could be carried out for the investigation and analysis of one's portfolio. This refers in particular to the study of different scenarios for the future development of the portfolio, which is absolutely crucial for a better understanding of the parameters and impact of the chosen methods on the outcome of the development. The limited number of scenarios usually leads to a restriction to comparatively few, well-defined scenarios—to keep the computing time in an acceptable range.

The reduction of the computing time per scenario through the efficient use of the new technological means by several orders of magnitude leads to a much greater degree of freedom with respect to choosing scenarios. The computing time becomes much less a limiting factor or can become practically irrelevant. One then has the opportunity to choose the values of parameters and/or the methods much more freely, or to put it simply: the scenario-based investigation of a portfolio becomes more like a playground, where even spontaneous ideas for a scenario can be tested and analyzed immediately.

Arguably this is the most important key characteristic, since the other two key characteristics are dependent on it and in practice do not make sense without it.

2.2 Interactivity

Interactivity means that a modern dashboard is used for the analysis of the results of an existing scenario and for the initiation and (at least nearly) immediate analysis of completed scenarios. Interactivity is linked to real-time capability since it only makes sense if the computation time for a new calculation can be considered negligible. The dashboard should of course have a suggestive (graphic-based) user interface for the easy analysis and change of parameters and the methodology, triggering new real-time calculations. Together with this real-time capability, this can greatly improve both the communication with and within management and, thus, decision-making in banks.

2.3 Methodological and Infrastructure Flexibility

Methodological and infrastructure flexibility refers to the following three aspects:

- Methodological flexibility refers to the fact that for the calculation part various modern methodologies can be used and exchanged in an ad hoc manner. This comprises both modern methodologies, such as machine learning and agent-based modeling, and more conventional methods, such as logistic regression. This possibility of an ad hoc exchange of an entire model can be seen as a modeling of higher order, since one can now compare fairly easily the influence of, and the results obtained with, different methods (but with exactly the same input data). Thus, flexibility

here refers to the property that the exchange of a method can be carried out as easily as a change of the values of input parameters.
- Infrastructure flexibility (in the narrower sense) means that the conceptual framework is independent of the specific tool or application. For example, it is not limited to the use of a specific in-memory database, a specific type of distributed computing, or a specific dashboard. Therefore, the conceptual framework allows the use of different in-memory databases, types of distributed computing, different dashboards, different open source software, and even different standard software.
- Infrastructure flexibility (in the wider sense) means that the conceptual framework can be applied by a single bank, a banking group, or a central bank. This only means that the types of model and data will be different, but the principal functioning is essentially the same. In brief, the conceptual framework can cover the viewpoint of individual banks, banking groups, and central banks.

2.4 Architecture-Based Modularization

Architecture-based modularization is the only one of the key characteristics that is not directly related to the technological means, but instead refers primarily to the business side. This means that the whole methodology is to be subdivided into well-defined, encapsulated functions, where each of the functions transforms a well-defined input according to a well-defined methodology into an equally well-defined output. This subdivision first must be carried out from a business point of view, and subsequently must be mirrored on the implementation side. In brief, it simply means that one has structured a complex calculation stringently and transparently for the sake of clarity. This is a prerequisite for an organized, easy way to exchange and replace certain functional pieces of the whole methodology. In other words, it is another, in this case non-technological, prerequisite for methodological flexibility. The architecture-based approach is already explained in a different article of this book and, thus, it is simply referenced from here (Merkt et al. 2021). Modularization is exemplified in the subsequent chapter.

3 Framework Application

The application of the conceptual framework is exemplified for the credit risk. Accordingly, in the following subsections, it is explained how the individual key characteristics of the conceptual framework can be realized for the benefit of credit risk management.

3.1 Basic Situation

As mentioned, the illustrative example refers to the portfolio credit risk. In this example, the following basic situation is assumed for the determination of the portfolio credit risk (Fig. 1):

- The **viewpoint** of our Credit Risk determination is that of an individual (model) bank. This means it is an individual bank that must determine and monitor its portfolio credit risk. Note in this context that the framework would also allow to account for, for example, a parent institute of a banking group or for a central bank. This would just require considering both the separation and aggregation of the different portfolios of different individual banks (the banks within a banking group or the banks under the supervision of a central bank).
- The credit risk taken by the bank is due to granting loans of certain types to their clients. Three types of **loans** are considered (without loss of generalization): (unsecured) corporate loan, (unsecured) retail loan/consumer credit, and mortgage loan. Other types of exposures can of course be

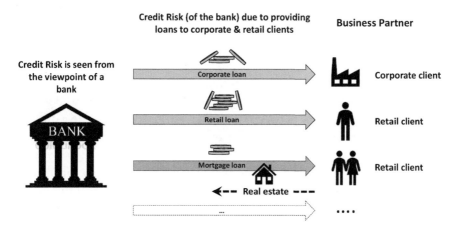

Fig. 1 Depiction of the basic model situation (© ifb SE)

considered. This would just mean that some additional modeling is required (e.g., specific EAD determination for derivatives, in case of inclusion of derivatives).
- The bank's **business partners** are corporate and retail clients, to whom the loans are granted. The different types of business partners can be distinguished through their classifying attributes. The model bank does grant loans to different business partners, and a business partner may have loans with different banks.
- For mortgage loans, there are **collateral instruments** in the form of real estate to be considered. In the model, there is always a one-to-one relationship between an exposure (in the form of a mortgage loan) and a collateral instrument in the form of real estate.

The enterprise-architecture-based approach here finds its expression in the formalization of the business entities mentioned in the form of four types of business object: Exposure (E), Business Partner (B), Collateral Instrument (C), and Portfolio (P). The latter represents an entity on its own due to the specific granularity of the portfolio information (and the specific aggregation methodology). As a consequence, every single piece of information can in each case be uniquely attributed to one of these three business objects (e.g., product type and exposure-at-default are attributes of the exposure). To indicate this, the attributes have a superscript in the form of the business object abbreviations (e.g., $EAD^{(E)}$ or Exposure-at-Default$^{(E)}$ denote the EAD of an exposure). The different business objects carry both static attributes (attributes whose values remain constant over time), such as the Industry_sector$^{(B)}$, and time-dependent attributes, such as the Probability-of-Default$^{(B)}$.

3.2 Thinking in Scenarios

A central feature of the model is the thinking in scenarios, which means that different future developments of the portfolio credit risk are considered. In this context, the difference between the two scenarios can be due to a different choice for (the values of) the model parameters and/or the use of partially different methods per scenario.

With regard to the values of the parameters, the scenarios refer to the (time evolution of the) macroeconomic indicators, or to phrase it differently: scenarios are macroeconomic scenarios. The macroeconomic scenarios reflect different possible outcomes for the future evolution of the macroeconomic indicators (e.g., economic downturn). Consequently, the time dependency of any of the other parameters is only due to a dependency on the macroeconomic indicators.

Two cases can be distinguished: In the first case, the values of the macroeconomic indicators are calculated per scenario for all (future) time steps (see next subsection). In the second case, arbitrary values for the values of the macroeconomic indicators can be chosen. Thus, the values are not then explicitly calculated.

In the following, a specific scenario is indicated by $s = 0, \ldots, S$. Here $s = 1, \ldots, S$ indicates the calculated scenarios (first case), and $s = 0$ indicates a scenario where the values of the macroeconomic indicators are simply set.

3.3 Temporal Structure

The forecasting for the macroeconomic indicators and, depending on these, the portfolio credit risk key figures is time discrete. This means the results are obtained for predefined points in time. The forecasting is based on historical information, which itself is available for discrete past points in time. The transition between the past and the future is the (in principle arbitrary) observation point. This means that information up to the observation point is considered as simply being given and from the observation point on the information is unknown and to be determined (unless it is static information). This results in a temporal or tenor structure, which can be described as follows: Let $T = \{t_{-L}, \ldots, t_{-1}, t_0, t_1, \ldots, t_U\} : t_{-L} < \cdots < t_{-1} < t_0 < t_1 < \cdots < t_U$ be the ordered set of all discrete points in time, for which either historical information is available or for which credit-risk-relevant information is to be forecast. Here, t_0 denotes the observation point in time, $L + 1$ is the number of (past) points in time for which historical information is available (including the observation point in time) and U denotes the number of (future) points in time for which the forecast has to happen. Neighboring points are assumed to be equidistant: $t_{-L+1} - t_{-L} = \cdots = t_0 - t_{-1} = t_1 - t_0 = \cdots = t_U - t_{U-1}$. Note that neither the equidistance, nor the length of the time intervals, nor the number of time intervals are necessary conditions. The past (including the observation point in time) is then represented by $T^{(-)} = \{t_{-L}, \ldots, t_{-1}, t_0\}$ and accordingly the future is represented by $T^{(+)} = \{t_1, \ldots, t_U\}$ and, thus, $T = T^{(-)} \cup T^{(+)}$. Based on these considerations and the scenario-based thinking, the following notation is used (Table 1):

Table 1 Symbols and their explanations © ifb SE

Symbol	Description
$x^{(M)}_{m;s;\tau}$	Value of the m-th macroeconomic indicator (M), according to scenario s, at time step t_τ
$x^{(B)}_{i;s;\tau}$	Value of an attribute of the i-th business partner (B), according to scenario s, at time step t_τ
$x^{(E)}_{ij;s;\tau}$	Value of an attribute of the j-th exposure to the i-th business partner (B), according to scenario s, at time step t_τ
$x^{(EP)}_{ij;s;\tau;0}$	Value of an attribute of the unsecured part of the j-th exposure to the i-th business partner (B), according to scenario s, at time step t_τ
$x^{(EP)}_{ij;s;\tau;1}$	Value of an attribute of the secured (by either residential real estate or commercial real estate) part of the j-th exposure to the i-th business partner (B), according to scenario s, at time step t_τ
$x^{(C)}_{k;s;\tau}$	Value of an attribute of the k-th collateral instrument, according to scenario s, at time step t_τ
$x^{(P)}_{s;\tau}$	Value of an attribute of the whole portfolio, according to scenario s, at time step t_τ

i: number of business partners; j: number of exposures; k: number of collateral instruments; m: number of macroeconomic indicators; s: number of scenarios

3.4 Business Capabilities

As already mentioned, as a general (construction) principle an architecture-based modularization is applied to the whole calculation. The results are clearly defined functional pieces with their input and output attributes. On the uppermost level the functional pieces are the following (Fig. 2):

- The **Macroeconomic Indicator determination** carries out the forecast of the values of some macroeconomic indicators, e.g., the unemployment _rate$^{(M)}$, for a set of future time steps, given by the tenor structure of the calculation (see Sect. 3.3 "Temporal Structure"). The forecasting for the different points in time is carried out for different scenarios, where the stochastic dependency between the various macroeconomic indicators is taken into account.
- The **PD determination** is a forecasting of the Probability-of-Default$^{(B)}$ and the Rating$^{(B)}$ per client in the portfolio, based on the forecast values of the macroeconomic indicators and on idiosyncratic attributes. The Probability-of-Default$^{(B)}$ and the Rating$^{(B)}$ are related by a simple mapping.

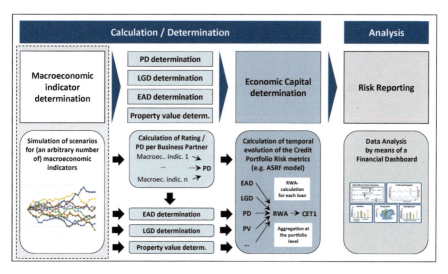

Fig. 2 Functional modules and their input–output relationships (black arrows) (© ifb SE)

- The **LGD determination** determines the Loss-Given-Default$^{(E)}$ (this means per loan/exposure) and the Loss-Given-Default$^{(C)}$ (this means per collateral instrument). The determination is essentially a simple derivation.
- The **EAD determination** means the determination of the future values of the Exposure-at-Default$^{(E)}$ per loan (exposure). The determination is dependent on the forecast values of the macroeconomic indicators and on the Rating$^{(R)}$ per business partner (for all business partners). It takes into account both the repayment of loans and the origination of new loans.
- The **Property Value determination** carries out forecasting of the Property value$^{(C)}$ per collateral instrument (in the form of real estate), securing the mortgage loans. The determination explicitly depends on the forecast macroeconomic indicators.
- The **Economic Capital determination** takes the forecast values for the Exposure-at-Default$^{(E)}$, the Probability-of-Default$^{(B)}$, the Loss-Given-Default$^{(E)}$ and Loss-Given-Default$^{(C)}$, and the Property_value$^{(C)}$ in conjunction with static business partner and loan information and determines the future values of portfolio credit risk key indicators as the Credit Value at Risk$^{(P)}$, the Unexpected Loss$^{(P)}$, etc.
- **Risk reporting** consumes the information from the calculation modules for interactive reporting in a financial dashboard. This means that the results of a calculation can be analyzed within, and new calculations can be triggered from the dashboard.

The different modules and their functioning will be explained in greater detail in the following subsections.

3.4.1 Macroeconomic Indicator Determination

The Macroeconomic Indicator determination is the determination of the future values of a chosen set of macroeconomic indicators, which for the purpose of the model are considered to sufficiently reflect the macroeconomic state. The determination of the macroeconomic indicators plays a special role among all functional modules, since two fundamentally different modes are considered (Fig. 3):

- In the first mode, a number of different scenarios are calculated (by taking into account stochastic dependencies between the different indicators). This can and is actually carried out independently and prior to the rest of the calculation, simply due to the fact that the macroeconomic indicators serve as input parameters. The result data per scenario is stored and serves as input for the rest of the calculation.
- In the second mode, the values of the macroeconomic indicators are simply set for one particular time step or for several future time steps based on expert knowledge. In this case, there is only a predefined set of values for the macroeconomic indicators and no calculation in the narrower sense. This expert choice of values is considered a determination in the wider sense.

Referring to the first mode, the following general statements may be made:

- It is based on the idea that historical data of the relevant macroeconomic indicators is used for the calibration of the respective model. Fortunately,

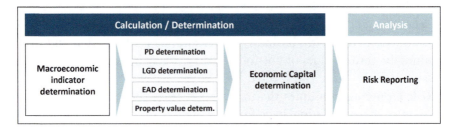

Fig. 3 Macroeconomic indicator determination (© ifb SE)

macroeconomic data is a form of market data. For this reason, long time series of this data is available for macroeconomic indicators.
- The calibrated model carries out the forecast for the values of the macroeconomic indicators for certain well-defined future time points (e.g., month end dates for the coming three years). The simulation for the set of macroeconomic indicators is carried out in a way that dependencies between the different indicators are taken into account and different scenarios are considered.

The central results of the determination are the values of all the macroeconomic indicators per scenario (in the first mode) or the predefined values (in the second mode), and per future time step.

Thus, the function takes as its input the historical values of the M macroeconomic indicators of each time step of the set $T^{(-)}$, which in matrix notation reads as follows:

$$\begin{pmatrix} x_{1;-L}^{(M)} & \cdots & x_{1;0}^{(M)} \\ \cdots & \cdots & \cdots \\ x_{M;-L}^{(M)} & \cdots & x_{M;0}^{(M)} \end{pmatrix}$$

Equation 1: Future values of the macroeconomic indicators (general)

In the example setup $M = 3$ macroeconomic indicators are used, namely the Gross Domestic Product ($x_1^{(M)}$ = GDP), the Unemployment Rate ($x_2^{(M)}$ = UER), and the Interest Rate ($x_3^{(M)}$ = INR). The historical values comprise $L = 113$ time steps and refer to annual quarters. Thus, the tenor structure T consists of past (and future) end dates of annual quarters. The historical values can be obtained, for example, from the Federal Reserve Bank of St. Louis and are publicly available (Federal Reserve Bank of St. Louis 2018). For the forecasting, one can choose between different methods, which express the methodological flexibility aspired to:

- Vector autoregression (VAR)
- Multi-GARCH (M-GARCH)
- Recurrent Neural Network (RNN).

The function produces as its output the forecast values of the M macroeconomic indicators per scenario for the set $T^{(+)}$ of future time steps, which in matrix notation reads as follows:

$$\begin{pmatrix} \text{GDP}_{s;1}^{(M)} & \dots & \text{GDP}_{s;U}^{(M)} \\ \text{UER}_{s;1}^{(M)} & \dots & \text{UER}_{s;U}^{(M)} \\ \text{INR}_{s;1}^{(M)} & \dots & \text{UER}_{s;U}^{(M)} \end{pmatrix} \forall s, \tau \in \mathbb{N}, 1 \le s \le S, 1 \le \tau \le U$$

Equation 2: Future values of the macroeconomic indicators (actually used for the example)

This information is used by the Probability-of-Default determination, the EAD determination, and the Property Value determination.

3.4.2 Probability-of-Default Determination

This function determines both the Rating$^{(B)}$ and the Probability-of-Default$^{(B)}$ per obligor and per future time step. As is quite common in credit risk management, the determination is split into two parts, where in the first part the determination of the Rating$^{(B)}$ happens, and in the second part the Probability-of-Default$^{(B)}$ is derived in the form of a simple mapping (using a look-up table). Both Rating$^{(B)}$ and Probability-of-Default$^{(B)}$ are dependent on both macroeconomic and idiosyncratic information. The macroeconomic inputs are the forecast values of the M macroeconomic indicators (see output of function "Macroeconomic Indicator determination"). The idiosyncratic inputs are (time-independent) attributes of the business partner. Note that there is no principal reason why time dependent idiosyncratic attributes could not be used, but this would just require the use of an additional module for the respective forecasting of the idiosyncratic variables (Fig. 4).

For the determination of the values of the Probability-of-Default$^{(B)}$ of all business partners and per future time step, one can choose between different methods, which is another expression of methodological flexibility:

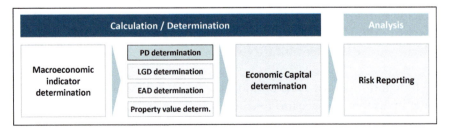

Fig. 4 Probability-of-Default determination (© ifb SE)

- Logistic Regression
- Random Forests
- Deep Learning.

The outputs of the PD determination are the future values of the Rating$^{(B)}$ and the PD$^{(B)}$ for each of the obligors and for each of the future time steps, which in formal notation reads as follows:

$$\begin{pmatrix} R^{(B)}_{1;s;1} & \cdots & R^{(B)}_{1;s;U} \\ \cdots & \cdots & \cdots \\ R^{(B)}_{I;s;1} & \cdots & R^{(B)}_{I;s;U} \end{pmatrix}, \begin{pmatrix} \text{PD}^{(B)}_{1;s;1} & \cdots & \text{PD}^{(B)}_{1;s;U} \\ \cdots & \cdots & \cdots \\ \text{PD}^{(B)}_{I;s;1} & \cdots & \text{PD}^{(B)}_{I;s;U} \end{pmatrix} \forall i, s, \tau \in \mathbb{N}, 1 \leq i \leq I, 1 \leq s \leq S, 1 \leq \tau \leq U$$

Equation 3: Future values of the Rating and the Probability-of-Default

This Rating part of the output is used by the EAD determination, and the PD part of the output is used by the Economic Capital determination.

3.4.3 Loss-Given-Default Determination

The Loss-Given-Default determination uses a simple derivation with prescribed values for the Loss-Given-Default$^{(E)}$ of an (unsecured) loan and for the Loss-Given-Default$^{(C)}$ of a collateral instrument in the form of residential real estate and commercial real estate, respectively. This reads as follows (Fig. 5, Table 2):

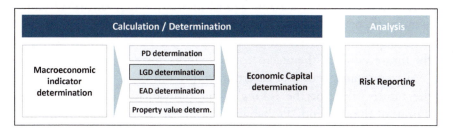

Fig. 5 Loss-Given-Default (© ifb SE)

Table 2 Determination of the Loss-Given-Default © ifb SE

	No collateral	LGD$^{(E)}$ = 100%
Collateral instrument	Collateral_type$^{(C)}$ = "Residential real estate"	LGD$^{(C)}$ = 35%
	Collateral_type$^{(C)}$ = "Commercial real estate"	LGD$^{(C)}$ = 40%

Note that there is no principal reason to use a much more complex model. This would just require a more comprehensive module, which for the purpose of this article (the illustration of the conceptual framework) would add unnecessary complexity.

The input for this function is the Loan_type$^{(E)}$ of a loan and the Collateral_type$^{(C)}$ of a collateral instrument. The outputs of this function are the (time-independent) values of the Loss-Given-Default$^{(E)}$ per loan and the Loss-Given-Default$^{(C)}$ per collateral instrument:

$$\begin{pmatrix} \text{LGD}_1^{(E)} \\ \ldots \\ \text{LGD}_J^{(E)} \end{pmatrix} \forall j \in \mathbb{N}, 1 \leq j \leq J, \begin{pmatrix} \text{LGD}_1^{(C)} \\ \ldots \\ \text{LGD}_K^{(C)} \end{pmatrix} \forall k \in \mathbb{N}, 1 \leq k \leq K$$

Equation 4: Future values of the Loss-Given-Default

This output is used by the Economic Capital determination and by risk reporting.

3.4.4 Exposure-at-Default Determination

This function determines the EAD$^{(E)}$ for each of the time steps of the set $T^{(+)}$. For this forecasting the following two time-dependent aspects are considered: Firstly the development of the Exposure-at-Default$^{(E)}$ of exposures already existing at the observation point in time and secondly the origination of new exposures, each one representing a new Exposure-at-Default$^{(E)}$. The major input parameters for this function are (Fig. 6):

- the future values of the macroeconomic indicators (see output of function "Macroeconomic Indicator determination") and
- the future value for the Rating$^{(B)}$ per individual business partner (see output of the function "Probability-of-Default determination").

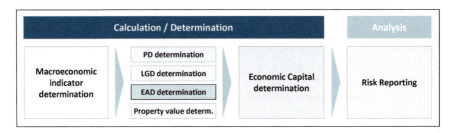

Fig. 6 Exposure-at-Default determination (© ifb SE)

The development of the Exposure-at-Default$^{(E)}$ of an existing exposure is comparatively easy to model, since only loans are considered, and for them simple analytical expressions in the form of monotonically decreasing analytical functions are used. As was already mentioned earlier, there are no principal reasons to include other products with a more complex (e.g., also non-deterministic) behavior. Much more demanding is a modeling of the (temporal evolution of the) origination of new loans for the following main (interdependent) reasons, which are both explicitly considered for this functional module:

I. The origination of new loans is dependent on factors intrinsic to the (model) bank in the form of the preferences for granting loans varying between, for example, different rating classes, client types, etc.
II. The development also depends very much on factors extrinsic to the bank in the form of the bank's environment in a twofold sense, specifically the macroeconomic situation and the behavior of the banks competing for clients with one's own bank on the financial market.

The second aspect is particularly complex since it considers the competing/concurrent but at the same time interdependent actions of several market players against the background of the macroeconomic situation. The following different types of market players (also called "agents") and types of actions are to be considered:

- The **clients** of banks **have loans** with different banks and/or **apply for and potentially get new loans**. In addition, they **repay those loans** that already originated at a certain point in time.
- Different **banks** (including the model bank) **offer and grant loans** according to their current status and their strategic preferences, in this respect competing with each other.
- On the **financial market**, the request for new loans by the clients on the one hand and the offering of loans by the competing banks on the other are **matched**.

In this context note that both the behavior of the banks and the clients depend on and happen against the background of the macroeconomy. To fully account for the complexity, one must explicitly determine the development of not just one's own bank, but jointly of the competing banks as well, this means without prescribing the behavior of the latter and the development of the market. It is easy to imagine that even with just a handful of agents the matching can become very complex, and is solvable only numerically, requiring considerable computing power. One fundamental (often unspoken) model paradigm of the vast majority of risk models of individual banks is that for the risk calculation the environment (macroeconomy, competing banks, etc.) is only entered in the form of parameters or prescribed behaviors, but is not in itself a subject or target of the model, and there is no dynamic feedback and interdependency between banks and their environment. Arguably a comprehensive determination in the sense described above would represent a significant softening of this fundamental paradigm, since determining the development also of the competing banks means to a certain extent determining a part of the macroeconomy as well. In the following, this will be called "comprehensive approach."

The immense computational power and the considerable computing times required for this kind of simulation are probably the main reason why banks have chosen different approaches in the past: some banks merely use expert knowledge for their own portfolio forecast with underlying assumptions about the exogenous macroeconomic development (and the behavior of the competing banks). Other banks use calculations, with the decisive restriction that the development of the competing banks (and of the market) in itself is not a result of the calculation but exogenous to the model (based on expert judgments).

An adequate methodology for the comprehensive approach is agent-based modeling (ABM), since this aims to determine the evolution of a system consisting of autonomous entities (called "agents"), interacting with each other and with a dynamic environment. The individual agents can be regarded as abstractions from real-world objects (e.g., banks, clients), with certain characteristic properties and a rule-based behavior (Schinckus 2019). In the context of the Exposure-at-Default determination, it is a bottom-up approach due to its explicit reference to the granular level of agents as autonomous business entities. In this context, an abstraction is used to define the granularity of the model, e.g., real-world entities such as banks and clients are stripped of their irrelevant properties, or several real-world entities are aggregated into one agent, etc. The applicability of agent-based modeling is similar to Artificial Neural Networks in the following sense: the latter gained widespread popularity only when sufficiently large networks could be used, and the former provides benefits only in case of a sufficiently large number of agents and evolutionary inhomogeneity in their individual states and behaviors. Due to the recent technological advances, this is now possible.

Against this background, two different approaches can be applied to arrive at a quantitative predictive model: on the one hand, one can apply an expert estimate, where one would have to prescribe the temporal evolution of one's own portfolio (e.g., according to an analytical function) and different scenarios can be considered that represent external influences. On the other hand, agent-based modeling can be used to model external influences explicitly and determine the future development of the portfolio. Since agent-based modeling will be explained in detail in a separate chapter of this book (Liermann and Dittmar 2021), only the principal functioning of the model is described here (see also subsequent figure):

- Both one's **own bank and the competing banks are treated equally as agents**, offering loans to potential clients in the financial market. This means from a methodological point of view there is no principal difference between one's own bank and a competing bank. As already mentioned, the explicit consideration of all banks from the economic system point of view is strikingly different to the vast majority of existing models.
- The **banks are characterized by certain static and dynamic attributes**, such as bank type (universal bank, mortgage bank, retail bank) and **by a specific behavior**, which consists of various actions they take upon impulses from their environment. The principal behavior of offering and providing loans to the clients on the market is characteristic for a bank. In addition, each bank is characterized by specific preferences and restrictions with regard to the successive order in which loans are granted to clients.
- The **business partners/clients of the banks are the second type of agents**. They differ from the banks as they apply for new loans and repay existing loans. Also, they are characterized by different attributes such as client type (retail client, corporate client) and debt ratio. They also have specific preferences and restrictions with regard to the acceptance of loan offers, which are also expressed by suitable functions.
- The third type of agent are the markets on which the banks and the **business partners meet, and where the supply and demand of loans are matched**, according to a market-specific matching methodology. The market agents play a coordinating role, are able to make decisions based on aggregated information and reduce the number of messages that need to be exchanged between individual agents.

On the one hand, agent-based modeling jointly determines the temporal evolution of the portfolios of all banks, and on the other it is the development of one's own portfolio that matters and, thus, will be used in the subsequent calculation steps (Fig. 7).

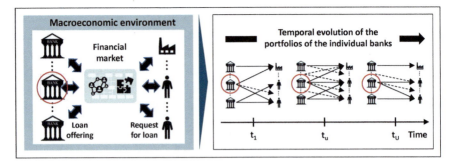

Fig. 7 Sketch of the determination of the temporal evolution of the portfolios (red circle: own bank) (© ifb SE)

The outputs of the EAD determination are the future values of the EAD$^{(E)}$ per loan of the bank's own portfolio, per scenario and for each of the future time steps, which in formal notation reads as follows:

$$\begin{bmatrix} \text{EAD}^{(E)}_{1;s;1} & \cdots & \text{EAD}^{(E)}_{1;s;U} \\ \vdots & \ddots & \vdots \\ \text{EAD}^{(E)}_{J;s;1} & \cdots & \text{EAD}^{(E)}_{J;s;U} \end{bmatrix} \forall j, s, \tau \in \mathbb{N}, 1 \leq j \leq J, 1 \leq s \leq S, 1 \leq \tau \leq U$$

Equation 5: Future values of the Exposure-at-Default

This output is used by the Economic Capital determination and by risk reporting.

3.4.5 Property Value Determination

This function determines the Property value$^{(C)}$ for a collateral instrument in the form of residential real estate and commercial real estate, respectively, for each of the time steps of the set $T^{(+)}$. The function uses as its major input parameters the Collateral_type$^{(C)}$ and the future values of the macroeconomic indicators (see output of function "Macroeconomic Indicator determination"). For the forecasting of the Property value$^{(C)}$ an expert estimate is used, where the development is prescribed functionally, dependent on the macroeconomic variables. Note that other more sophisticated methodologies could also be included in this context (Fig. 8).

The outputs of the function are the future values of the Property value$^{(C)}$ for each collateral instrument and for each of the future time steps, which in formal notation reads as follows:

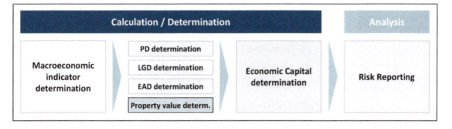

Fig. 8 Property value determination (© ifb SE)

$$\begin{bmatrix} \text{Property\_ value}_{1;s;1} & \cdots & \text{Property\_ value}_{1;s;U} \\ \vdots & \ddots & \vdots \\ \text{Property\_ value}_{K;s;1} & \cdots & \text{Property\_ value}_{K;s;U} \end{bmatrix} \forall k,s,\tau \in \mathbb{N}, 1 \leq k \leq K, 1 \leq s \leq S, 1 \leq \tau \leq U$$

Equation 6: Future values of the property value

This output is used by the Economic Capital determination and by risk reporting.

3.4.6 Economic Capital Determination

The Economic Capital determination is the last calculational step, where the results from the previous modules become combined and aggregated into measures for the portfolio credit risk. The main inputs for this function are the future values of the Probability-of-Default$^{(B)}$ for each business partner (see output of function "Probability-of-Default determination"), the Loss-Given-Default$^{(E)}$ per exposure and the Loss-Given-Default$^{(C)}$ per collateral instrument (see output of function "Loss-Given-Default determination"), and the Exposure-at-Default$^{(E)}$ for each of the exposures of the reference bank (see output of function "Exposure-of-Default determination"). In principle, various credit portfolio models could be used, for example of the Asymptotic-Single-Risk-Factor (ASRF), Credit Risk+ or Credit Metrics type. For the illustrative purpose of this article an ASRF model is chosen, since it is widely known (due to its relevance in the regulatory context) and has an analytical form. In addition, the portfolio credit risk measures are also available on the most granular level (collateralized or blank exposure part). The corresponding analytical functions for the corporate and retail loans correspond to those for regulatory reporting (European Union 2013), with just slight modifications. The outputs of this function are the future values of the EL$^{(E)}$ (EL: expected loss) and the UL$^{(E)}$ (UL: unexpected loss) for each exposure part,

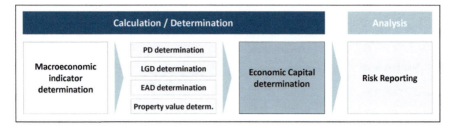

Fig. 9 Economic Capital determination (© ifb SE)

per scenario, and for each of the future time steps, which in formal notation reads as follows (Fig. 9):

$$\begin{bmatrix} \mathrm{EL}^{(E)}_{1;s;1} & \cdots & \mathrm{EL}^{(E)}_{1;s;U} \\ \vdots & \ddots & \vdots \\ \mathrm{EL}^{(E)}_{J;s;1} & \cdots & \mathrm{EL}^{(E)}_{J;s;U} \end{bmatrix}, \begin{bmatrix} \mathrm{UL}^{(E)}_{1;s;1} & \cdots & \mathrm{UL}^{(E)}_{1;s;U} \\ \vdots & \ddots & \vdots \\ \mathrm{UL}^{(E)}_{J;s;1} & \cdots & \mathrm{UL}^{(E)}_{J;s;U} \end{bmatrix} \quad \forall j, s, \tau \in \mathbb{N}, 1 \leq j \leq J, 1 \leq s \leq S, 1 \leq \tau \leq U$$

Equation 7: Future values of the expected loss and the unexpected loss

Note that for the secured loans a splitting of the loan into a not secured and a secured part is carried out, and for each part the $\mathrm{EL}^{(E)}$ and the $\mathrm{UL}^{(E)}$ are separately determined. Per loan the sum of the blank and the secured part then gives the corresponding result for the loan. It must be kept in mind that a secured loan is secured by just one collateral instrument, and a collateral instrument can only collateralize one loan (see Sect. 3.1 "Basic Situation").

The output is used together with the output from the other functions by risk reporting.

3.4.7 Risk Reporting

From an abstract point of view, the meaning of risk reporting (within the conceptual framework) is twofold (Fig. 10):

- Firstly, it means the (primarily) graphical visualization and the analysis of the results obtained in the preceding calculational steps, on the basis of a highly suggestive dashboard.
- Secondly, it refers to the initiation of completely new calculations with changed model parameters and/or a changed methodology.

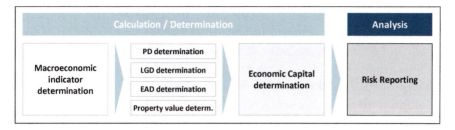

Fig. 10 Risk reporting (© ifb SE)

Fig. 11 Example interactive dashboard (© ifb SE)

The subsequent figure shows an actual realization of a dashboard (here: SAP Analytics Cloud), which can pass as a concrete realization of this kind of risk reporting (Fig. 11).

The concrete structure of the dashboard and the concrete types of graph displayed will definitely be specific to the particular bank that applies the framework and uses the dashboard. Thus, the dashboard shown here is just an example realization. It consists of three distinct parts: the Control Parameter unit, the Scenario Information unit, and the Model Result unit.

The **Control Parameter unit** can be seen in the left part of the dashboard. This is the place where the essential model parameters are displayed and can be adjusted. The model parameters are, on the one hand, the macroeconomic parameters and, on the other, the various methods used for the calculation. The calculation results, which can be seen in the result unit, are determined based on and always refer to the settings in the control unit. Once any of the parameters in the control unit are changed, a new full calculation of the portfolio is immediately initiated, and the results of the new calculation can (almost) immediately be seen in the result unit of the dashboard. In this context, almost arbitrary combinations of changes of parameters and methods are possible. The immediate initiation of a new calculation due to a change of the model parameters is what makes the framework interactive, the (almost) immediate display of the results is what gives it its real-time character, and the possibility to exchange a whole model ensures its methodological flexibility. The change of the input parameters in the form of the macroeconomic indicators (Unemployment Rate, Key Interest Rate, and Gross Domestic Product) simply happens by using the respective different slider in the Control Parameter unit. One can also choose between different methodologies for each of the different parts of the calculation (Macroeconomic Indicator determination, Probability-of-Default determination, etc.) by simply selecting a certain model out of a drop-down menu in the Control Parameter unit (see lower left part of the dashboard). Concerning the setting of the macroeconomic indicators there are two general options:

- In the uncorrelated case (Correlation "off"), one may set the values of the macroeconomic indicators arbitrarily, this means not assuming any decisive stochastic dependency between the macroeconomic indicators. This case could be interesting for the study of the influence of exceptional macroeconomic situations, such as a financial crisis (where the dependencies between different macroeconomic indicators are practically unknown).
- In the correlated case (Correlation "on"), the macroeconomic indicators cannot be set independently, since by definition they are interdependent. In this case, one chooses a particular calculated scenario for the interdependent evolution of the macroeconomic indicators (by setting one of the macroeconomic indicators as "Active Parameter" and setting a specific value for the indicator).

The **Scenario Information unit** refers specifically to the macroeconomic indicators and shows how the values of the indicators change with time. The part of the graph highlighted in gray shows the historical values (this means for time steps within $T^{(-)}$), whereas the remaining values to the right are the forecast values (this means for time steps within $T^{(+)}$). The forecast values were determined with a particular methodology and for a particular scenario. The methodology used for the forecasting and the scenario chosen are displayed in the control unit and were set there. The Scenario Information unit was integrated into the dashboard to visually link the macroeconomic indicators (and their evolution) to the results information in the result unit.

The **Model Result unit** can be seen in the lower right half of the dashboard. Here, the results of the calculation are displayed, based on the settings seen in the Control Parameter unit. Once the settings within the control unit are changed, a new calculation starts and the results within the Model Result unit are updated. The types of graph to be shown in the Model Result unit of course depend on the preferences of the individual bank, and even on different groups of users within the bank. Apart from the fact that the information to be displayed in the result unit should be available in the data model, there is a large degree of freedom for the definition of the graphs. In the dashboard shown above, there are four different graphs, displaying key results of the calculation on an aggregated level, e.g., the distribution of the unexpected loss (determined in Economic Capital determination) over the different rating grades.

4 Implementation

The central statement of this article is that the recent technological leaps enable banks to conduct their overall bank management in a much more modern manner. The central goals underlying the associated conceptual framework are real-time capability, interactivity and methodological flexibility.

4.1 Technological Means

The technological means for the realization of the conceptual framework and in particular its central goals (see above) are the following:

- **Real-time capability** can be achieved by using an in-memory database and/or distributed computing (distributed data storage and processing). For specific reasons, it can make sense to combine the two different technological means within one IT architecture. Note that there are also other modern technological means imaginable (e.g., quantum computers), but in-memory databases and distributed computing are currently seen as the best options, since they are readily available and two of the pillars of digitalization.
- **Interactivity** is a combined feature of a modern dashboard and the underlying database. The dashboard must enable the change of parameters and the subsequent immediate initiation of a new calculation. This requires

in turn that there is an appropriate bi-directional interface between the dashboard and the database.
- **Methodological flexibility** is not directly associated with another technological means but builds largely upon the technological means already mentioned. Therefore, in the dashboard it must be possible to change not just values of parameters, but also methods. Of course, this also requires an appropriate modular organization and structuring of the whole methodology.

There are numerous ways to use and combine the new technological means to meet these central goals (at least to a considerable degree), and the different ways correspond to different (target) IT architecture scenarios. The main reasons for the many different imaginable IT architecture scenarios are the following:

- The revision of the IT architecture must be carried out against the background that for well-considered reasons some of the existing IT systems may not be removed and, thus, must be integrated into a new IT architecture.
- There are usually different standard software applications from different vendors, which serve the goals equally well and differ only in, for example, the functional details.

Among other things, the scenarios differ by the location of the different business capabilities. Here "location" means in which IT system a specific business capability is actually realized (implemented). The location of the different business capabilities has important implications for the interfaces, how the data is to be exchanged between the different systems.

Against this background, an example IT architecture is described, which has actually been implemented and tested. In addition, alternative scenarios are briefly discussed. The description of the scenario is structured according to the different types of software involved ("Components") and to the principal functioning of a whole calculation and reporting process. The ultimate starting point for the description of the principal functioning of the architecture scenario is always the dashboard since new calculations are initiated from there.

4.2 Example IT Architecture Scenario

In the scenario, standard software applications (SAP and Simudyne) are combined with open source software (Python and R). The scenario mirrors a situation where a bank, on the one hand, has a modern central in-memory database in place (SAP HANA), but on the other wants to use a standard software for agent-based modeling (Simudyne SDK). A bank might have made the decision for different software products from different vendors on the basis of the functional sophistication of the software in its respective field of application (Fig. 12).

4.2.1 Components

The **principal input data** (business partner data, loan data, collateral instrument data, market data) **and the result data** are stored in an **SAP HANA database**, which is an in-memory database and the technological basis to perform real-time calculations (in the context of this architecture scenario).

The **business capabilities** (Macroeconomic Indicator determination, Probability-of-Default determination, Loss-Given-Default determination, Economic Capital determination, Property Value determination) are coded **in Python and R**. The only exception is the "Exposure-at-Default determination" (see next point). The Python and R code is efficiently integrated within SAP HANA.

The **business capability "EAD determination"** is implemented **on the basis of Simudyne SDK** as a powerful standard software dedicated especially to agent-based modeling (and artificial intelligence). Simudyne SDK runs on a Hadoop cluster.

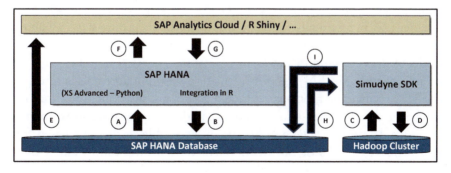

Fig. 12 Sketch of the example IT architecture scenario (© ifb SE)

Interactive **risk reporting** can be realized by using frontends, such as **SAP Analytics Cloud or R Shiny** (see general statements above).

4.2.2 Principal Functioning

The macroeconomic scenarios are calculated prior to the calculation of EAD time series. That means their dynamics are decoupled from the evolution of the EAD time series. Of course, it is a valid consideration to make the macroeconomic evolution an endogenous part of future extensions of the EAD model, but one should note that it is not trivial to calibrate macroeconomic dynamic processes with real data. Therefore, historical time series of the macroeconomic indicators are read from persistent SAP HANA tables and are sent to a separate R server (R installed on Linux host[2]), together with the R code for time series forecasts via a stored procedure (A). The result data in the form of the forecast values of the macroeconomic indicators is sent back to SAP HANA. This data exchange is efficient due to the similarities of data structures in SAP HANA and R and, thus, it offers a performance advantage over standard SQL interfaces.

A calculation of the portfolio credit risk is then initiated from the dashboard. Within SAP HANA, the calculation functions by using a HANA calculation view. To have control over the business capabilities, i.e., to alter model parameters, the HANA calculation view is equipped with a set of input parameters, which, when accessed from the reporting frontend, automatically trigger a new calculation (G) upon change. Therefore, upon change of any parameter in the control unit of the dashboard, the SAP HANA calculation view consumes the macroeconomic forecasts and uses them for the execution of the Probability-of-Default (and Rating), the Loss-Given-Default and the Property Value determination. The macroeconomic forecasts and the R script for the calculation of PD/Rating, LGD and the property value are sent to the R server (A), in essentially the same way as in the preceding step (see above). The result data is sent back to SAP HANA and is incorporated in the data model of the calculation view.

Subsequently, the SAP HANA calculation view initiates a Scala script (H) that (1) executes the agent-based model as a Spark-distributed job that runs on the Hadoop cluster (C,D), and (2) performs post-processing to make the result data on the Hadoop file system accessible to the SAP-based frontend. The key results of the ABM calculation are the future values of the EAD for all exposures, generated as Parquet files. These Parquet files are then

---

[2] This interface uses the well-known RSERVE bridge (Urbanek 2020).

linked to a HBASE table, which can be accessed by the SAP HANA calculation view (I). On the SAP HANA side, the communication with a Hadoop cluster is enabled through so-called smart data access (SDA), so that from the perspective of the calculation view the HBASE table is just a remote data source.

Then, once again, basic data and result data (PD, LGD, EAD, property value) are sent to the R server (A), this time for the Economic Capital determination as the last calculation step. As in the previous steps, the result data is sent back to SAP HANA and becomes incorporated in the data model of the calculation view.

The SAP HANA calculation view is read regularly (according to a specified frequency) by the dashboard in a fully automated manner (F). Each read triggers the full process chain described above in real time using filter and model parameter values selected by the user. Therefore, the data displayed in the dashboard is always up to date. Apart from the data in the calculation view, other data can of course also be retrieved directly from the SAP HANA database and combined with the calculation data (E).

4.3 Alternative IT Architecture Scenarios

As indicated, there are several different IT architecture scenarios imaginable, which meet the central goals to a similar degree. With the same components as in the example scenario (see preceding subsection), one can think of other combinations such as the following:

- Instead of using both an SAP HANA database and a Hadoop cluster, one can decide to just use the former as the ultimate data source (and sink). This would mean that all functional modules run on an SAP HANA database. On the one hand, this would facilitate the exchange of data between the different components, since an interface between SAP HANA and a Hadoop cluster is omitted. On the other hand, agent-based modeling (with Simudyne SDK) runs best if the computational processes are highly parallelized. This is the reason why it is particularly well suited for Hadoop clusters. Thus, in this case one would simplify the interfaces and the data exchange but would have to use a highly parallelized machine.
- One could also imagine using just a Hadoop cluster without an in-memory database such as SAP HANA. This would mean that all functional modules run on a Hadoop cluster. On the one hand, this would facilitate the exchange of data between the different components, since the interface between the Hadoop cluster and the SAP HANA database is omitted.

In addition, this is well suited for running agent-based modeling (with Simudyne SDK), since a Hadoop cluster is by definition intended for distributed computing (parallelization of processes and/or distributed data storage). On the other hand, SAP HANA comprises an infrastructure for the orchestration of processes and the administration of the different methods (versioning, governance, etc.). In addition, content in the sense of a predefined data model and corresponding predefined performant views of the data is available. Therefore, in this case as well one would simplify the interfaces and the data exchange, but in contrast to the first case one would not have the infrastructure and the data model content available.

Thus, even just taking the components of the example scenario into account, different scenarios can be imagined, each with pros and cons. It is obvious that the decision for a certain IT architecture scenario strongly depends on the preferences and strategic goals of the particular bank, financial corporate or insurance company. This will be addressed (among other things) in the next chapter.

5 Practical Guidelines

Since the conceptual framework represents a fairly new view of how to conduct overall bank management, it must have consequences for the mindsets, the governance and the processes in different ways, which will be explained in the following paragraphs.

  I. The decision to apply the conceptual framework has a definite strategic character. Thus, the ultimate prerequisite for a realization is that there is a clear and strategic decision that such a framework is to be realized in principle, and to what extent it is to be realized. In this context, the following aspects must be considered:

   - The decision is to be made against the background of a (usually) already existing IT landscape, where at least some of the applications are intended to be kept. This could (but not necessarily has to) restrict the extent to which real-time calculations, interactivity, and methodological flexibility can be realized.
   - The decision must take into account that the corresponding change not only refers to the IT architecture, IT systems and IT processes, but must have an impact on business processes and the methodologies

used as well. One can argue that a changed mindset is required (see II).

- The decision must also take into account the implications for the interpretability of results, in case complex new (families of) methods such as machine learning are used extensively (see III).

II. Since the conceptual framework by definition entails significantly enhanced possibilities for the overall bank management, all people using these means must first be carefully guided on how to use the new means and how to principally interpret and communicate the results. For example, the CEO of a bank might want to initiate a calculation from his tablet computer, to spontaneously investigate the influence of a specific macroeconomic situation on the credit risk of the portfolio. The result (since calculations are performed in real time) is almost immediately available and can be seen and analyzed on the tablet computer, and possibly the result is surprising and unexpected. On the one hand, such a usage of the new means is absolutely desirable and intended by the conceptual framework, since it greatly helps bank management to better understand the dependency of the portfolio on the macroeconomy. On the other hand, this might result in frequent consultation of the Credit Risk Management department with a request for help to interpret the results. The Credit Risk Management department might become overwhelmed by the number, frequency, and complexity of requests of this kind. Consequently, the **usage of the new means must become channeled and organized**, where the following aspects must be considered:

- The dashboard tool should comprise means for a traceability of the results in the sense that the setting of the parameters for a calculation, initiated via the use of the dashboard, can be stored and easily transmitted to others. There must be a process with a corresponding governance in place, which defines the recipient(s), the type and the format of information to be transmitted, etc.
- There must be careful training of those people who are intended to use the new means. As a minimum, this must cover an understanding of how the new conceptual and IT framework works in principle, what it offers and also what kind of restrictions there are, and what (new or revised) processes one must follow for the usage.

III. From a **methodological point of view, one must address the traceability of the result** received with complex (families of) methods, such as machine learning and agent-based modeling. This is to be done against the background that machine learning methods, for example, are considered a "black box" by some. Among other things, this also means integrating methods and processes for the traceability of the results. There are now approaches available that explicitly account for much better traceability. These approaches are sometimes subsumed under the term "model forensics."

IV. For the use of the conceptual framework by a specific bank, a considerable amount of **expert knowledge is required**. This is due to the considerable degree of freedom associated with the different functional components. Thus, on the one hand, one must define not just the values of the model parameters but also certain functional relationships (e.g., between the credit demand and the macroeconomic indicators in the Portfolio Credit Risk determination). On the other hand, the choices made are no less "definite" in the sense that any calculation (since it can be carried out in real time) does not consume much time, and, thus, calculations with different functional forms could be conducted.

6 Summary

It has been argued that the recent technological advances (e.g., in-memory databases and distributed computing) can be considered a true (technological) leap, enabling banks to conduct their overall bank management in a manner which seemed practically impossible a few years ago. With the Financial Navigator, a conceptual framework for this new way has been described. The key goals of the framework are real-time capability, interactivity and methodological flexibility (which builds upon the two former). Real-time capability means that complex and comprehensive calculations can be carried out in a very short timeframe (at least nearly real time). Arguably, this is the most important technological advance, since so far computing time has been and is the most important limiting factor for exploring the parameter space and for trying out new methods. To gain a better insight into the basic functioning of the conceptual framework, an illustrative example from portfolio credit risk has been described from a business and IT architecture point of view, including a discussion of the pros and cons of different IT architecture scenarios, against the background of the key goals.

Acknowledgement The author would like to thank his colleagues Marcus Jenderka, Harro Dittmar and Volker Liermann for fruitful discussions and helpful comments.

Literature

European Union. 2013. "Capital Requirements Regulation." *Official Journal of the European Union*, Art. 153–154.

Federal Reserve Bank of St. Louis. 2018. *Economic Research*. https://fred.stlouisfed.org/.

Goodfellow, Ian, Yoshua Bengio, and Aaron Courville. 2016. *Deep Learning*. Cambridge, MA: The MIT Press.

Kopic, Teschome, Schneider, Steurer, and Florin. 2019. "In-Memory Databases and Their Impact on Our (Future) Organizations." In *The Impact of Digital Transformation and Fintech on the Finance Professional*. Cham: Palgrave Macmillan.

Liermann, Volker, and Harro Dittmar. 2021. "BSDS—Balance Sheet Dynamic Simulator (Application ABM)." In *The Digital Journey of Banking and Insurance, Volume I—Disruption and DNA*, edited by Volker Liermann and Claus Stegmann. New York: Palgrave Macmillan.

Liermann, Volker, Sangmeng Li, and Johannes Waizner. 2021. "Distributed Calculation Credit Portfolio Models." In *The Digital Journey of Banking and Insurance, Volume II—Digitalization and Machine Learning*, edited by Volker Liermann and Claus Stegmann. New York: Palgrave Macmillan.

Merkt, Rainer, Markus Thiele, and Florian Dinges. 2021. "Digitalization Landscape Banking." In *The Digital Journey of Banking and Insurance, Volume I—Disruption and DNA*, edited by Volker Liermann and Claus Stegmann. New York: Palgrave Macmillan.

Schinckus, Christophe. 2019. "Agent-Based Modelling and Economic Complexity: A Diversified Perspective." *Journal of Asian Business and Economic Studies* 26 (2): 170–188.

Thiele, Markus, and Harro Dittmar. 2019. "Internal Credit Risk Models with Machine Learning." In *The Impact of Digital Transformation and FinTech on the Finance Professional*, edited by Volker Liermann and Claus Stegmann. Cham: Palgrave Macmillan.

Urbanek. 2020. "Rserve: Binary R Server." *The Comprehensive R Archive Network*. October 15. https://cran.r-project.org/web/packages/Rserve/index.html.

Wikipedia. 2021. *Agent-Based Model*. Accessed February 12, 2021. https://en.wikipedia.org/wiki/Agent-based_model.

Actuarial Data Science

Susanne Brindöpke

1 Introduction

New technological inventions and new data sources drive digitalization, which in these times is certainly one of the most important drivers for almost every business sector, not only in financial companies. It will change the way we learn and study, how we communicate privately or with clients, how we do business, how we do shopping and banking, etc. It will fundamentally change our lives.

The insurance sector has always been a data-driven business. The key function of an insurance company is to take on the risk of an event that a single entity (person or company) could not bear by itself. To do so it must analyze (a great deal of) data to understand the risks and consequences of such events, that is to say what determines the occurrence of the risk and how likely it is to occur in the future. The fundamental principle thereby is collective risk coverage, e.g., individual policyholder risks are pooled together with the risks of other policyholders, so that the premiums of all policyholders in this so-called insurance collective are used to compensate for the occurrences of individual claims within this collective.

S. Brindöpke (✉)
ifb SE, Grünwald, Germany
e-mail: Susanne.Brindoepke@ifb-group.com

The insurance business offers a variety of digitalization use cases, e.g., the fundamental change of the distribution of insurance policies or the way claims are processed. However, the focus in this chapter is on applications in the traditional fields of work of actuaries, such as pricing, reserving, investment,[1] or risk management.

This chapter gives an overview of the concept of actuarial data science from the business perspective rather than mathematical or technological presentations of the ML models and their performance. It frames the concept of actuarial data science as an interdisciplinary field of work and provides an overview of the recent research that has been conducted by means of potentially promising use cases.

1.1 The Definition of Actuarial Data Science

Advancing digitalization in many fields and the resulting shift to data-based business models most likely also impact the work of most actuaries, because their daily business is usually to analyze data and to develop and maintain models based on data. Pricing, reserving, investment, and risk management are traditional fields of work of actuaries that might benefit from the technological shift and Big Data.

Although there is no generally valid definition of data science, it is usually seen as an interdisciplinary field between statistics (stochastics included) and computer science (Wikipedia 2020). But statistics and computer science in turn need a context or domain to have a content-related meaning at all. In the case of actuarial data science, the context-related expert knowledge will be in the broadest sense the insurance business or strictly speaking the actuarial sciences.

The actuarial data science working group of the German Actuaries Association (DAV) even extends this concept to include capabilities in data management, the consideration of the social, ethical, and legal environment and the communication, visualization, and the target group-specific presentation of the results. Summarizing, there are particularly high requirements imposed on the actuarial data scientist in terms of knowledge, experience, and professionalism.

In the following, we use the term "machine learning" or the methods themselves as a reference to actuarial data science.

---

[1] Machine learning techniques for investment or asset portfolio management are not addressed in this chapter as this has a much wider range of application and is not restricted to actuarial practice.

1.2 Why It Matters

There is already a lot of pressure on insurance companies' profits due to the ongoing low-interest phase and the costs of implementing rapidly changing regulatory requirements. Additionally, new market participants, e.g., insurtech companies and big technology enterprises, put further pressure on the existing business models of insurance companies, as they might "demonstrate that certain processes within the insurance value chain can be carried out cheaper, more efficiently and more effectively with new technologies" (EIOPA 2020). Hence, the central function of an insurance company, namely the highly regulated pooling and covering of risks, becomes a key aspect in competing with other insurance companies as this function will be kept at regulated entities.

Another key aspect is increasing customer expectations to offer products that are tailored to their specific needs and are changeable as their life changes, e.g., adjustable premiums or insured amounts, insurance on-demand, or variable policy durations. This requires more advanced predictive models and the consideration of various external data sources as the current available sources and resulting features are certainly not sufficient for future use cases.

Customers are also more informed, for example, the comparison of insurance products from different insurance companies via online platforms is already commonplace for many products. Many customers today, especially younger ones, expect digital products: they want to buy the insurance, file claims, and cancel the protection if no longer required via mobile phone in just a few steps. The improvement of the customer experience is also a major factor in competition.

(Albrecher et al. 2019) predict that parts of the value chain of insurers will be attacked by newcomers as a result of ongoing digitalization, with profit margins decreasing and cross-subsidies across the value chain becoming more difficult to achieve. However, the clear advantage lies in the long history of insurers dealing with the specific actuarial risks that startups are not willing to put on their balance sheet because of the high regulatory capital required. They believe the decisive competitive edge comes from efficient risk and capital management, with an understanding of the value drivers of the risk-taking business an important part of it.

1.3 Structure of the Chapter

In Sect. 2, typical use cases of actuarial data science are discussed, from general applications like fraud detection or lapse rate modeling, to life and non-life insurance-relevant use cases.

For non-life insurance, interesting research on machine learning was recently published for the optimization of product pricing and for reserving. Of course, pricing and reserving are also important in life insurance, but the payment amount in case of a claim is deterministic, so the modeling is limited to whether there will be a claim or not, i.e., whether the insured person dies or not. Furthermore, there are specific legal requirements on how to calculate premiums and provisions. Hence, for life insurance, the modeling and forecasting of the mortality rate are of crucial importance. Although insurance companies also take advantage of publicly available mortality tables, they are well advised to model mortality rates on their specific collective of customers. Another promising use case in life insurance is the computationally challenging estimation of capital requirements.

The third section focuses on challenges and critical aspects that have to be considered when implementing machine learning algorithms. The requirements on data availability and processing as well as interpretability or explainability issues are addressed in other chapters of this book. This section focuses on ethical aspects that arise when machines are used more and more to make decisions and the impact on risk management.

2 Applications of Machine Learning Techniques

2.1 Introduction

Spindler and Hugo Hoffmann (2019) found in their interviews that two basic value drivers are contributing to the change in business due to digital transformation in insurance companies. The first is process automation (see Soybir and Schmidt [2021]), which in their opinion is often falsely regarded as the traditional use case of machine learning.[2]

Claims processing, for example, is a typical application of process automation. Besides distribution and underwriting, claims processing is indeed a key business function of an insurance company. The turnaround time for each

---

[2] An interesting combination of RPA and machine learning can be found in (RPA—Use Case SPPI see [Gabriel 2021]).

single claim is a significant part of the operational costs. Hence, it is vital to improve this process to make it as efficient as possible.

Although process automation does not necessarily require artificial intelligence, merely simple, recurrent processes, machine learning algorithms may support and enhance traditional methods (see Soybir and Schmidt [2021]).

But the second value driver, to enhance the predictions an insurance company has to make, e.g., for pricing and reserving, is extremely important because covering risks is the core business function as it is the purpose of an insurance company in the first place. If the predictions on future claims or risks are poor, the insurance company will most likely face bankruptcy or will not be able to meet the capital requirements.

The following sections give an overview of the recently discussed machine learning use cases in actuarial science. It is not a complete list, as the publications and research on this topic are rapidly increasing.

The possible application fields are not presented from a mathematical foundational perspective, but rather from the business-related view. Please refer to the relevant chapters in the 2019 book (Liermann et al. 2019) to learn more about the specific algorithms.

2.2 General Applications

2.2.1 Fraud (Claims)

One of the most prominent applications of machine learning in insurance is most likely the detection of fraud. Compared to other industries, insurance fraud has unique properties. First of all, insurance fraud is difficult to model because the exact cases of fraud are unknown as a lot of insurance fraud goes undetected. Insurance fraud can furthermore be committed by many different parties: the insurance applicant, the policyholder, third parties who receive compensation in case of an injury or damage, service providers who help fix the damage or physicians/physiotherapists in healthcare insurance, etc. Finally, insurance fraud may be committed by individuals who would never break the law in a traditional way as it may be seen as a minor offense. Hence, there are many different types of insurance fraud and so fraud data is quite heterogenous.

Traditionally, fraud detection systems are based on implemented rules and a violation of one of the rules will trigger a manual audit process to check if a claim is fraudulent or not. Of course, the rules are fixed, at least for a certain period of time, until a new type of fraud is detected and specific rules for the detection of the "new" fraud type are implemented. Manual auditing of course is a time-consuming process and puts a lot of pressure on the operational costs. As estimated by the National Health Care Anti-Fraud Association (NHCAA),[3] there is a financial loss from tens of billions of dollars to 300 billion dollars each year for the healthcare sector alone, and the Federal Bureau of Investigation (FBI) estimates that over 40 billion dollars a year are lost through fraud across all non-health insurance.

Modern machine learning models can greatly cut auditing costs by automatically screening incoming claims and flagging up those that are deemed to be suspicious. It is common knowledge that criminals quickly adapt to changes in fraud detection. Hence, detection of new or emerging patterns is vital. This can either be done with adaptive unsupervised methods or continuous updating of the training data in supervised methods (Ekin 2019). Most research on fraud has been conducted in the healthcare sector.

Fraud detection is a field of application for machine learning which is often mentioned and could lead to major improvements in claims processing and the costs involved. For a practical example of the fraud application of supervised learning, please refer to (Enzinger and Li 2021) in this book.

2.2.2 Lapse Rate Modeling

Lapse risk carries substantial financial risk as it affects pricing, reserving, profitability, liquidity, risk management, as well as the solvency of the insurance company. Lapse risk is indeed the most significant life underwriting risk according to the European Insurance and Occupational Pensions Authority's Quantitative Impact Study QIS5 (Loisel et al. 2019).

Lapse is also important in P&C insurance[4] as the competition in this market is fierce. Few new customers are entering the P&C insurance market per year, so the only possibility for growth is to steal market share from other insurance companies (Super 2019). Customer retention, especially high-value customers, e.g., in terms of higher premiums, fewer claims or more insurance products, becomes crucial to keep up with competitors.

As some factors that lead to cancel an insurance policy may be unavoidable, the sensitivity of insurance policyholders to such a cancelation may be found in the data the insurance company has already collected. In the recent literature, the factors that trigger a cancellation are divided into two categories: external or environmental factors, for example interest rates, unemployment rates, returns in capital markets, or the external visible properties of the

---

[3] https://www.nhcaa.org/resources/health-care-anti-fraud-resources/the-challenge-of-health-care-fraud/.
[4] Property and casualty insurance.

insurance company, and internal or micro-oriented factors coming from the behavior of the policyholders or the specific characteristics of the insurance product. It is obvious that external factors can hardly be controlled by an insurance company, but competitors cannot influence these factors either.

For the modeling of the lapse rate or the binary version of whether a lapse occurs or not, general linear models (GLMs) have been the state-of-the-art method, as for many other tasks in typical actuarial applications. However, there are certain preconditions for the use of GLMs that may not hold for the specific task, e.g., that the lapse rate follows a certain distribution.[5] Classification and Regression Trees (CART) and the proportional hazards model, a class of survival models which relate to the time that passes until the lapse occurs, have also been applied. Generally speaking, ML algorithms perform better, sometimes only to a minor extent, but sometimes they even outperform traditional models.

An interesting approach is provided by (Loisel et al. 2019), who not only model the classification problem of distinguishing loyal customers from those who are likely to cancel,[6] they also developed a profit-based loss function that creates a link between the insurance companies' costs and profits. The classification considered by itself might lead to incorrect steering in case the customer is not worth retaining. An extension to a gain regression where profits are maximized is therefore a reasonable enhancement. In this study, the combination of the classification and profit maximization led to much better results when using ML approaches.

To summarize, modeling the lapse rate or the occurrence of lapse is another possible field of application for machine learning. Because not every customer lapse has the same undesired impact, a combinatorial analysis with the profits involved should be favored over pure classification models.

2.2.3 Wearables

The emergence of wearable technology and IoT (Internet of Things) can provide insurance companies with non-traditional data which can be used for various purposes. Wrist-worn wearables or medical devices are already widely used across life and health insurance to gather additional data, engage with customers, incentivize or educate customers to live a healthier lifestyle, and assist with underwriting.

---

[5] In GLMs the response variable comes from an exponential family distribution, for example Normal, Exponential, Binomial or Poisson distribution.
[6] The ML approaches applied were Extreme Gradient Boosting and Support Vector Machines.

Fitbit, Garmin, Apple, and Xiaomi as the largest wearables providers offer more or less the same measurements, such as movement, heart performance, heart rate, body temperature, blood oxygen levels, and more on an ongoing basis. Via machine learning, these measurements are analyzed continuously and improve the understanding of health- and mortality-related risk factors. Early intervention in case of a deterioration of certain measurements, for example, is probably less cost-intensive than curative treatment after a further progression of disease.

It is worth mentioning that customers must be willing to share this very personal information in the first place. To support this, insurance companies can either offer financial reimbursements (discounts or non-cash rewards) or hand over data for information, for example sharing recommendations about sports training or nutrition. In any case, the insurance company must treat the data with a high degree of discretion within the specific data protection laws.

The additional data gathered by wearables might lead to more individualized, granular pricing with a reduction in adverse selection.[7] In most cases, this is seen as a desired outcome as customers are paying premiums closer to their "fair price" that truly reflect their risk. Low-risk customers will therefore benefit from a more enhanced pricing, but other individuals, who were previously being subsidized by the low-risk customers and are actually most in need of insurance coverage, might face disadvantages up to a withdrawal of coverage (SOA [Society of Actuaries] 2020).

An insurance company must take into account these implications when incorporating new data in its pricing models to keep its reliability, trustworthiness, and its responsibility considering the social value of insurance coverage. Of course, in an environment of competition this role must be supported by regulators, who set up a framework for data responsibility in an ethical manner. Further details on the data perspective can be found in (Floß and Velauthapillai 2021).

---

[7] Adverse selection is defined as the information asymmetry between the policyholder and the insurance company.

2.3 Non-Life

2.3.1 Pricing

Pricing or ratemaking in the non-life sector is a two-step modeling problem. Firstly, it has to be modeled how likely it is that a claim will occur and, secondly, in the event of a claim, what will the exact amount of the claim be. Although there are frequently contractual arrangements that aim to restrict the payment liabilities of insurance companies, for example maximum payments for compensation or deductibles of the policyholder, a claim amount may vary significantly.

The development of adequate prices requires extensive statistical analysis of relevant data. This is, in particular, the various properties of the insured object, the policyholder, and the property region, the so-called inventory data, and, secondly, information about historical claim frequencies and amounts. For example, in motor insurance, this will include the car properties such as type, horsepower, year of construction, and mileage, but also policyholder features, especially age, accident-free years, profession and, possibly, additional drivers.

Traditionally, simple heuristic or distribution-free methods have been used that split the overall claim amount into certain risk classes, which are represented by risk factors as combinations of features. Practically, the number of features and their possible combinations can rapidly lead to huge numbers of (poorly represented) risk classes. In motor insurance, for example, several million different risk classes may result. General linear models (GLM) that are today in widespread use and state of the art for premium calculations have mostly replaced heuristic methods. The disadvantages of GLM include strong distributional assumptions that could not be met practically, which results in lower predictive power.

Modern machine learning methods can reveal complex interrelationships in the data that GLM cannot detect (ADS 2019) to price risks more accurately and to learn about risk-relevant customers' behavior. For example, data about competitors' prices on aggregator platforms can be analyzed and used to optimize one's own policy prices in a dynamic way. Another example is the use of telematics for real-time monitoring of a driver's behavior in motor insurance, where premiums can be set by pay-as-you-drive features.

Research on pricing in non-life insurance is rapidly evolving and the advantages seem to prevail over the traditional approaches. The data handling and analyzing capabilities will have a major impact on the business success to generate competitive advantages, especially in an environment where policies are concluded online.

2.3.2 Reserving

Another interesting application is reserving. Loss reserves are a major item in the financial statement of an insurance company and in terms of how it is valued from the perspective of possible investors. The development and the release of reserves are furthermore important input variables to calculate the MCEV (market consistent embedded value), which "provides a means of measuring the value of such business at any point in time and of assessing the financial performance of the business over time" (American Academy of Actuaries, Members of the Life Financial Reporting Committee 2011). Hence, the estimates of unpaid losses give management important input for their strategy, pricing and underwriting. A reliable estimate of the expected losses is therefore crucial.

Traditional models of reserving for future claims are mainly based on claims triangles (e.g., Chain Ladder or Bornhütter-Ferguson as distribution-free methods) or distribution-based (stochastic) models with aggregated data on the level of the gross insurance portfolio or on the level of a sub-portfolio as the methodology requires the use of portfolio-based parameters, e.g., reported or paid losses, a priori expected parameters like losses or premiums. The reserving amount can be influenced by many factors, for example the composition of the claim, medical advancement, life expectancy, legal changes, etc. The consequence is a loss of potentially valuable information on the level of the single contract as the determining drivers are entirely disregarded.

Furthermore, the traditional methods have some disadvantages, e.g. they respond too sensitively when it comes to outliers or they require a priori estimates of model parameters that could be biased. Another problem is described by (John and Wiedemann 2018), who state that actuarial reserving is somewhat separated from the operational claims processing process, which means that the expert knowledge of the loss adjuster is not considered in the loss reserving amount, although it could provide valuable information, also for business steering.

Recent research on loss reserving, for example (Gabrielli et al. 2020; Wüthrich, Neural networks applied to chain–ladder reserving 2018; Wüthrich, Machine Learning in Individual Claims Reserving 2017; Baudry and Robert 2019; and Kuo 2019), confirms that ML techniques can lead to estimates of higher accuracy compared to the sole use of traditional claims models, either by embedding traditional models into a neural network model (so-called nesting) or by applying neural networks exclusively. However, the scientific articles also state that further research must be done, e.g., how to assess the forecast quality and how to evaluate the stability of these techniques.

2.4 Life

2.4.1 Mortality Rates

Mortality rates play a significant role in many fields of insurance companies' work, for example in pricing, product development, reserving, or capital requirement calculation. Mortality rates are constantly subject to change and the mortality of a certain collective of one particular insurance company might differ essentially from the mortality of the portfolio of another insurance company, even in the same country.

Although certain public or private institutions provide mortality tables[8] that contain current mortality rates of the overall population in a specific country and, where appropriate, future evolutions, an insurance company is nevertheless interested in the mortality rates of its own portfolio. Even in case the mortality tables serve as the calculation basis for the fields of application mentioned above.

The modeling and forecasting of mortality rates have been subject to extensive research in the past as they are nontrivial. The most prominent and widely used approach is the stochastic Lee-Carter Model (Lee 2015) with its numerous extensions. More recent approaches involve non-linear regression and generalized linear models (GLM). The importance of the knowledge of which features of the insurance collective determine future mortality and the power of machine learning algorithms to detect (unknown) patterns have led to more research in this field.

Levantesi and Pizzorusso (2019), for example, introduced a machine learning estimator to improve the forecasting quality of the standard Lee-Carter Model, where decision trees, random forests, and gradient boosting were used as supporting tools to retain the explainability of the results. (Perla et al. 2020) generalized the Lee-Carter Model with a simple convolutional network. While a pure implementation of these networks did not lead to enhanced predictions, the generalization of the Lee-Carter Model

---

[8] See, for example, Society of Actuaries (SOA): https://mort.soa.org/ or the Social Security Administration (SSA): https://www.ssa.gov/OACT/STATS/table4c6.html.

"produced highly accurate forecasts on the Human Mortality Database, and, without further modification, generalizes well to the United States Mortality Database," the authors stated.

Other research into machine learning in this field mainly comes from traditional models and attempts to enhance them instead of replace them. The reason for this could be the requirement for comprehensive knowledge of what determines the mortality rates because of their particular importance. Machine learning algorithm results may sometimes be difficult to understand.

2.4.2 Capital Estimation

The concept of capital, whether regulatory or internal capital, is fundamental when it comes to risk management and valuation of an insurance company. The amount of capital available, i.e., excess of assets over liabilities currently held, and the amount of capital needed i.e., required excess of assets over liabilities to withstand future adverse outcomes, mostly in a period of one year, are the most important key metrics to evaluate solvency and robustness. Applications of economic capital are, according to (SOA 2016), for example, capital adequacy and allocation and risk appetite, performance measurement, strategic planning, pricing, and mergers and acquisitions.

Whereas the current capital amount can be obtained through simple summation, the calculation of capital needed is a quite sophisticated task, particularly for life insurance companies with long-term liabilities. For regulatory capital under the European Solvency II regime, for example, different approaches exist, from a given standard formula to partly internal models to fully internal models. In the latter case, most models are computationally exhaustive. To calculate the capital needed with an internal model, a loss distribution must be derived which can be obtained, for example, via Monte Carlo simulations by preparing several thousand balance sheet valuations in various economic scenarios. Of course, this is a very time-consuming task, especially for life capital projections with cash flow models. To overcome this computational burden, most large life insurance companies use proxy models (Kopczyk 2018), which can still be time-consuming, especially where non-linear structures (typically for life insurance cash flows) are modeled with linear proxies, which is often the case.

The application of machine learning algorithms has been picked up for this use case as it is expected to resolve several obstacles at once, including feature engineering and selection as well as a reduction of the computational burden. (Krah et al. 2020), for example, present and analyze various adaptive machine learning regression approaches for proxy modeling in life insurance with potential for both performance and computational efficiency. (Fernandez-Arjona 2020) analyzed neural networks as a proxy model, also performing very well even with small training samples. Furthermore, they found neural networks to be even simpler compared to traditional methods from a qualitative point of view.

The results show that life capital estimation as a highly non-linear modeling task is a particularly promising field of application for various machine learning techniques.

3 Challenges for the Implementation of Machine Learning

3.1 General Preconditions

The use of modern machine learning techniques requires certain knowledge that may not yet be available in the company. Actuarial associations worldwide addressed this issue by establishing special data science courses as an extension of the traditional actuarial education.

Furthermore, machine learning relies on the availability of sufficient data, which must be available on a regular basis as required for the particular task. The quality required must also be ensured at all times. Of course, not all new data might be relevant, which means that data collection and data cleansing ought to be highly automated processes, otherwise they just pose new obstacles and hurdles to the use of machine learning algorithms. On the other hand, not all data that is relevant can or should be used due to legal restrictions or ethical reasons. Data protection is addressed in (Czwalina et al. 2021).

Besides the changing data environment, another important issue is the lack of interpretability and explainability of the models, which is often argued in connection with machine learning. It has become quite common to hear people refer to machine learning algorithms as "black boxes," which is probably valid for some approaches, but not in general. The chapter (Methods Machine learning [Liermann et al. 2019]) discusses this challenging topic.

In the following sections we will address two further important issues. One is the increased role of ethics, which is especially vital for actuaries and their reputation as highly moral, reliable persons. The other is the impact on risk management that a widespread application of modern machine learning systems consequently has and the process adjustments necessary.

3.2 Ethics

Regulators,[9] large insurance companies and the actuarial associations[10] worldwide have recognized the ethical relevance of machine learning systems. Especially when they are used to make decisions, they have a profound impact and should consequently be valued in terms of ethical and moral considerations. The number of ethical guidelines in connection with artificial intelligence[11] has increased substantially over recent years, many of them defining a set of principles to act upon.

One example in the insurance business is life risk, where health and lifestyle sensors or wearables provide data on numerous health indicators that can be used for predictions (see Floß and Velauthapillai [2021]). Or insurance companies might want to use a genetic test result for underwriting, or other medical or family history data. For example (Tiller et al. 2019) found evidence of genetic discrimination by Australian insurance companies. Consumers with cancer-predisposing variants experienced difficulties obtaining insurance. Price optimization based on the profiling of customers is also found in property and casualty insurance, where using telematics can also result in anti-selection as human failure is the main cause of car accidents.

Not every use case has to be viewed from an ethical point of view. For example, a picture of damage to a car after an accident can be evaluated by machine algorithms and the claim reimbursed without anyone from the insurance company being involved in the process at all. Another example is Aerobotics providing drone footage of crop land to see what might have been damaged in a drought or in a flood. But when it comes to human beings and utilizing people and their features as data points, ethical considerations have to be taken into account. In particular, discrimination and bias can lead to unethical decisions that have an enormous impact on the policyholder or insurance applicant.

Machine learning algorithms should therefore also be approved in terms of the ethical application. (Loi and Christen 2019) propose ethical guidance for the application of non-discriminatory algorithms for risk prediction for private insurance. (Lindholm et al. 2020) introduce a simple formula, where certain discriminatory information about the policyholder is not allowed in insurance pricing.

---

[9] For example, EIOPA has established an Expert Group on Digital Ethics in Insurance: https://www.eiopa.europa.eu/content/eiopa-establishes-consultative-expert-group-digital-ethics-insurance_en.

[10] For example, the European Actuary Association (EEA) recently hosted the Data Science & Data Ethics e-Conference in June 2020: https://actuarial-academy.com/seminars/seminar?No=E0192.

[11] https://inventory.algorithmwatch.org/.

Insurance companies are aware that unethical principles pose substantial reputational and legal risks and implement guidelines that are mainly based on ethical principles. Nevertheless, these ethical principles in machine learning still have to be operationalized.

3.3 Impact on Risk Management

Certainly, the new technologies and the availability of more data must have an impact on the way insurance companies perform risk management. Because sophisticated models are most likely already in use, e.g., for pricing, it is important to have a closer look at the natural alterations that will follow for the risk processes.

Spindler and Hugo Hoffmann (2019), for example, anticipate a shift from a backward-looking top-down risk management approach based on internal data and statistical modeling to a forward-looking bottom-up approach based on both internal and external data and a machine learning and data analytics framework.

In the past, statistical models like all types of regressions or general linear models (GLM) or stochastic approaches have mainly utilized contract characteristics and (historical) claims to derive predictions about future claims or the evolution of single parameters that impact the risk distribution of an insurance company. This static approach is expected to shift to a much more dynamic process where, in addition to the internal data sources, various external data sources can be on- and off-boarded at minor cost and machine learning algorithms replace statistical models.

Naturally, in most cases new technologies not only offer opportunities but can also pose new risks and uncertainties for the current business that have to be addressed and taken into account. As Big Data and machine learning algorithms "present particular challenges due to complexity, self-calibration, autonomy and the potential for unexpected results and unforeseen impacts" (Forum 2019), an appropriate and, for the purpose of machine learning, extended model risk management framework must be in place before the use of the algorithms can be envisaged. Machine learning algorithms for pricing might lead to fully personalized insurance if real-time data becomes available. This will definitely challenge the traditional way of how risks are assessed because then the analysis of probability distributions becomes obsolete (Spindler and Hugo Hoffmann 2019). At this point, the mandate of insurance companies to pool risks is questioned.

In any case, the company must evaluate the costs of implementing and maintaining machine learning compared to the benefits it delivers. The benefits can either be the number/quality of insights, the potential additional predicting power or the reduction in operating costs due to faster or better predictions.

4 Summary

The chapter introduced the term actuarial data science and explained the importance for expanding the knowledge of actuaries to include data science capabilities. It demonstrated some promising use cases for machine learning in actuarial sciences, and showed that there is a significant chance to enhance the predictive power of models built by actuaries.

There are many possible applications of data science in the typical tasks of actuaries, such as pricing, reserving, and capital or risk management. Even fields of work where actuaries are not normally present, such as claims processing and sales, can make use of the mathematical knowledge of actuaries, for example in fraud detection or lapse rate modeling.

The chapter also dealt with challenges in adopting machine learning techniques. In addition to the knowledge required, the existence of various data sources and the capability to strip off the "black box" coat of these, the last section focused on ethics and the necessary adjustments to risk management practices.

Literature

ADS, Fachgruppe. 2019. "Wie Big Data und Machine Learning die Schadenversicherung verändern." *Aktuar Aktuell*, September: 10–11.

Albrecher, Hansjörg, Antoine Bommier, Damir Filipovic, Pablo Koch-Medina, Stephane Loisel, and Hato Schmeiser. 2019. "Insurance: Models, Digitalization, and Data Science." *European Actuarial Journal*, May.

American Academy of Actuaries, Members of the Life Financial Reporting Committee. 2011. *Market Consistent Embedded Values*, March. https://www.actuary.org/sites/default/files/files/MCEV%20Practice%20Note%20Final%20WEB%20031611.4.pdf/MCEV%20Practice%20Note%20Final%20WEB%20031611.4.pdf.

Baudry, Maximilien, and Christian Y. Robert. 2019. *A Machine Learning Approach for Individual Claims Reserving in Insurance*, May 2. https://doi.org/10.1002/asmb.2455.

Czwalina, Marie Kristin, Matthias Kurfels, and Stefan Strube. 2021. "Data Protection Regulation." In *The Digital Journey of Banking and Insurance, Volume III—Data Storage, Processing, and Analysis*, edited by Volker Liermann and Claus Stegmann. New York: Palgrave Macmillan.

EIOPA. 2020. *(Re)Insurance Value Chain and New Business Models Arising From Digitalisation*, April 14. https://www.eiopa.europa.eu/sites/default/files/publicati ons/consultations/discussion-paper-on-insurance-value-chain-and-new-business-models-arising-from-digitalisation.pdf#page=11&zoom=100,72,66.

Ekin, Tahir. 2019. *Statistics and Health Care Fraud: How to Save Billions*. Boca Raton: Chapman and Hall/CRC.

Enzinger, Philipp, and Sangmeng Li. 2021. "Fraud Detection Using Machine Learning Techniques." In *The Digital Journey of Banking and Insurance, Volume II—Digitalization and Machine Learning*, edited by Volker Liermann and Claus Stegmann. New York: Palgrave Macmillan.

Fernandez-Arjona, Lucio. 2020. *A Neural Network Model for Solvency Calculations in Life Insurance*, May 5. https://arxiv.org/pdf/2005.02318.pdf.

Forum, CRO. 2019. *'Machine Decisions': Governance of AI and Big Data Analytics*. https://www.thecroforum.org/wp-content/uploads/2019/05/CROF-Machine-Decisions-Governance-of-AI-and-Big-Data-Analytics.pdf.

Gabriel, Jens. 2021. "RPA Use Case—"IFRS 9/SPPI"." In *The Digital Journey of Banking and Insurance, Volume II—Digitalization and Machine Learning*, edited by Volker Liermann and Claus Stegmann. New York: Palgrave Macmillan.

Gabrielli, Andrea, Ronald Richman, and Mario V. Wüthrich. 2020. "Neural Network Embedding of the Over-Dispersed Poisson Reserving Model." *Scandinavian Actuarial Journal*, 1–29.

John, Daniel, and Marcel Wiedemann. 2018. "Actuarial Data Analytics—der Weg zur Einzelschadenreservierung." *Der Aktuar*, April: 5.

Kopczyk, Dawid. 2018. *Proxy Modeling in Life Insurance Companies with the Use of Machine Learning Algorithms*, November 16. http://dkopczyk.quantee.co.uk/wp-content/uploads/2019/03/doc.pdf.

Krah, Anne-Sophie, Zoran Nicolic, and Ralf Korn. 2020. "Machine Learning in Least-Squares Monte Carlo Proxy Modeling of Life Insurance Companies." *Risks* 79.

Kuo, Kevin. 2019. *DeepTriangle: A Deep Learning Approach to Loss Reserving*, September 16. https://doi.org/10.3390/risks7030097.

Lee, Ronald. 2015. *The Lee-Carter Model: An Update and Some Extensions*, Setember 7. https://www.cass.city.ac.uk/__data/assets/pdf_file/0009/293 229/Lee-RON-LC_Presentation_v.pdf.

Levantesi, Susanna, and Virginia Pizzorusso. 2019. *Application of Machine Learning to Mortality Modeling and Forecasting*, February 26. https://doi.org/10.3390/ris ks7010026.

Liermann, Volker, Sangmeng Li, and Victoria Dobryashkina. 2019. "Mathematical Background of Machine Learning." In *The Impact of Digital Transformation* and Fintech on the Finance Professional, edited by Volker Liermann and Claus Stegmann. New York: Palgrave Macmillan.

Lindholm, Mathias, Ronald Richman, Andreas Tsanakas, and Mario V. Wüthrich. 2020. *Discrimination-Free Insurance Pricing*, February 10. https://papers.ssrn.com/sol3/papers.cfm?abstract_id=3520676.

Loi, Michele, and Markus Christen. 2019. *Insurance Discrimination and Fairness in Machine Learning: An Ethical Analysis*, September 14. https://papers.ssrn.com/sol3/papers.cfm?abstract_id=3438823.

Loisel, Stéphane, Pierrick Piette, and Cheng-Hsien Jason Tsai. 2019. *Applying Economic Measures to Lapse Rate Management with Machine Learning Approaches*, December 27. https://hal.archives-ouvertes.fr/hal-02150983v2.

Perla, Francesca, Ronald Richman, Salvatore Scognamiglio, and Mario V. Wuthrich. 2020. *Time-Series Forecasting of Mortality Rates using Deep Learning*, May 6. https://papers.ssrn.com/sol3/papers.cfm?abstract_id=3595426.

SOA. 2016. *Economic Capital for Life Insurance Companies*, October. https://www.soa.org/globalassets/assets/Files/Research/Projects/research-2016-economic-capital-life-insurance-report.pdf.

SOA (Society of Actuaries). 2020. *Actuarial Practice Innovation*, April. https://www.soa.org/globalassets/assets/files/resources/research-report/2020/actuarial-practice-innovation-essays.pdf.

Soybir, Sefa, and Christopher Schmidt. 2021. "Project Management and RPA." In *The Digital Journey of Banking and Insurance, Volume I—Disruption and DNA*, edited by Volker Liermann and Claus Stegmann. New York: Palgrave Macmillan.

Spindler, Christian, and Christian Hugo Hoffmann. 2019. *Data Logistics and AI in Insurance Risk Management*, August. https://www.internationaldataspaces.org/.

Super, Tom. 2019. *The Next Insurance Battleground: High-Value Customers*, May 8. https://www.insurancejournal.com/news/national/2019/05/08/524950.htm.

Tiller, Jane, Susan Morris, and Toni et. al Rice. 2019. *Genetic Discrimination by Australian Insurance Companies: A Survey of Consumer Experiences*, July 29. https://www.nature.com/articles/s41431-019-0426-1.

Velauthapillai, Jeyakrishna, and Johannes Floß. 2021. "Special Data for Insurance Companies." In *The Digital Journey of Banking and Insurance, Volume III—Data Storage, Processing, and Analysis*, edited by Volker Liermann and Claus Stegmann. New York: Palgrave Macmillan.

Wikipedia. 2020. *Data Science*, October 20. https://en.wikipedia.org/wiki/Data_science.

Wüthrich, Mario V. 2017. *Machine Learning in Individual Claims Reserving*, March 29. https://papers.ssrn.com/sol3/papers.cfm?abstract_id=2867897.

Wüthrich, Mario V. 2018. "Neural Networks Applied to Chain–Ladder Reserving." *European Actuarial Journal*, October 28: 407–436.

BSDS—Balance Sheet Dynamics Simulator (Application ABM)

Volker Liermann and Harro Dittmar

1 Introduction

The future development of the balance sheet structure of a bank is an important ingredient of bank risk management for a single bank as well as on a systemic level (banking system). On a single-bank level, the balance sheet structure is derived from a bottom-up planning process. The bottom-up planning process steps are performed in silos which avoid the integrated view of market dynamics introduced by systematic shocks or fundamental changes in behavior. The document describes a prototype of a Balance Sheet Dynamics Simulator (BSDS) using agent-based modeling (ABM) for composing the dynamics in the banking market.

1.1 Traditional Stress Test

Our times are characterized by continuous and sometimes disruptive change. The well-established VUCA[1] acronym points out the setting we live in (truly not only for the financial industry). Given the dynamics in the

---

[1] VUCA—volatility, uncertainty, complexity, ambiguity.

V. Liermann (✉) · H. Dittmar
ifb SE, Grünwald, Germany
e-mail: volker.liermann@ifb-group.com

market, it has become common to strongly alter the evaluation parameters (like interest rates or credit rating) which lead to the well-established stress testing frameworks (EBA stress test[2] in the European Union and DFAST[3] and CCAR/CLAR[4] in the United States). The European stress test initiatives assume a static balance sheet with an undetailed replacement logic for expiring loans (including the defaulting of a certain portion of the loan, the balance volume will decline in this modeling). The US stress test initiative is more realistic, but the balance sheet development is defined by banks. This bank-defined development enables design leeway.

Some of the risk dynamics we are facing in the coming years will be the result of the credit portfolio composition. Margin pressure (low-interest rates) and competition (foreign banks, fintech companies, and in particular the Big Techs[5]) can force weak banks to invest in problematic client groups and can provide an incentive to concentrate portfolios. The credit risks of corporate clients especially and, to an even greater extent, the mid-tier corporates are hard to transfer at reasonable cost, implying that a bank sticks to its portfolio for a longer period.

1.2 Balance Sheet Dynamics

Given the long-term nature of the corporate credit risk business, it becomes more and more important in these days of rising competition to have a forward-looking view of the exposure and the associated risk. A major challenge is to find a stable portfolio that responds slowly enough to allow the adaptation to a changing environment. Competition narrows down the alternatives to keep the balance sheet volume and structure stable and affects all traditional banks.

In a competitive environment it is important to acknowledge that some of the credit decisions made today can be irreversible. The art of risk management is to anticipate the coming development to avoid the situation of the mouse in Kafka's Little Fable (Kafka 1933).[6]

Dynamic changes in the environment, such as the creditworthiness of clients, which depends heavily on macroeconomic developments, are subject

---

[2] European Banking Authority stress test (see European Central Bank 2020), for the methodology in 2021 see European Banking Authority (2020).
[3] DFAST—Dodd-Frank Act Stress Test, part of the Dodd-Frank Act (see US Congress 2010).
[4] Comprehensive Capital Analysis and Review (see BOARD OF GOVERNORS of the FEDERAL RESERVE SYSTEM 2015) and the unpublished Comprehensive Liquidity Analysis and Review.
[5] GAFAM & BATX.
[6] At the end of the Little Fable the mouse gets trapped and eaten by the cat.

to the well-established stress test frameworks already mentioned. The ifb Financial Navigator (Thiele, Financial Navigator—A Modern Approach to Analytical Banking 2021) includes a comprehensive example of a stress test framework that aims to embed balance sheet dynamics. Section 2.2 provides a condensed introduction to the idea of the Financial Navigator.

In this chapter, we will focus on the modeling of balance sheet dynamics within the agent-based model (ABM) paradigm. For an introduction to ABM see Bookstaber, The End of Theory: Financial Crises, the Failure of Economics, and the Sweep of Human (2017), Turrell (2016) and Bookstaber et al., An Agent-based Model for Financial Vulnerability (2017).

1.3 Structure of the Chapter

This chapter is structured as follows: Sect. 2 gives a business-driven motivation of the context where the Balance Sheet Dynamics Simulator could be used and what it contributes to these contexts. The third section provides a general overview of agent-based models. Section 4 introduces—based on the business requirements—a minimum set of components needed to perform the simulation. Section 5 focuses on the model defining interaction and communication between the agents and Sect. 6 summarizes and gives an outlook of model extensions.

2 Business-Driven Motivation

A robust stress test observes the development of a bank's risk within multiple dimensions that can be categorized as follows: (A) macroeconomic parameters and market data for the modeling of interdependencies with general or sector-specific changes and (B) the portfolio in terms of concentration and composition of the client and product types.

Common procedures for the incremental development of business models are typically limited to a time scale that can lag behind possible disruptive changes in the environment. Expert-based planning for future portfolio compositions is limited in its responsiveness to unforeseen developments on a shorter time scale.[7] Considering the possibility of rare but significant disruptive events, the general assumption of the continuity of the current

---

[7] Some banks still rely on a yearly planning process with forecast adjustments on a quarterly basis. They do not consider many well-known dependencies of macroeconomic dynamics on demand and supply.

situation should be challenged by simulations that promise a more realistic risk projection into the future.

2.1 Value-Driver-Oriented Planning

In the planning process, many banks have moved to a more advanced, data-driven, and dynamic approach: value-driver-oriented planning. The idea behind this method is to identify the drivers of the dynamics in the planning process. Based on the company's performance indicators, the key influencing factors are analyzed, and their dependencies are modeled so that they both can be integrated into the planning process. A detailed introduction to and explanation of the concept is given in Valjanow et al., Digital planning—driver-based planning leveraged by predictive analytics (2019) and Valjanow et al. (2021).

In the value-driver-oriented planning concept, the influencing factors are analyzed and reviewed at a high frequency. The deeper the analysis, the closer one can approach a supply and demand calculus that represents the observed dynamics ideally. ABMs are a suitable tool to carry out such an analysis.

2.2 Financial Navigator—Idea

The Financial Navigator has two application environments: (A) a central bank that seeks to explore possible developments of a financial system and ensure its stability and (B) a bank or financial institution that likes to know more about the development of its risks. The common idea behind these possible applications is the projection of the risk situation as described in (Liermann and Viets, Predictive risk management 2019). Projecting the risk for a future point in time, given different market data and model-exogenous scenario developments in combination with different developments of the portfolio structure, offers the chance to analyze the paths leading to a dead end for the institution.

The Financial Navigator framework can be broken down into two stages: (1) the risk calculation and (2) data analysis of the generated risk data (see Fig. 1). The data analysis is performed by a dynamic dashboard (see Liermann and Li, Dynamic Dashboards [2021] for detailed information on dynamic dashboards).

The risk calculation itself can be separated into four blocks (left side of Fig. 1). The first block models the dynamic of the general macroeconomic

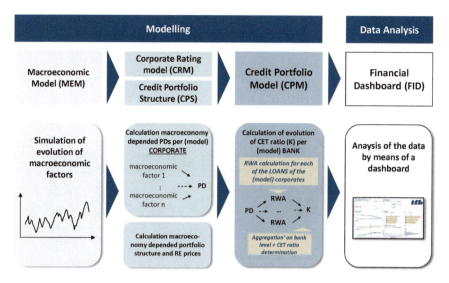

Fig. 1 Overview financial navigator (© ifb SE)

development (with models like VAR[8] M-GARCH Model[9] or RNN[10]). The rating model is part of the second block of the risk calculation. The other parameters of the credit portfolio model are assumed to be constant (not depending on macroeconomic changes, an assumption that can be easily adjusted). The proposed models for the rating range from simple logit/probit models like the classical Altman-model,[11] to random forest,[12] up to deep learning models (FNN[13]). A discussion on rating models in the deep learning context can be found in (Thiele und Dittmar, Credit risk models and Deep learning 2019). The last block is the credit portfolio model, which identifies the concentration in the client portfolio, with models like Credit Metrics (for the original paper see Gupton et al. 1997) and update in RiskMetrics Group (2007) and CreditRisk$^+$ (see Wilde 1997). The Financial Navigator uses the parallelization technology of Spark to allow real-time calculations (see Liermann et al., Distributed Calculation Credit Portfolio Models 2021). In

---

[8] Vector Auto Regression Model (see Lütkepohl 2005).

[9] Multivariate GARCH Model (see Bauwens et al. 2006).

[10] Recurrent Neural Network (see Section 3.2 in Liermann et al., Deep Learning—an Introduction 2019).

[11] See Altman, Financial Ratios, Discriminant Analysis and the Prediction of Corporate Bankruptcy (1968) for the original paper and (Altman et al. 2014) for a more recent analysis.

[12] See Section 3.7.1 in Liermann et al., Mathematical Background of Machine Learning (2019).

[13] Feedforward neural network (see Section 2.1.2 in Liermann et al., Deep Learning—an Introduction 2019).

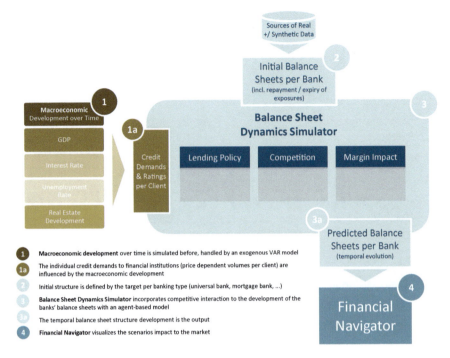

Fig. 2 Balance sheet dynamics simulator—overview (© ifb SE)

some contexts, it might also be sufficient to use the simplified RWA[14] calculation (standard approach or IRB approach see Basel Committee on Banking Supervision [2017]).

Along with the rating simulation (second block in the risk calculations on the left-hand side of Fig. 1), the Financial Navigator translates the macroeconomic dynamics into impacts on the client portfolio structure of each bank (in the central bank setting).

Figure 2 gives a detailed overview of the interfaces between the Financial Navigator and the BSDS, which will be described in Sect. 3. On the left-hand side of Fig. 2, we see the macroeconomic factors that influence the credit demand and supply. At the top, we see the initial balance sheets of the banks. Combined with the banks' target exposures that are defined by their desired growth, the resulting exposure gap translates to the supply for new loans in the following period. In the lower right-hand corner, we see the loan data (or the simulated balance sheet for future points in time) passed back to

---

[14] Risk weighted assets.

the Financial Navigator to be used in its third block of the risk calculation (credit portfolio model).[15]

The macroeconomic development (1) is represented by time series of the GDP,[16] the interest rate, the unemployment rate, and the development of the real estate sector. They are the output of a separate macroeconomic model (exogenous to the BSDS) and they influence the credit demand of the non-financial sector, which contains corporate, commercial real estate, residential real estate, and retail clients (1a). The details of the actual balance sheets with maturity structure are used to initialize the model (2). The clients' individual credit demands for new loans, as well as the credit supplies for new loans by the banks are then matched during the simulation (3). During this matching, preferences like lending policy, competition situation, or margin impact are taken into consideration. Finally, the results can be aggregated over all banks to obtain a prediction of how the average balance sheet structure changes over time (3a). In (4), the simulated balance sheet structure is further processed in the Financial Navigator to calculate the future credit risk by either calculating RWA (regulatory view) or calculating a real Credit Value at Risk by a credit portfolio model (economic view).

3   Agent-Based Modeling

Provided with the necessary computational resources, numerical models can deepen our understanding of complex systems by representing the essential aspects of their states and dynamic behavior. Models play several different roles in the development of what-if scenarios or the abstract representation of a complex real system. Some examples for useful simulation results are:

- fundamental insight into the collective behavior of entities and emergent phenomena,
- causality and relevance of system elements for a specific macroscopic behavior,
- conditions for equilibrium and critical states (effective regulatory measures), or
- the assessment of the evolution of a system in realistic best/worst-case scenarios and in response to shocks.

---

[15] In an early stage of the Financial Navigator, the balance sheet was assumed to be constant like in the EBA stress test, by replacing the matured loans.

[16] Gross domestic product, the most common indicator for the macroeconomic development.

The models that contribute to a better understanding of a system can be:

- **exploratory**: start from a plausible composition of the system: "Keep it descriptive, stupid!" (KIDS) philosophy (Edmonds and Moss 2004),
- **descriptive**: fundamental science and rigorous math leading to abstract/stylistic representations and analogies that typically follow the "Keep it simple, stupid!" (KISS) philosophy, or
- **predictive**: applied science that depends on a significant amount of calibration data and always builds upon prior fundamental research on the topic.

Generally, there are unavoidable tradeoffs between model **realism, precision and generality**, which have been discussed in a paper by Michael Weisberg (Weisberg 2006) among others. To make a model predictive, a thorough knowledge of the system states that are possible in theory is essential for proper calibration. Thus, the natural order of research efforts is exploratory, descriptive, predictive.

With the BSDS we intend to explore how a simple matching algorithm that generates the temporal evolution of artificial loan portfolios responds to different exogenous macroeconomic scenarios. As described in Sect. 4.3, we initialize the system with a combination of synthetic and real input data. Since we do not have access to the data that would be required for the calibration of a predictive model, we stick to a high level of simplification and abstraction. Accordingly, the BSDS can be categorized as the concept for an exploratory "minimal viable model," which is not meant to give the impression of a finished tool for scientific research at this stage. One advantage of the design of an ABM is that it facilitates gradual extensions that make the model more realistic, which shall become clearer in the following sections.

3.1 Role of Bottom-Up Dynamics Simulations

It is not easy to choose a suitable modeling approach that achieves the compromise sought between realism, precision, and generality. One key question is whether reliable first principles and available calibration data that form the basis for the model development imply a top-down approach, such as system dynamics, or a bottom-up approach, such as agent-based modeling. Naturally, one starts with the side that can be verified with observable data and/or benchmarked with conventional existing models, and then attempts to harmonize it with more detailed or generalize it to more abstract representations. Depending on the available references to previous research on the system of interest, one must also decide which logical form (**deduction/induction/abduction**) fits the motivation that envisions improvements toward higher realism, precision, or generality. The success of rigorous deduction relies on proper assumptions. However, the identification and abstraction of the most significant parts of a complex system that support those assumptions can be challenging, and exploratory abduction can help to identify the elements that are worth a closer look. Figs. 1 and 3 illustrates how different approaches complement each other during the development of a robust descriptive or predictive model.

Top-down and bottom-up approaches both play an important role in the exploration of the behavior of complex dynamic systems from a variety of disciplines. Numerous examples exist for the application of ABMs to molecular, biological, social, and economic systems (Hamill and Gilbert 2015), as well as abstract problems such as the origins of evolution, altruism, or complexity. The key strengths and weaknesses of a bottom-up approach like ABM are summarized in the following two paragraphs. Some key criteria are related to the successful implementation of an ABM as a scalable **actor-model** (Roestenburg et al. 2017).

ABM treats constituents of the system as discrete autonomous entities, which provide a high flexibility during model development. This design also

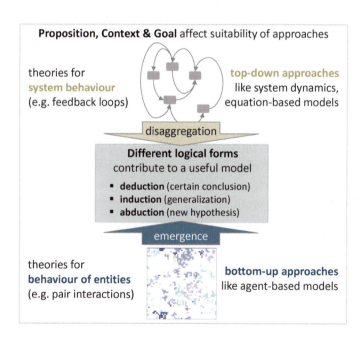

Fig. 3 Preliminary considerations for the modeling of complex systems (© ifb SE)

makes ABMs very scalable, which can in turn improve the performance for large system sizes that benefit from the possibility to utilize distributed computing infrastructures. Scalability requirements can be driven by the computational load and/or the amount of the data, which sparked our interest in the ABM approach for the balance sheet dynamics simulation: we want to have the option to consider many banks and clients. Parallelizable and distributable code not only enables larger systems, but also complex or adaptive agent behavior that may involve machine learning algorithms. At the same time autonomous entities bring a conceptual advantage, as their design facilitates gradual refinements of a working model, which is especially useful if one wishes to test a minimal viable product and make it more realistic later. Another advantage is that autonomous entities enable the efficient simultaneous consideration of agents that act on multiple time scales, especially when the ABM is programmed as an actor model. For example, one might want to simulate the macroeconomic development using a country agent that updates environmental factors once a year, while individual trading agents interact in that country on a daily basis. In summary, the inherent distributability of agents in a computational network enables the efficient use of computational resources for a dynamic number of agents, interaction topology and for agents with inhomogeneous behavior. For example, in cellular automata, regions of dead cells only require reserved memory, but their presence in an inactive state does not slow down the propagation of the system through time.

There are possible drawbacks that should be kept in mind: modeling a system with many autonomous entities should be justified by its possible size and complexity, for example, due to the anticipated inhomogeneity of the agents' states and their behavior (O'Sullivan et al. 2012). If the simulation can be run on a single computer and the agents' activities are not very different, an ABM may not be the best performing solution, as action codes must be copied to each autonomous instance of an agent class, which increases memory requirements. Furthermore, in an actor-oriented ABM, information is only accessible via messaging, which can cause an unnecessary computational overhead if the computing infrastructure does not actually depend on it.

3.2 Elements of an Agent-Based Model

There are several ABM frameworks available that make this versatile method more accessible by taking care of general requirements for graph computation and the use of distributed infrastructures (Railsback and Grimm 2019; Harmon and Lyon 2019). Some frameworks like NetLogo or MASON also

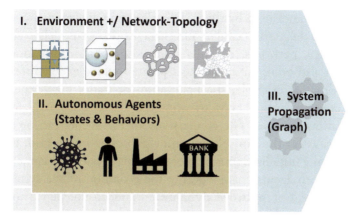

Fig. 4 ABM—essential elements (© ifb SE)

provide libraries of sandbox models that may serve as starting points. As summarized in Fig. 4, there are three essential ingredients that need to be defined in an ABM for a specific use case:

I. the **agent classes**,
II. the **environmental definitions**, and
III. rules for the **system propagation**.

Agents are defined as **autonomous computational entities** that interact with their environment (including other agents) according to algorithmically encoded behavior, thereby changing states of themselves and other agents. The state of an agent can consist of several features, some of which may be static constants that are set once during the initialization of the model, and some of which are dynamic variables that change during the simulation run. Examples of agents in the context of economic systems are traders, banks, or a stock exchange. Agents can be implemented as objects or as actors. Actors only become active when they receive at least one message from another agent in the computation graph, which saves computational resources in systems with many agents. For example, only a few retail clients may participate in trades for most of the time, while the rest of them are mere savers, but all of them can be activated during rare systemic events, such as bank runs.

The essential environmental definition of an ABM is the **framework for possible agent interaction** or communication, in other words the topology that specifies which other agents any given agent interacts and exchanges information with. Dynamic rules on how the links between agents change during the evolution of the system are the subject of the field of network dynamics and are not used by the BSDS. Common environments for ABMs include lattices (e.g., of cellular automata or Ising models), continuous Euclidean space, networks, or grids from geographic information systems (GIS). It can also be useful to define separate topologies for different types of interactions: for example, the finalization of trades may depend on an electronic communication network while the delivery of goods depends on geospatial infrastructures. The connectivity of the agents can be static and homogenous, as for the Von Neumann neighborhood on a grid, but it may also be randomly initialized and/or evolving dynamically. Dynamic rules how the links between agents change during the evolution of the system are the subject of the field of **network dynamics**[17] and do not play a role for the BSDS. However, it should be noted that, depending on the use case, the focus of an ABM may be the evolution of the states of the agents, or the evolution of a network. Another optional aspect is global environmental variables that represent properties of the framework, such as drag factors of a spatial grid on which agents move. Global variables of a spatial environment that are influenced by agents could in principle be implemented as the properties of an "environmental agent" that remains linked to all other agents throughout the simulation. However, the environment is typically treated as an exclusive model element that differs from agents in several aspects of its implementation.

The third essential element of an ABM is the **definition of an action and messaging sequence** that is used to coordinate the agents' behavior and propagate the system from one time step to the next. In an ABM that is implemented as an actor model, messages trigger agents to perform actions (see Pregel approach to graph processing [Malewicz et al. 2010]). These actions can involve calculations that update state variables, such as loan repayments of a borrower that affect their balance, and the transmission of messages that trigger subsequent actions of other agents. The result is a systematic cascade of parallel and/or serial calculations that can be repeated to propagate the system through time. An action sequence may also involve the spawning of new or deletion of existing agents, accompanied by a dynamic allocation of computational resources. This enables an efficient shared use of resources when the size and complexity of the system increases or decreases.

---

[17] More information on application of networks can be found in Enzinger and Grossmann (2019).

4 Model Initialization

This section will outline the proposed data that would be needed to initialize the core elements and entities used to carry out the balance sheet dynamics simulation. This includes data that describes the exogenous macroeconomic environment and granular information on the individual agent states and properties.

4.1 Macroeconomic Scenario Data

The environmental definitions of the BSDS do not include any spatial elements, meaning that the environment of an agent is defined by the links to the agents it communicates with. Another environmental element is the time series of an exogenous simulation of the macroeconomy, which can be accessed globally, but remains unaffected by the agents, meaning it follows its own, decoupled dynamics.

The analysis of the stability of a financial sector carried out in the Financial Navigator (see Thiele, Financial Navigator—A Modern Approach to Analytical Banking 2021) is based on a set of twenty scenarios generated by a macroeconomic model.[18] Every macroeconomic scenario is composed of three-time series that describe the predicted evolution of the GDP,[19] interest rate and unemployment ratethree to five years in a quarterly frequency. For the BSDS, one scenario is selected to set the (exogenous) scene for the dynamic evolution of the balance sheets.

Figure 5 shows the historic development of the three macroeconomic parameters (shaded) and the prediction for one scenario from 2018 to 2022. The data is to be used as an exogenous influence on the client ratings, the target debts of the clients, and the target exposures of the banks.

The balance sheet dynamics can be carried out for any of the macroeconomic scenarios. Due to the possibly sensitive dependence on the (partly synthetic) initial conditions, one should also perform multiple runs for the macroeconomic scenario focused on, using different hypothetical initial states with varying portfolio details. Another reason to perform multiple runs can be stochastic elements of the matching process that result in a certain variance between the system trajectories of each simulation run.

---

[18] The Financial Navigator can use a Vector Auto Regression Model (VAR), an M-Garch model and an LSTR Neural Network to generate scenario paths for the major macroeconomic indicators and is flexible to incorporate other models.

[19] Gross domestic product.

Fig. 5 Development of the macroeconomic indicators. Historical data is shaded in grey (© ifb SE)

Table 1 Example target credit rating structure by client type for the distribution of exposures (© ifb SE)

	AAA (%)	AA (%)	A (%)	BBB (%)	BB (%)	B (%)	CCC	Total by rating (%)
Corporates	5	20	60	10	5			100
CRE			30	40	30			100
RRE	40	50	10					100
Retail	15	20	25	20	15	5		100

4.2 Business Model Parameters

These parameters describe properties of bank agents but are universal (global) in the sense that they do not vary between individual banks. We refer to them being defined on a model level as opposed to the agent level. One such parameter is the bank-type-specific maximum growth of the balance sheet, e.g., 15% per year.[20]

Another universal set of parameters is the target credit rating structure the banks are trying to establish by reporting corresponding fractions of their total supply to the market. A corresponding example matrix with the dimensions rating and client type is shown in Table 1.

Similarly, there is a client type structure that describes how the total exposure should be distributed among the rows of Table 1. Note that despite the simplifying assumption of universal structures that only depend on the bank type, the distinction of 3 bank types, 4 client types, and 7 rating classes corresponds to 3*4*7 = 84 parametric values in principle. Because it is unlikely that such a high level of detail is justified by either the general realism of

---

[20] The maximum growth of a bank's balance sheet per year could be derived for the macroeconomic development.

the model or the significance of this detail for the general system behavior, it is sensible to make further simplifying assumptions, such as the bank-type independence of rating structures.

4.3 Agent-Specific Data

This section summarizes the minimum agent-related information needed for the model. The simple and rather stylistic properties that define the states of the agents are defined simply enough to justify the decision to initialize the system with a combination of synthetic and real input data. The intention is that the model can be tested without the need for real balance sheets or features for the client rating. The BSDS has three major agent types: banks, clients, and markets.

4.4 Client and Bank Data

For natural system trajectories, the clients must differ in their initial credit demands, which are assumed to correlate with their assets, or "sizes," abstractly speaking. If no real client data is available, one might consider generating artificial clients, but ideally with a distribution of demands that mimics real distributions. To create clients of different sizes and credit demands, one possibility is to reconstruct them from an income distribution.

Besides the client size, the main characterizing information is the creditworthiness of the client, expressed in a credit rating. The rating development over time is coupled to the exogenous macroeconomic dynamics and depends on the rating model.

Just like the clients, the banks have individual "sizes" that are assumed to correlate with their assets and/or equity, and that define how much exposure they can tolerate, in other words which credit supplies they offer on the markets. This is the only characteristic variable that describes an individual bank, while its other parameters are inherited from the business model of the respective bank type.

4.4.1 Account Data and Product Parameters

The account data links banks, clients and exposure amounts with loans. The loan data defines which clients contribute which amounts to the total exposure of the banks, and how these individual contributions mature over time. To keep the model simple, we only consider one type of loan per client type, specified by only three parameters: (1) the minimum loan amount that is accepted by the banks, (2) the term length or frequency of reduction of the loan amount, and (3) the total duration of the loan. As the simulation proceeds, maturing exposures contribute to the credit supplies that become available for the creation of new loan agreements. In other words, the initial loans, the simulated loans of previous periods and their exposure profiles (maturity) give the setting for the potential of new loans for banks and clients.

In the initial state, the outstanding amounts and maturity profiles differ between clients. The product parameters for new loans that are generated during the simulation should be able to reproduce the full variety of products and maturity profiles that are present in the initial state.

One should note that the topology of the model is static (see Sect. 5.1) and not linked to the dynamic loan data. While the loan data represents agreements that connect banks and clients without a technical counterpart, the topology of the computing graph used to propagate the system only involves direct communication between banks and markets and clients and markets.

5 Methods and Interactions

The last section of the model description describes the behavior of bank, client, and market agents and their interaction.

5.1 Connection Between Clients and Banks (Markets)

Figure 6 illustrates a simple topology with only one market. The banks with their credit supply (exposure gap) are on the left-hand side, while the clients

Fig. 6 BSDS—Agents—Simple setting (© ifb SE)

BSDS—Balance Sheet Dynamics Simulator (Application ABM) 153

Fig. 7 BSDS—Agents—Elaborate setting (© ifb SE)

with their credit demand are on the right-hand side. The arrows indicate that banks communicate their supplies to the market, while the clients communicate their demands. Figure 7 shows a slightly more complex topology with four markets, corresponding to the four different client types on the left-hand side (corporate, CRE,[21] RRE,[22] and retail clients[23]). Similarly, there are also banks of different types (e.g., universal bank, mortgage bank and retail bank) on the right-hand side. This elaboration of the topology does not require significant changes of the logic of the matching algorithm: the matching is now simply carried out simultaneously by each of the four markets.

In one setting, all clients are associated with the market relevant for their client group.[24] The members of a banking group can act in different markets (e.g., a retail bank can provide loans to the retail market and to the RRE market).

5.2 Bank Business Models/Credit Supply

The credit supply in the model is provided by the banks. At the beginning of a period, each bank has a current exposure profile, given by the initial loans (at the model start) and/or simulated new loans of previous periods. The total supply (or exposure gap) of one bank corresponds to the difference between the existing exposures from current loans and the targeted total exposure that

---

[21] Commercial real estate.

[22] Residential real estate.

[23] The retail sector is only modeled by groups of clients because a modeling of each retail client would lead to a system size with huge computational effort.

[24] A more sophisticated setting would even allow the clients to act in different markets simultaneously (e.g., a retail client can demand installment loans and a mortgage).

is calculated with a bank-type-specific growth formula. The credit supply on a given market and in each rating category is then obtained by multiplying this total supply with the respective fractions of the credit rating and client type structures specified in the bank business model.

5.3 Application Behavior/Credit Demand

The bank and client classes differ considerably in their actions: while banks try to grow and establish a certain portfolio structure, clients merely seek a certain total amount of credit depending on individual desired debt ratios and the global macroeconomic situation.

The credit demand is linked to the macroeconomic development (e.g., the general economic growth expressed in the GDP[25] growth). To define the micro-based dynamics of the credit demand in a market, clients must be equipped with a mechanism to translate the macroeconomic dynamics to their credit demand.

As a first step, one could define a balance sheet total and a targeted debt ratio for each client and calculate the credit demand as their product minus the amounts of existing loans. To make the demand dependent on the macroeconomy, one could let the balance sheet total grow proportionally to the GDP growth. A next step could be adding some dynamics to the borrowed capital ratio.

5.4 Balancing and Matching Credit Demand/Supply

The balancing and matching of individual credit supplies and demands is the core aspect of the model that changes the balance sheets directly and therefore governs the behavior of the system as a whole. While there are many possibilities to configure this matching (e.g., random pairing versus combinatorial optimization, with or without partition of demands), this chapter explains only the general mechanism and not how its efficiency can be maximized or how it could mimic natural limitations of the combinatorial set.

Fig. 8 shows the simplest matching of supply and demand (without margin and credit interest rate) as an illustrative example. First, the credit supplies and credit demands that have been reported to the market are collected ① and then aggregated by client type and rating (considering only banks that are active in this segment) ②. In each category, the imbalanced total amounts are

---

[25] Gross domestic product.

Fig. 8 Aggregation supply and demand and client matching (© ifb SE)

equalized by rescaling all supplies and demands with universal opposed price sensitivity functions[26] ③. Finally, an attempt is made to match the discrete rescaled individual supplies and demands, thereby creating new loans ④. In the simple example illustrated in Fig. 8, this match is exhaustive as it depletes the full amount, and it results in four loans: credit A (bank B1 to client C1), credit B (bank B1 to client C2), credit C (bank B2 to client C1) and credit D (bank B2 to client C3). One should keep in mind, however, that matching the discrete amounts that exist in a system with a broad range of bank and client sizes is typically not exhaustive and the success of the matching depends on combinatorial optimization algorithms.

If one wishes the model to include a price differentiation on an agent level, the exercise shown in Fig. 8 must be carried out for each price. One prerequisite of price-based matching (and getting the match volumes in ③) is to translate individual bank margins into a credit interest rate. A common approach would use the following margin components: (1) risk-free interest rate, (2) funding cost, (3) standard risk costs (expected default cost derived from the rating or a PD[27]), (4) capital or equity costs (derived from an RWA or an unexpected credit default risk), (5) standard unit costs, and (6) the margin.[28] The sum of these six components can be used for a standard price-based supply and demand pattern as illustrated in Fig. 9.

---

[26] In this simple model, we wish to account for the mere existence of a price dynamic, but we are not interested in the equilibrium price and its realistic contributions that are mentioned in the following paragraph.

[27] Probability of default.

[28] To understand the potential of ABM, it is an easy thought experiment to alter the first five components by banking group and see how this will affect the market structure in the future periods (e.g., what happens when the funding costs for smaller banks rise? Will the smaller banks lose market share?).

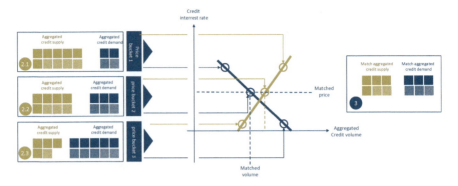

Fig. 9 Supply and demand matching with prices (© ifb SE)

On the left side of Fig. 9 we see the aggregated supply and demand by price bucket (and client type, rating). This information is compressed in the supply and demand graph in the middle of Fig. 9, and the optimal[29] price bucket is identified (price bucket 2 with six units). In price bucket 1, the credit volume would only be five units (because the banks are only willing to provide a maximum of five credit units). In bucket 3, the credit volume would only be four units (because the clients are only willing to demand for a maximum of four credit units).

6 Summary

In this article we proposed a concept for a dynamic model that can be used to simulate the evolution of the balance sheet structures of banks by letting them compete for clients under the influence of an exogenous macroscopic development. Agent-based modeling, as a bottom-up method, might complement the understanding of the balance sheet dynamics and their stability under pre-defined macroeconomic scenarios. While the common parameter stress test approach has reached a certain maturity, the transaction scenarios are often borrowed from the standard planning process and are therefore always subject to bias by those involved in the planning process. Good risk management relies to a large extent on independent options. The Balance Sheet Dynamics Simulator is a building block for a forward-looking stress test and risk management infrastructure.

The model presented in this chapter is meant as a starting point for further development aimed at the exploration of the dynamics in markets. Model

---

[29] The price bucket where the biggest credit volume is transacted.

extensions can incorporate new market participants entering the market and fish dry the market of the profitable (and high-margin) clients. These participants can be spawned as new agents providing credit supply. They can focus on better rating classes, leaving the established players behind with the low-margin and less reliable clients and causing a significant change in the market and the client structure for each bank's credit portfolio.

An initial implementation based on the concept for the Balance Sheet Dynamics Simulator uses the software development kit of Simudyne (see Liermann and Dittmar, BSDS—Balance Sheet Dynamic Simulator (Implementation ABM in Cloudera/Simudyme) 2021), can run on a Hadoop cluster to handle large system sizes, and enables the Financial Navigator (see Thiele, Financial Navigator—A Modern Approach to Analytical Banking, 2021) to provide performant risk analysis with complex models for the balance sheet development.

Literature

Altman, Edward I. 1968. "Financial Ratios, Discriminant Analysis, the Prediction of Corporate Bankruptcy." *Journal of Finance* 23: 589–610.
Altman, Edward I., Małgorzata Iwanicz-Drozdowska, Erkki K. Laitinen, and Arto Suvas. 2014. *Distressed Firm and Bankruptcy Prediction in an International Context: A Review and Empirical Analysis of Altman's Z-Score Model*. New York: Stern School of Business, New York University.
Basel Committee on Banking Supervision. 2017. *Basel III: Finalising Post-Crisis Reforms*. Basel: Bank for International Settlements.
Bauwens, Luc, Sébastien Laurent, and Jeroen Rombouts. 2006. "Multivariate GARCH Models: A Survey." *Journal of Applied Econometrics* 21: 79–109.
Board OF Governors of the Federal Reserve System. 2015. "Comprehensive Capital Analysis and Review 2015." *BOARD OF GOVERNORS of the FEDERAL RESERVE SYSTEM*, March 18. https://www.federalreserve.gov/bankinforeg/stress-tests/CCAR/201503-comprehensive-capital-analysis-review-preface.htm.
Bookstaber, Richard. 2017. *The End of Theory: Financial Crises, the Failure of Economics, and the Sweep of Human*. Prinston, NJ: Princton University Press.
Bookstaber, Richard, Mark Paddrik, and Brian Tivnan. 2017. "An Agent-Based Model for Financial Vulnerability." *Journal of Economic Interaction and Coordination* 13 (July 1): 433–466.
Edmonds, Bruce, and Scott Moss. 2004. From KISS to KIDS—An 'Anti-Simplistic' Modelling Approach. *Lecture Notes in Computer Science* 3415: 130–144.
Enzinger, Philipp, and Stefan Grossmann. 2019. "Managing Internal and External Network Complexity." In *The Impact of Digital Transformation and Fintech on the Finance Professional*, edited by Volker Liermann and Claus Stegmann. New York: Palgrave Macmillan.

European Banking Authority. 2020. "European Banking Authority." *European Central Bank—Banking Supervision*, November 13. https://www.eba.europa.eu/eba-publishes-methodology-2021-eu-wide-stress-test.

European Central Bank. 2020. "Stress Tests." *European Central Bank—Banking Supervision*, December 15. https://www.bankingsupervision.europa.eu/banking/tasks/stresstests/html/index.en.html.

Gupton, Greg, Christopher Finger, and Mickey Bhatia. 1997. *CreditMetrics—Technical Document*. New York: J.P.Morgan & Co., Inc.

Hamill, Lynne, and Nigel Gilbert. 2015. *Agent-Based Modelling in Economics*. UK: Wiley.

Harmon, Richard, and Justin Lyon. 2019. *Computational Simulation—The Next Frontier for Better Decision Making*. Bluepaper, London: Simudyne.

Kafka. 1933. *A Little Fable*. London: Martin Secker.

Liermann, Volker, and Harro Dittmar. 2021. "BSDS—Balance Sheet Dynamic Simulator (Implementation ABM in Cloudera/Simudyme)." In *The Digital Journey of Banking and Insurance, Volume II—Digitalization and Machine Learning*, edited by Volker Liermann and Claus Stegmann. New York: Palgrave Macmillan.

Liermann, Volker, and Nikolas Viets. 2019. "Predictive Risk Management." In *The Impact of Digital Transformation and Fintech on the Finance Professional*, edited by Volker Liermann and Claus Stegmann. New York: Palgrave Macmillan.

Liermann, Volker, and Sangmeng Li. 2021. "Dynamic Dashboards." In *The Digital Journey of Banking and Insurance, Volume II—Digitalization and Machine Learning*, edited by Volker Liermann and Claus Stegmann. New York: Palgrave Macmillan.

Liermann, Volker, Sangmeng Li, and Johannes Waizner. 2021. "Distributed Calculation Credit Portfolio Models." In *The Digital Journey of Banking and Insurance, Volume II—Digitalization and Machine Learning*, edited by Volker Liermann and Claus Stegmann. New York: Palgrave Macmillan.

Liermann, Volker, Sangmeng Li, and Norbert Schaudinnus. 2019. "Deep Learning—An Introduction." In *The Impact of Digital Transformation and Fintech on the Finance Professional*, edited by Volker Liermann and Claus Stegmann. New York: Palgrave Macmillan.

———. 2019. "Mathematical Background of Machine Learning." In *The Impact of Digital Transformation and Fintech on the Finance Professional*, edited by Volker Liermann and Claus Stegmann. New York: Palgrave Macmillan.

Lütkepohl, Helmut. 2005. *New Introduction to Multiple Time Series Analysis*. Berlin: Springer.

Malewicz, Grzegorz, Matthew Austern, Aart Bik, James Dehnert, Ilan Horn, Naty Leiser, and Grzegorz Czajkowski. 2010. *Pregel: A System for Large-Scale Graph Processing*. Google.

O'Sullivan, David, James Millington, George Perry, and John Wainwright. 2012. Agent-Based Models—Because They're Worth It? In *Agent-Based Models of*

Geographical Systems, edited by Alison Heppenstall, Andrew Crooks, Linda See and Michael Batty, 109–123. Netherlands: Springer.

Railsback, Steven, and Volker Grimm. 2019. *Agent-Based and Individual-Based Modeling: A Practical Introduction*. Princeton: Princeton University Press.

RiskMetrics Group, Inc. 2007. *CreditMetrics™—Technical Document*.

Roestenburg, Raymond, Rob Bakker, and Rob Williams. 2017. *Akka in Action*. NY: Manning.

Thiele, Markus. 2021. "Financial Navigator—A Modern Approach to Analytical Banking." In *The Digital Journey of Banking and Insurance, Volume I—Disruption and DNA*, edited by Volker Liermann and Claus Stegmann. New York: Palgrave Macmillan.

Thiele, Markus, and Harro Dittmar. 2019. "Credit Risk Models and Deep Learning." In *The Impact of Digital Transformation and Fintech on the Finance Professional*, edited by Volker Liermann and Claus Stgemann. New York: Palgrave Macmillan.

Turrell, Arthur. 2016. "Agent-Based Models: Understanding the Economy from the Bottom Up." *Bank of England Quarterly Bulletin*, 173–188.

US Congress. 2010. *Dodd–Frank Wall Street Reform and Consumer Protection Act*. Washington, DC: US Congress.

Valjanow, Simon, Philipp Enzinger, and Florian Dinges. 2019. "Digital Planning—Driver-Based Planning Levaraged by Predictive Analytics." In *The Impact of Digital Transformation and Fintech on the Finance Professional*, edited by Volker Liermann and Claus Stegmann. New York: Palgrave Macmillen.

Valjanow, Simon, Philipp Enzinger, Daniel Suttner, and Maik Alexander Schmidt. 2021. "Value-Driver-Oriented Planning—Management-Oriented Design and Value Driver Identification." In *The Digital Journey of Banking and Insurance, Volume I—Disruption and DNA*, edited by Volker Liermann and Claus Stegmann. New York: Palgrave Macmillan.

Weisberg, Michael. 2006. Forty Years of 'The Strategy': Levins on Model Building and Idealization. *Biology and Philosophy* 21: 623–645.

Wilde, Tom. 1997. *CreditRisk+ A Credit Risk Management Framework*. Zurich: CSFB.

Breaking New Grounds in Non-Financial Risk Management

Volker Liermann, Nikolas Viets, and Davin Radermacher

1 Introduction

1.1 Financial Risk vs Non-Financial Risk

Enterprise risk management has traditionally focused on market risk, credit risk, and liquidity risk, i.e., so-called financial risk management. This has particularly been the case for financial institutions, who are also subject to regulatory requirements when it comes to measuring and withstanding financial risks.

However, in the recent past more and more risks have gained weight, and thus attention, that are not directly linked to a financial risk context. Some of the prominent drivers for this development include litigation due to misconduct, organizational inefficiencies, an increase in working from home during the Covid-19-related restrictions by authorities, and many more. Indirectly,

---

V. Liermann (✉) · D. Radermacher
ifb SE, Grünwald, Germany
e-mail: Volker.Liermann@ifb-group.com

D. Radermacher
e-mail: Davin.Radermacher@ifb-group.com

N. Viets
ifb International AG , Zürich, Switzerland
e-mail: Nikolas.Viets@ifb-group.com

and with a time delay, these occurrences also lead to quantitative, i.e., financial, damages, often accumulating and with potentially negative effects on operations (e.g., due to loss of reputation or even business license).

A distinguishing feature of non-financial risks is their strong mutual interdependence. They tend to have a low to very low probability of occurrence and their effects often materialize only after years, but they can still have devastating consequences.

Another aspect of non-financial risks is that, somewhat in contrast to mere operational risks, they are hard to quantify in monetary terms. Traditional operational risk management aims to estimate possible losses in order to quantify the capital required for the survival of the bank. Non-financial risk management, however, focuses on the determination of the threat level of certain events or conditions, rather than quantifying a loss (which is often tricky if not impossible).

Nonetheless, no particular method has been established yet to manage non-financial risks. With the framework presented in this article we try to contribute to filling this gap.

The high level of uncertainty as well as dynamic changes (think of "VUCA"[1]) underline the importance for enterprises of taking immediate action in order to (a) become aware of the non-financial risks they are exposed to and (b) address them as part of a comprehensive and systematic model framework.

1.2 NFR and Big Data

The traditional approach to quantifying possible losses, like the one used by financial institutions in "OpRisk Management," entails applying a probability to a specific loss amount (we leave aside the question of whether this heuristic is even appropriate) and cannot be applied to all aspects and risk categories of NFR.

In the context of most non-financial risk categories, a quantification of expected losses is somehow challenging, if not impossible. But this approach could be misleading anyhow because NFR events only occur at low frequency but with an enormous impact on the organization (financial or reputational).

However, there is usually data available (even in appropriate frequency and granularity) that allows for model-driven analyses and can be used to determine the threat level. This kind of quantification is often more useful and can therefore contribute to better risk management (Fig. 1).

---

[1] Volatility, uncertainty, complexity, and ambiguity.

Fig. 1 Initial situation and motivation (© ifb SE)

Example: Cyber risk

The estimation of cyber-risk-induced losses is challenging: cyber risks are rare but can be devastating, sometimes even jeopardizing the existence of the organization. The dollar estimation of the loss will be based on more or less uninformed guesses, making the entire "expert estimate" meaningless.

However, the number of computers that have not installed the latest security update within the past 10 working days (or the aggregate days-past-due of the organization with respect to mandatory security updates) is a straightforward indicator for the level of threat that the organization's IT is exposed to. This figure does not try to estimate any financial damage but instead provides an insight into the threat situation originating from the company's technical infrastructure. It can easily be applied to different legal entities or departments as a means of benchmarking or be observed over time in order to evaluate cyber risk management improvements. An estimate of expected financial loss is not required since everybody should know that security gaps could lead to the worst damage imaginable. Plus, there is obviously no mathematical correlation between the dollar amount of damage and, for example, the number of computers missing the latest patches.

The preceding example shows that even if there is no meaningful way of modeling risk in financial terms, we often actually do have quite useful data (or can produce it easily) required to quantify the risk situation.

To summarize: If there is data, there is hope.

In the section on risk-category-specific models (see Sect. 4), we will pick up this idea to illustrate the approach by discussing different key risk indicators (KRI) by NFR category. It is far more promising to find key indicators to illustrate the threat situation than trying to estimate a loss based on doubtful statistical numbers (statistically rare probabilities, which induce a high level of uncertainty).

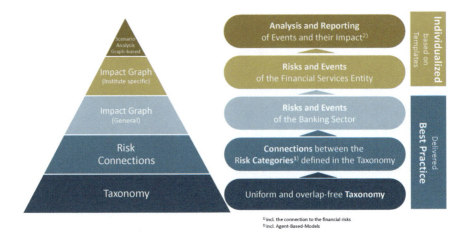

Fig. 2 NFR approach/structure (© ifb SE)

1.3 Structure of the Article

After this short introduction to management and quantification of non-financial risk the rest of the article is structured as follows: In Sect. 2 we present a new framework for assessing non-financial risks. After establishing a common taxonomy, we will explain the concept of impact graphs as a means of systematizing and visualizing risk exposure. Section 3 provides a brief discussion of integrated versus risk-type-specific models, the latter being subject to detailed analysis in Sect. 4. We add to the framework some thoughts on NFR reporting in Chapter 5 before concluding the chapter with a brief summary.

2 NFR—Introducing a New Framework

2.1 Framework Overview

Our NFR model follows a pyramid structure: the taxonomy provides a common foundation upon which the model is built. Within the taxonomy, all risk types are connected, creating a hierarchy of risk types and sub-risk types. This allows each risk type to be uniquely located in the taxonomy without creating any overlaps regarding its definition (Fig. 2).

We organized NFR into risk categories to establish a structure that can be followed by responsibilities (departments, teams, persons) and reporting structures to sort the subject. Nonetheless, these categories are highly interconnected. We will use impact graphs to discover the connections between risk categories.

Intertwined with the *risk connection graph* is the *general impact graph*, adding event chains to the model. Events represent exogenous influences on the materialization of a given risk and may also stand for any chain of events or decision process leading to a particular outcome.

Up to this point, the model is standardized. For the specific organization to which it is applied, an individual impact graph may be specified. It could be the result of the business model, specific portfolio characteristics (in case of financial institutions), or other individual considerations.

The final step is the actual analysis. Since NFR are not as easily quantifiable as financial risks due to lack of data, the goal is to simplify the complex system of events and decisions which influence the materialization of risks. Therefore, it is useful to divide the system into its single components. Since these individual components are more well-known than the entire chain of events, adequate risk assessment is possible and can be based on available data more easily.

2.2 Risk Categories

The groundwork for any successful NFR implementation is a meaningful risk taxonomy. In Fig. 3, risk categories of the ifb taxonomy are illustrated for a financial institution. The overview distinguishes between three risk categories. On the left side (in gold), we define risk categories whose characteristics are primarily triggering (these risks are located at the beginning of an impact graph). Located on the right-hand side of Fig. 3 (in dark blue) are risk

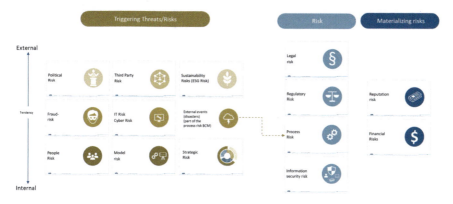

Fig. 3 Overview of example risk categories (© ifb SE)

categories where the impact on the organization is observable, i.e., the risk materializes.[2] The light blue risk categories connect the triggering events and the materialization of the risks (in terms of the impact graphs).

Risk categories in the upper part of Fig. 3 tend to have external causes while risks in the lower part are usually driven by internal factors of the enterprise.

2.3 Taxonomy

The risk categories illustrated in Fig. 3 are reorganized in Fig. 4 (while maintaining the color code). The figure breaks down every risk category into three or four subcategories to present more detail

Figure 4 presents a condensed overview of the variety of risk categories and subcategories. A discussion of definitions and causalities on a subcategory level is beyond the scope of this article. The taxonomy graph illustrates quite vividly the number of aspects covered in a landscape of NFR.

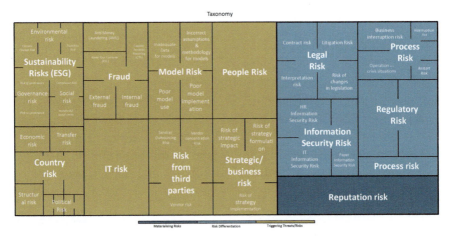

Fig. 4 NFR taxonomy (© ifb SE)

---

[2] Financial risks could be further divided into credit risk, market risk, and liquidity risk.

The most obvious approach to address these aspects in terms of the organization is to attach the different NFR categories to a specific organizational unit or even one person. This approach is driven by the extremely varied nature of each risk category which, together with the structural differences of the NFR categories, usually requires profound expert knowledge.

However, all risk categories do have in common that they can be best described in terms of risk events and the triggering impact from or to other risk events. An analysis of risk events has the advantage of being able to provide insights beyond individual NFR category silos and instead offers a holistic view of the network of risks and their dependencies.

Our implementation experience shows that risk events and their impacts are best addressed, analyzed, and documented by impact graphs.

2.4 Impact Graphs

Impact graphs are a very efficient means of documenting the triggers and interactions of a variety of risk events, without being restricted to a single risk category. In addition, impact graphs allow a committed and realistic discussion across the organizational risk category silos (e.g., commodity risk, liquidity risk, and interest rate risk in many companies).

A visualization[3] of a model impact graph is shown in Fig. 5 for ESG risk as an example. The graph shows the risk events (red nodes), the connections

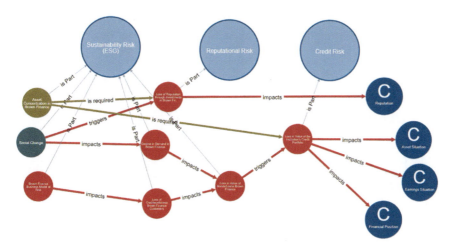

Fig. 5 Example impact graph (in Neo4J) (© ifb SE)

---

[3] The graph was generated with the graph database Neo4j (see Neo4j, Inc 2020).

(impacts) to each other, and that each risk event is associated with a risk category. By using a directed graph, an analysis of risk driver (or sources of risk) functions as an entry point to the observed system and up to the spot where the risk materializes. The sources (a node where only directed edges go out) and sinks (a node where edges only go in) correspond to risk drivers and materialized risk spots.

2.4.1 Types of Edges and Nodes in an Impact Graph

In Fig. 6, different types of nodes and edges are described in more detail. For the classification of risk events we use three levels:

- Risk domain (financial risk and non-financial risk), risk category, and sub-risk category (blue)
- Events, sub-events, and materialized events (green)
- Risk events, sub-risk events, and materialized risk events
- Preconditions and vulnerabilities as well as given preconditions and vulnerabilities

The distinguishing factor between event and risk event is that an event can have a positive and a negative impact, while a risk event always has a negative impact on the organization. A "materialized" event/risk event is an event/risk event that has already occurred.

Risk domains and (sub)-risk categories are connected by the edge type "isSubRisk." Risk categories are linked to different types of events and risk

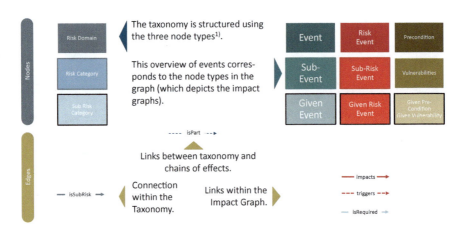

Fig. 6 Impact graphs—nodes and edges (© ifb SE)

events as well as the variations of preconditions and vulnerabilities by the edge type "isPart."

All nodes connected to events and risk events are linked by three edge types:

- "impacts": link from one risk event to another, with direct impact on the following risk event ("direct" meaning unconditional)
- "triggers": link between two risk events (directed), requires a vulnerability to be effective
- "is required": connection between a vulnerability and a risk event

The starting point of an impact graph is the risk drivers (sources in terms of the directed graph vocabulary), normally risk events or vulnerabilities. The endpoint of the impact graph is the negative effects on a company's viability. Negative effects can be measured in terms of:

- financial position: net assets at a given date,
- liquidity: cash flow during a specific period (e.g., represented by cash flow statement),
- financial performance: earnings during a specific period, and
- the institution's reputation.

The first three (accounting-driven) negative effects and reputation are shown in Fig. 7. It is important to distinguish between reputation and reputational risk. The latter is a risk category and is assigned to risk events while reputation is an endpoint and a negative effect on the organization.

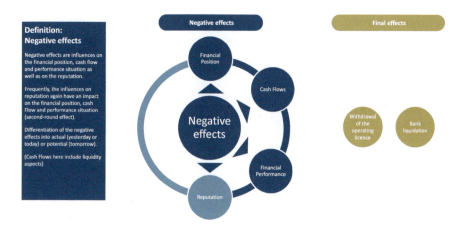

Fig. 7 Negative effects (© ifb SE)

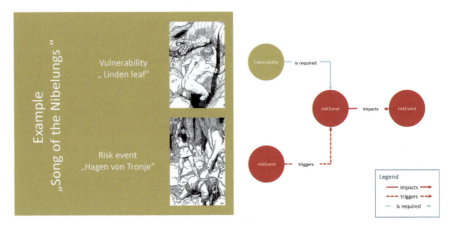

Fig. 8 Vulnerabilities—definitions (© ifb SE)

2.4.2 A Special Node Type: Vulnerabilities

The differentiation between risk events and vulnerabilities is introduced to develop sector standards for the impact graphs which can be adopted to the situation of a specific bank.

The idea behind the vulnerabilities can be easily explained with the "Nibelungenlied" (translated: "The Song of the Nibelungs", see anonymous 1200), an epic poem written in Middle High German around the year 1200. As illustrated in Fig. 8, the linden leaf[4] is the vulnerability of Siegfried, which was irrelevant because the corresponding risk event Hagen von Tronje does not trigger the risk event of being punctured by a spear.

The same pattern can be applied to events and preconditions.

A hypothetical analysis is enabled with the node types "vulnerability"/ "precondition" and the "materialized" event type. In general, all events in the graph have not occurred yet, but the occurrence of the event in the near or far future is possible. By marking an event (or vulnerability/precondition) as materialized, the occurrence can be documented in the graph and has a probability of 100%.

---

[4] In short: Siegfried, crown prince of Xanten, killed a dragon and bathed in its blood. This made him invulnerable except for a single spot on his back. There, a leaf from a linden tree had fallen on Siegfried's back giving him his well-known vulnerability.

2.4.3 Example: ESG Risk Impact Graph

To develop a better understanding of how the impact graphs work and how they serve as a tool to disclose the interconnectedness of the risk categories, we next look at a real-world example from the ESG context (Fig. 9).

In Fig. 10, the impact graph illustrates some risk events in the ESG context. We start in the lower left-hand corner with the risk event that companies with a brown finance business model face a couple of challenges in the current situation. This impacts the reduction in creditworthiness of such companies and can further lead to a loss in the value of a company's bond or a loan to the company.

The same event (loss in bond value) can also be a trigger itself. The ESG example is used to illustrate the logic. The risk events ("Loss of creditworthiness brown finance customers," "Decline in demand for brown finance,"

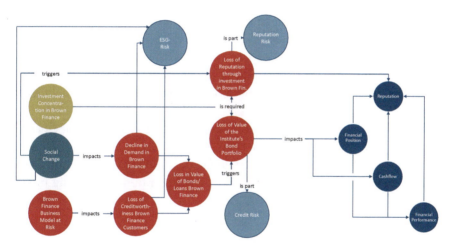

Fig. 9 Example impact graph—ESG—stylized design (© ifb S)

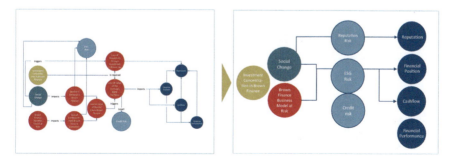

Fig. 10 Impact graph—collapse (© ifb SE)

"Loss of reputation through investment in brown finance," "Loss of value of the institute's bond portfolio," "Loss in value of bonds/loans brown finance") are connected to one node mapping the associated risk categories ("ESG risk," "reputation risk," and "credit risk") to this node.

The risk driver ("Investment concentration in brown finance," "Social change," "Brown finance business model at risk") and the negative effects ("asset situation," "financial situation," and "earnings situation") remain unchanged.

3 Coexistence of Integrated Models and Risk-Category-Specific Models

The impact graphs and their ability to carry out further analyses are a toolset to develop a holistic view of the NFR. This is precisely the motivation and one major advantage of using this framework. The impact graphs can also be employed differently: as a starting point for stress testing by using established risk estimation approaches like credit risk models. The risk events in the impact graph trigger the parameter adjustments for the renewed (stressed) calculation of the model (with the altered parameter, e.g., probability of default).

The starting point for a transition to an existing model can be the financial risk as well as in the non-financial risk domain. In financial risk management, traditional risk models are often applied, while in the non-financial risk domain machine learning and other statistical or pattern-recognizing models come into effect (Fig. 11).

Fig. 11 Coexistence of integrative and detailed analyses (© ifb S)

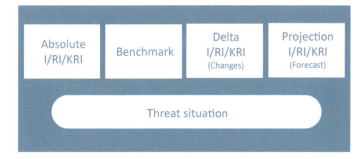

Fig. 12 Other dimensions in assessing indicators and risk indicators (© ifb SE)

Figure 12 shows how the impact graphs as a subject in the top area of the NFR pyramid are the takeoff point for risk-category-specific models (financial and non-financial risk) or for an integrated and interconnected view of the risk events structured by the impact graphs.

4 Risk-Category-Specific Models

The impact graph framework helps in developing an overview of connections and dependencies. Even though one models on a micro level, analysis is still possible on a large scale and provides a broader view of NFR. The entry level (in terms of granularity) is the risk event. A frequent analysis and risk management on the level of risk events is reasonable only in specific situations (HIFLI—high frequency, low impact).

In NFR, the rare but impactful events (LFHI—low frequency, high impact) are challenging. In the following section we show how a loss estimation could be conducted by looking at the approaches used in traditional operational risk management.

4.1 Loss Estimation and Impact Graphs

At the end of the 1990s, operational risk came into the focus of bank risk managers, driven by the first consultation paper for Basel II. The main objective was to quantify the possible losses driven by operational processes and to hold capital against these losses (both expected and unexpected—Value at Risk concept).

Risk managers used similar patterns to estimate risk as was common in market risk and credit risk management. Loss was calculated by few statistical key figures, first trying to estimate the probability of the event and then assigning a possible loss amount. In most of these models the stochastic parameters (probability and loss) are subject to variation, usually expressed in terms of statistical distributions. The approaches differ in complexity and the way that connections (mostly by modeling the statistical correlation) are established but they all try to estimate a loss amount.

Developing the relative probability and absolute amount of loss and the corresponding distributions has proven to be difficult in risk management practice.

4.2 Threat Level

Due to the difficulties highlighted in the previous chapter, in many of the NFR categories a different mindset prevails among risk practitioners. Rather than estimating the possible loss, the risk managers seek to find meaningful indicators to illustrate and document the threat level in an NFR category or for a specific event in an NFR category.

One possible example of an indicator is the employee termination rate in the context of person risk. An absolute figure is always hard to interpret without expert knowledge. A common concept is to view the absolute value in different lights or dimensions. The first idea—cross-section—is to compare the absolute indicator with benchmarks inside the organization (divisions, departments, teams, or legal entities) or outside (other companies or even the industry segment). Another approach—time series analysis—extends the view by a time component, which means the indicator is compared to data from previous periods (weeks, months, or years).

In Fig. 12, an additional dimension is introduced: the projection. In risk management, it can be important to calculate a forecast of the indicator to establish an anticipatory perspective helping to broaden the options for reaction.

Using all dimensions mentioned leads the risk manager towards a better understanding of the threat level and the opportunity to communicate and document his views and findings. We introduced these extending dimensions for general indicators (I) but the dimension can be applied accordingly to risk indicators (RI) and key risk indicators (KRI) which are introduced in the following section.

4.3 Threshold Values—Transition from Indicators to Risk Indicators

Another way to help interpret the absolute indicator is to define buckets using thresholds. The buckets can, for example, be labeled with "low risk," "moderate risk," "medium risk," and "high risk." The limits for the buckets are expressed in thresholds. The multi-dimensional view (benchmark and time) introduced in the previous section can be used to define the thresholds.

> Definition: Threshold
>
> Threshold values are predefined numerical manifestations of any indicator or coefficient that signal a certain development and/or trigger a specific action. They can be derived from historical averages, comparisons between departments but also in comparison to other companies or industries. They are often the expression of the experience and value system of one or more experts.

If the threshold and the mapping are aligned across an organization, the value system for interpreting the categories can be homogeneous.

Figure 13 shows the example of the employee termination rate for a mapping into categories using thresholds. This mapping in a potential (homogeneous) category can be viewed as the transformation of the indicator to a risk indicator. Such indicators can be aggregated by summing up or calculating average or other meaningful statistical calculations.

If a risk indicator or the aggregation of a risk indicator is highly relevant, this figure can be emphasized and distinguished from other risk indicators by labeling it a "key risk indicator."

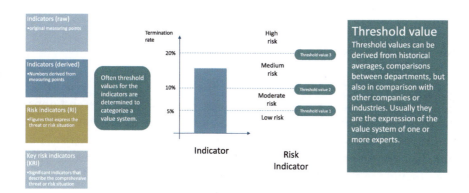

Fig. 13 Threshold values—transition from indicators to risk indicators (© ifb SE)

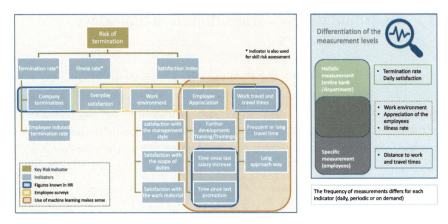

Fig. 14 Key risk indicator tree for person risk (© ifb SE)

4.4 KRI Trees

When we look at risk indicators and key risk indicators altogether, they often carry a natural order. The most important and telling RI and KRI are on the top of a hierarchy or tree. The different levels of the tree or hierarchy are defined by calculations (lower levels represent the input and higher levels represent the output of a calculation) or by explanatory power (Fig. 14).

Fig. 14 shows an example of a risk indicator tree in the context of people risk. The structure can be derived from calculations. Furthermore, it illustrates that the topmost indicators summarize the information of the indicators below them. A common approach is to take advantage of available high-frequency data to develop a model using machine learning to project the development of the KRI (e.g., the termination quota). The detailed procedure of developing such a model is described in (Schmüser et al. 2021).

4.5 Duality Between Key Figure Trees and Impact Graphs

Within the NFR framework, specific models, key indicator trees, and impact graphs are coexistent. The objective of risk indicators and key risk indicators is to support the risk manager by controlling and monitoring the risk situation. This controlling and monitoring can be achieved by estimating future losses (mainly in the operational risk area, especially in an HIFLI regime) or by showing the threat environment using RI or KRI on different levels of a

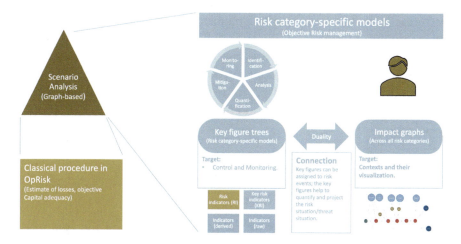

Fig. 15 Duality between key figure trees and impact graphs (© ifb SE)

key figure tree. Apart from the monitoring aspect, risk indicators can sometimes also be used to estimate the probability of a risk event (not applicable to all risk events).

Figure 15 shows the coexistence. The aspects in the topmost area of the NFR pyramid come with the highest complexity (left-hand side). The key figure trees (in the middle) aim to support the risk controlling and monitoring process, giving operational hints where threat levels are rising. The impact graphs on the right-hand side support the visualization and communication of the interconnectedness of the subject.

5 Reporting

5.1 The Importance of NFR Reporting

Risk management is all about good communication. In the course of the 2008 financial crisis, risk managers (hopefully) learned their lesson in financial risk management. The same is true for non-financial risks. Perhaps even to a greater extent, as non-financial risks are more difficult to communicate. Therefore, solid reporting is an important element of the entire NFR framework presented above.

NFR reporting aims to provide senior management with an insight into the company's risk exposure in terms of non-financial risk categories. As discussed earlier, for most NFR categories there is data available to illustrate the threat level, but only in rare circumstances is it advisable to project a dollar amount of losses.

Another characteristic of NFR is that they are highly interconnected, and one category can have a significant impact on other NFR categories. If, for example, the threat level of *person risk* rises, this affects the stability and the threat level of fraud risk, information security risk, and process risk, to name just a few.

5.2 Separation and Aggregation of Subjects and Dimensions

A typical challenge in any type of risk reporting is to find the appropriate degree of granularity for each report addressee within the organization. Senior management needs a holistic and therefore aggregated information level. In addition, a risk manager needs to have the opportunity to drill down even to the level of raw data used to determine the threat level in order to be able to justify and explain the determined threat level.

A natural structure comes from the NFR categories, as they look at risk of a similar nature. The next step is to then define the structure of the report within each NFR category. The risk and the threat level can and should vary between different NFR categories. Nonetheless, some structural dimensions for reporting can be used across NFR categories. In most companies, the threat level is not homogeneous across the organizational structure (e.g., internal business units or legal entities).

Internal and external organizational structures are available and appropriate for most NFR categories. The starting point for the specific structures of NFR categories should be value drivers or risk drivers, which can easily be derived from impact graphs (the risk drivers being the sources in the directed graph, see Sect. 2.4.1).

5.3 Example—Compliance Risk

In Fig. 16, an example report for compliance risk is shown in a simplified and abstract layout. The upper left box provides the summarized assessment for the NFR category with a status, a trend indicator, and a hint at the challenges in this NFR category.

The adjoining box in the upper row shows the connectedness with other NFR categories, and the aggregated threat level of these NFR categories. Next to this, risk events (and their actual threat level) within compliance risk are

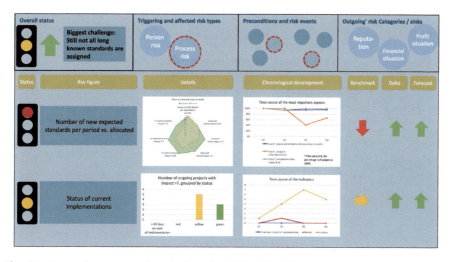

Fig. 16 Reporting approach – design sketch (© ifb SE)

shown. The box in the upper right corner shows additional impacted NFR categories.

The middle and lower parts of the report consist of a visualization of key risk indicators that best illustrate the threat level of the NFR category in focus. Besides the actual values in the middle section, the benchmark's development,[5] the chronological development (delta), and a forecast are shown.

The example shows that a balanced combination of qualitative and quantitative information offers a differentiated, but also sufficiently aggregated view of the risk profile in this NFR category.

5.4 Technical Infrastructure

Setting up technical infrastructure is a complex project. The example architecture in Fig. 17 shows the main components derived from the functional requirements from section to section. The main components are: (1) the graph database, (2) the raw and derived data for the key risk indicators by NFR category and (3) the forecasts or projections of the key risk indicators.

Implementing the required technical infrastructure is usually a complex project. The example architecture Fig. 17 shows the main components derived from the functional requirements laid out in Sects. 2 and 4 of this

---

[5] In this case, the benchmark is based on external peer groups but can be extended to internal structures like departments, business units, or legal entities.

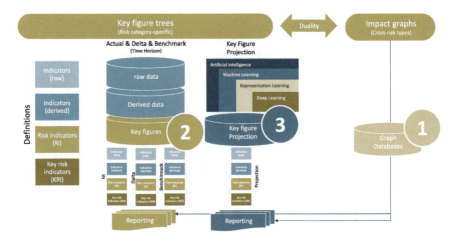

Fig. 17 Example system landscape (© ifb SE)

chapter. The main components are: (1) the graph database, (2) the raw and derived data for key risk indicators in each NFR category, and (3) the forecast or projection engine of key risk indicators.

The common basis to align different NFR categories is the graph database, which is optimized to store graphs (see Schröder and Tieben 2021). A graph database allows for insightful analyses about risk events and their connections and can provide an NFR category with overarching views and intelligence capabilities (Fig. 17).

Depending on the non-financial risk category, the raw data (2) can include huge amounts of data (Big Data). This highly granular data can use an existing data lake[6] or require setting up a data lake for NFR purposes. If high-frequency data exists in the NFR category, machine learning algorithms can be used to forecast the key risk indicators (3).

The connecting base to align the different NFR categories is the graph database, which is optimized to store graphs (see Schröder and Tieben 2021). A graph database allows interesting analyses about the risk events and their connection and can provide an NFR category with overarching views and analysis capabilities.

---

[6] Data lake: The term data lake is commonly used to describe a single data store that holds large amounts of raw data as well as processed data of an organization. It may include both structured and unstructured data objects.

6 Summary

6.1 The Need for Non-Financial Risk Management

This article tries to demonstrate the requirements for an integrated and connected (in terms of risk categories) non-financial risk management. Also, different NFR categories require individual key indicators and calculations. Impact graphs are the binding net that enables an integrated view.

Given the nature of non-financial risk (normally low frequency and high impact), the importance for risk management and corporate management altogether should not be underestimated. The continuously changing environment and the rarity of impactful events pose significant challenges for risk intelligence.

A key element to overcoming these hurdles is to work with what we have (or what is available on a reliable basis). Non-financial risk management is not improved by incorporating hard-to-estimate probabilities of events or other highly unstable parameters into pseudo-accurate risk models. However, it can be improved by incorporating the available data and modeling key risk indicators that serve as proxies for the threat level and the risk profile in a specific NFR category.

While continuous change is one of the rare stable patterns, the variety of new risks originating from the company's business model or its operational model will increase. These new risks will usually not be compensated with risk premia—in contrast to financial risks. Some of them can be insured but most must be taken and managed to the extent that they do not endanger the existence of the organization.

6.2 Outlook: Application of Machine Learning

Once the KRI trees are set up and the calculation methods are defined, the best practice in monitoring these KRI does not end with analyzing the status quo. It is important (a) to benchmark key indicators with internal (organizational) and external (peer groups) structures, (b) to monitor their development over time, and (c) to forecast key risk indicators in order to enable management to take appropriate action in a timely manner.

This forecasting requirement can be enabled or improved by machine learning and other big data technology. ML algorithms can support the recognition and continuation of patterns from raw data. By using projected raw data, the calculation of KRI can be performed for future points in time, thus helping management to anticipate the company's non-financial risk profile (see Schmüser et al. 2021; Schröder and Tieben Sentiment Analysis for Reputational Risk Management 2021).

Literature

Anonymous. beginning of 13th century. *The Song of the Nibelungs.*

Neo4j, Inc. 2020. *Home.* September 15. Accessed January 10, 2021. https://neo4j.com/.

Schmüser, Arne, Farah Skaf, and Harro Dittmar. 2021. "Use Case—NFR—HR Risk." In *The Digital Journey of Banking and Insurance, Volume II - Digitalization and Machine Learning*, edited by Volker Liermann and Claus Stegmann. New York: Palgrave Macmillan.

Schröder, Daniel and Marian Tieben. 2021. "Sentiment Analysis for Reputational Risk Management." In *The Digital Journey of Banking and Insurance, Volume II—Digitalization and Machine Learning*, edited by Volker Liermann and Claus Stegmann. New York: Palgrave Macmillan.

Culture and Projects

This part focuses on the cultural aspect: the project management culture. The chapters assembled here deliver insights into the culture needed for the transformation that an organization faces on the journey to become a digital company.

Fintech companies focus on the combination of financial services and technology. Why is it so hard for traditional banks to keep up with their challengers? It is not what they do, it is not the technology they use: it is the way they do it. The way of doing things does not actually differ fundamentally between fintech companies and Big Tech, so a more illustrative abbreviation would be FiCuTech, because the culture links the business to the technology in a unique way.

The COVID-19 pandemic has forced almost all tertiary sector workers to work from home, and in most contexts this worked well. The concept of remote work is not new, and the structures and tools have been available for quite some time. The challenges of COVID-19 forced us to find our way of working remotely. While everyone agrees that neither one hundred percent remote working nor zero percent remote working will be the future, the experience will impact project structures and the incorporation of remote components into the setting.

In Chapter 12 "Digi-Cultural Mindset" (Merkt, Lang and Schmidt, Digi-Cultural Mindset 2021), the impact and the potential of a digi-cultural mindset (DCM) is discussed, derived from the groundbreaking work in behavioral psychology. Furthermore, other models and concepts like SORC and SCRUM are discussed.

The next chapter "New Project Structure" (Akhgarnush, Bruse and Hofer, New Project Structure 2021) summarizes the tools and patterns of the already well-established world of agile project management. The chapter introduces the principles and values of agile project management followed by the Scrum framework with its roles and responsibilities as well as its specific events and periods. Over the course of the chapter, the best methods and tools to implement this way of project management are explored, and a side look is taken at other agile project management frameworks. The following third chapter in this part (Beister and Zeljkovic 2021) merges the agile and the waterfall project approach into one hybrid way of working. The chapter gives advice and hints at where to use either approach on its own, or where to merge them into a hybrid framework. Furthermore, four different variants of the hybrid approach are discussed. The fourth chapter (Akhgarnush, Bruse and Pott, Remote Projects 2021) shows a now well-established way of working (remote projects) and highlights the benefits of this different way of thinking. The chapter explores technological aspects (tools and the ability to scale) along with cultural aspects (virtual culture).

The fifth and last chapter puts a spotlight on project approaches and organizational patterns in the context of process optimization and RPA[1] in particular. The chapter splits up a standard RPA project into four relevant phases. It summarizes the main challenges posed by RPA projects and closes with a long-term integration perspective.

Literature

Akhgarnush, Eljar, Fabian Bruse, and Ben Hofer. 2021. "New Project Structure." In *The Digital Journey of Banking and Insurance, Volume I—Disruption and DNA*, edited by Volker Liermann and Claus Stegmann. New York: Palgrave Macmillan.

Akhgarnush, Eljar, Fabian Bruse, and Daniel Pott. 2021. "Remote Projects." In *The Digital Journey of Banking and Insurance, Volume I—Disruption and DNA*, edited by Volker Liermann and Claus Stegmann. New York: Palgrave Macmillan.

Beister, Uwe, and Milica Zeljkovic. 2021. "Hybrid Project Management." In *The Digital Journey of Banking and Insurance, Volume I—Disruption and DNA*, edited by Volker Liermann and Claus Stegmann. New York: Palgrave Macmillan.

Merkt, Rainer, Veronika Lang, and Anna Schmidt. 2021. "Digi-Cultural Mindset." In *The Digital Journey of Banking and Insurance, Volume I—Disruption and DNA*, edited by Volker Liermann and Claus Stegmann. New York: Palgrave Macmillan.

---

[1] Robotic Process Automation.

Digi-Cultural Mindset

Rainer Merkt, Veronika Lang, and Anna Schmidt

1 Introduction

Imagine you are just about to read the newspaper on a sunny Monday morning, when suddenly a topic strikes your attention: "Huge pandemic about to spread throughout the continent. The world we know today will change radically. Many companies all over the world are starting to shut down their offices, an era of a *new normal working mode* has arrived!". How will you react? How will you master the upcoming changes and shape the transformation process?

This message might sound familiar to you. In March 2020 an unknown virus called COVID-19 spread all over the world forcing us to change our daily lives. As much as it influenced our private lives—i.e., lockdown of most public places and activities as well as restricted travel and gathering opportunities—it caused a huge shift in the working mode within many companies.

R. Merkt (✉) · A. Schmidt
ifb SE, Grünwald, Germany
e-mail: Rainer.Merkt@ifb-group.com

A. Schmidt
e-mail: anna.schmidt@ifb-group.com

V. Lang
4ED1 GmbH, Berlin, Germany
e-mail: veronika@4ed1.com

One major challenge: enabling everyone to work remotely. Suddenly, working from home became the new normal. It forced companies to undergo a change toward a high level of digitally enabled work, as local work and local meetings were not possible anymore. The pandemic not only caused a superficial shift of working mode, but also affected the deeper, underlying structures of many organizations: culture. This includes:

1. (partly) unconscious culture of learning and coping with change as well as mental models about work,
2. interaction between employees and
3. other collective attitudes and activities.

This is not the only change that companies have been facing recently. In times of highly dynamic markets, driven by multiple factors like globalization or demographic change, companies are challenged to constantly review their status quo and refine their course. The acronym VUCA quite accurately characterizes the conditions of our current global situation: volatile, uncertain, complex, and ambiguous. Digitalization is another major driver for organizations and therefore part of the volatile, uncertain, complex, and ambiguous topics we are dealing with right now.

Thus, taking the time to investigate an organization's culture not only in times of change is highly recommended as it contributes to an organization's profits and productivity as well as influencing employee satisfaction (Berson 2008). Without a clear, holistic approach to managing these changes at all organizational levels, the risk of failing to adapt to current and future circumstances may pave the way to a loss of market position.

We propose that a key success factor in this context of cultural change is having a digi-cultural mindset. The ambition of this article is not only to introduce you to the theoretical background of organizational behavior but also to give you ideas and a few tools to initiate organizational change.

2 Digi-Cultural Mindset

> A fool with a tool is still a fool. (Grady Booch)

With regard to digitalization and culture, this chapter considers two connected aspects: technological and organizational change. Digitalization brings new technologies and players into the market and forces companies to investigate their competitiveness as a reaction to the changing needs of

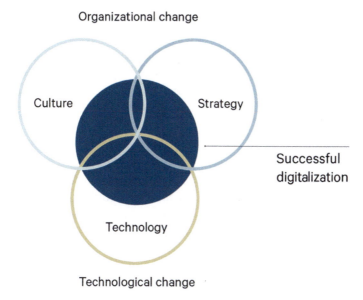

Fig. 1 Successful digitalization is where culture, business strategy and technology are aligned (© ifb SE)

customers—therefore it initiates a two-way change process within many organizations: top-down at a company's strategic level as well as bottom-up at a company's cultural level, mainly based on changing tasks involving changing expectations and needs of employees.

This chapter attempts to combine these two topics: the process of navigating through a transformation itself and defining a target vision in constantly changing circumstances. In our opinion, a successful digital transformation happens through the combination of strategic, cultural and technological aspects. Talking about successful digitalization, there is no technological change without an organizational change and vice versa. The following figure tries to illustrate this interplay (Fig. 1).

2.1 Let's Talk About Change

As you might have noticed, there is more to take care of than just the implementation of whatever new thing you want to introduce: the change process within the people working in this new environment. To be more precise, employees and leaders may need to develop and strengthen a learning-oriented mindset, free of resistance, fear, or ambiguous thoughts about change.

To master a transformation, all drivers of change need to be harmonized. It may sound a bit odd to you, but hopefully after reading this chapter you will have a better understanding of what a digitally mature company may look and feel like and how to get there yourself. This target vision of a company—from a holistic and people-centered point of view—is what we call a *digi-cultural mindset*. Within the following pages we will introduce you to what exactly this concept might be.

The first step on your way to a *digi-cultural mindset*: imagine you are an entrepreneur: what strategic changes based on a digitalization process can you think of that initiate not only a new process, product, or client base but also changes within your workforce (e.g., within your employees, tasks, skills…)?

Here is a little illustration of different drivers of change:
External event initiating a change process:

- You have been selling chocolate for many years. In your early days, people of all ages came to visit your store. Now, mainly young children and older people buying chocolate for their grandchildren come to visit your store. But they are not the most generous buyers. You have realized: everyone else is working and therefore too busy to come to a specialized chocolate store, they simply buy their sweets online.

Strategic decision as a response to an external event: External event initiating a change process:

- Expansion of your business segment to online retail (new market & new client base)

Internal consequences of the decision to put change into practice:

- As more and more people use online shopping, you have decided to offer a special range of products that can only be bought online, next to another range of products that can only be bought in store (based on a changing market situation). This introduction of a new value chain initiates new workflows and therefore requires employees with specialized, new skills. You probably need to develop a training framework to enable your employees to handle an online shop and you probably need to rethink your hiring process. This training can either happen on the job or on a dedicated training course. It may also be necessary to align your employees' work environment as some of them will have to sit more in front of laptops to maintain your website.

There are many more things to be considered, for sure. But as you have noticed, there are multiple aspects influencing a successful business within the context of a digitalization process that needs to be aligned: target vision of the leader, impact on the individual person, and impact on the working conditions and culture.

Let's start looking at impacts of a transformation like digitalization on the individual person, more precisely on a person's organizational behavior. This is observable and can therefore give information about how a person deals with a situation. Also, behavior can be shaped by taking some basic learning mechanisms into account. As every transformation is a change from a well-known situation to an unknown situation, a feeling of unease might be provoked. This is due to the fact that your brain classifies uncertain or ambiguous situations as unpredictable and thus unsettling. Furthermore, learning something new can feel like replacing something that was useful before with something unknown. This also may provoke a feeling of uncertainty. But going through a transformation is not as complicated as it seems to be! To prevent a reaction of fear or stress, some points of orientation and a vision about where we are heading are necessary to thrive on our transformation journey. Some orientation will be given to you next.

2.1.1 Orientation

> Organizational behavior is seen affecting and being affected by the participant's cognitions, the environment and the person-situation interaction. (Davis and Luthans 1980)

The following section of the chapter will deal with an individual person's perception processes to give you a basic understanding of how everyone of us deals with situations. Next, we will broaden the picture and have a look at factors outside of an individual, like the collaboration between individuals working in a team and how to foster a positive team atmosphere. Last but not least, some leadership qualities will be taken into consideration on our way to our target vision. Step by step, you will be approaching a digi-cultural mindset in all contexts in an organization (individual, team, and the sum of everything: the organization itself) (Fig. 2).

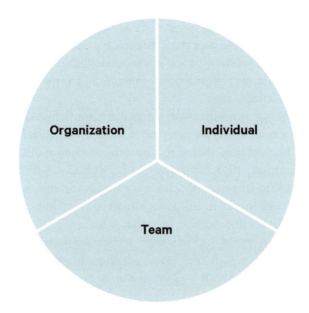

Fig. 2 Digi-cultural mindset spreads through all organizational contexts (© ifb SE)

2.2 Me, Myself and I—How We Perceive Change at an Individual Level

Here is a short introduction to how our general perception of the world around us usually influences how we act within this world—and thus influences to what extent we feel in control of a situation. It is in our nature that our thoughts and feelings drive and mutually influence our behavior. Therefore, what we perceive as a challenging or problematic event determines which options we see to master it. This mostly unconscious automatism is mainly driven by our (also mostly unconscious) basic beliefs and mental representations of the world, processes, and everything else interacting within this world. Investigating our thoughts, feelings, and behavior as well as their interaction can help us become more aware of them and therefore give us information about our mindset. This interdependence of thoughts, feelings and our behavior (Ellis 1957; Beck 1967) is visualized in this triangle, the mindset is constituted by these three interacting parts (Fig. 3).

Therefore, if we want to develop a certain mindset, we won't be able to do so without taking the interaction of our thoughts, feelings and behavior into consideration.

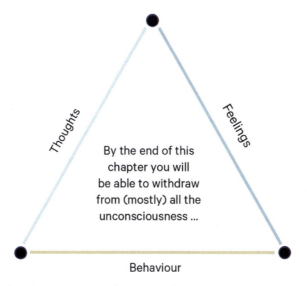

Fig. 3 A mindset is constituted of the interdependence of thoughts, feelings and behavior (© ifb SE)

2.2.1 To Start With: What Exactly Is a Person's *Mindset*?

There are multiple qualities summarized within this term: it describes a way of thinking, attitudes, mentality, ideology, self-perception, and more. Every person's mindset is different. A mindset can be somewhere between fixed and flexible, resistant toward change (fixed mindset) or agile: able to adapt to current circumstances by learning from experience. The latter is called a *growth mindset* (Dweck 2007). The following table gives you an overview of the characteristics of a fixed and growth mindset.

Fixed mindset	Growth mindset
Avoids challenges	*Embraces challenges*
Rather than risk failing and negatively impacting their self-image, having a fixed mindset will lead to avoiding challenges and sticking to what they already know they can do well	Focus on improvement; they embrace challenges because they know they will come out stronger on the other side
Ignores criticism or useful negative feedback	*Learns from criticism and negative feedback*

(continued)

(continued)

Fixed mindset	Growth mindset
"Criticism of my capabilities feels like criticism of me as a person"	= sources of information; they perceive negative feedback not as being directly about them as a person but rather about the current state of their abilities; it doesn't mean that all criticism is worth integrating or that nothing is ever to be taken personally
Intelligence and talent are fixed	*Intelligence and talent can be developed*
"We are the way we are," leads to a desire to look smart	Leads to a desire to learn, to improve; the brain is seen as a muscle that can be trained
Sees effort as fruitless or worse = shows less effort	*Sees effort as the path to mastery = shows more effort*
"What's the point of working hard and making effort if afterwards I might still be at square one?"	Effort seen as necessary to grow and master useful skills and knowledge; not turned away by fear knowing that failure is possible
Gives up easily when faced with obstacles	*Keeps trying and never gives up*
Obstacles are external forces that get in the way	External setbacks do not discourage them, self-image is not tied to their success or how they will look to others; failure is an opportunity to learn and so, whatever happens, they will win
Feels threatened by success of others	*Inspired by success of others*
When others succeed, they will try to convince themselves and the people around them that the success was due to either luck (because almost everything is due to luck in the fixed mindset world), or to objectionable actions	= sources of inspiration, information opportunities to learn; not a competitive, zero-sum game with others
"I'm a failure, I will never improve"	*Persists in the face of setbacks, will learn from failures*
Do not reach their fullest potential and their beliefs feed on themselves, forming negative feedback loops	They note their improvements, and this creates positive feedback loops that encourage them to continue learning and improving

Imagine a filter if you think about your mindset. It determines the quality of information you perceive and thus the behavior you show. Therefore, this is the key topic on your own transformation journey toward a *digi-cultural mindset*. In other words, our cognitions mediate between a situational event and our behavior.

> Here is an example, which should make it tangible for you:
> *Your team has been working with agile methods for a while. You are not familiar with the new meeting structure yet. However, during the first retrospective meeting your agile coach encourages everyone to speak openly about any dissatisfaction with their activities within the last sprint. Some do so openly, but you remain silent even though your head is full of proposals for improvement.*
>
> 1. What is discouraging you from sharing your ideas?
>
> *Previously, you have experienced negative reactions to your input. Colleagues have argued against your ideas and have even appeared annoyed. Moreover, their behavior reminded you of your school days – there you experienced similar reactions in class.*
>
> 2. How does this influence your self-perception?
>
> *You perceive yourself as a boring speaker never finding the right words and therefore avoid speaking publicly. You, speaking openly in front of a group, can only provoke negative reactions! You have nothing of importance to say.*
>
> **Result**
> This attitude was built over many years based on the experience of not being taken seriously. In the situation outlined above, the "example you" is consequently avoiding building more self-confidence and does not believe in the ability to change uncomfortable situations. By keeping quiet, you avoided having the experience of impacting your environment in a positive way. But enough self-pity! With this example, we only wanted to illustrate the interconnectedness between thoughts, previous experiences, current behavior and external factors like the work environment. Amongst others, all these factors together shape a company's culture.

2.2.2 Mind Full, or Mindful?

The good news here is that it is possible to change your world view (mindset). Our mindset is not only important with regard to learning a new skill or performing well at work. It is also of great importance for our general relationship with ourselves and others: trusting our capabilities, taking failure as an opportunity to learn instead of judging harshly, or feeling self-driven instead of helplessly controlled by external forces. These are only a few examples of how our mindset will drive us to our best or worst self (see table of fixed vs. growth mindset) and to more or less pleasant interactions with others. Being aware, i.e., mindful, of your thoughts, feelings, and behavior will lead to a deeper understanding of how your interactions work and can help you to actively foster better communication and pleasant relationships with others.

2.2.3 Excurse

Let's dive deeper into this circle of interaction to understand how we learned to react and therefore how to actively and successfully adapt to changing circumstances. Watch out for some historical information ahead!

In their early years, behavioral scientists saw the human mind as a "black box"—understanding our behaviors as a simple response to external stimuli but not questioning whether there was more influencing our behaviors, like feelings or thoughts. B.F. Skinner, one of the most popular behavioral psychologists (1904–1980), might have said something like "The brain is so complex we can't possibly understand it, so why bother? We know the inputs (stimuli) and we know the outputs (behavior) and isn't that enough?" (Meacham 2017). Skinner loved to experiment with animals, especially rats. He made it to become one of the—if not THE—most influential psychologists of the twentieth century (Haggbloom et al. 2002). By rewarding or punishing rats for their behavior, he showed that behavior could be influenced by consequences and that not all consequences automatically caused the same reactions within every individual (rat). He introduced the principle of reinforcement: if consequences of an action are perceived as negative, e.g., painful (a punishment), the action will not be repeated. Whereas, if consequences of an action are positive, the probability of an action increases. These mechanisms are also known as *operant conditioning* (McLeod 2018).

Furthermore, consequences do not always have to be externally controlled. Examples for self-produced consequences for one's own actions could include satisfaction from performing a task or developing new skills and therefore feeling more independent. The strength of reinforcement highly depends on individual preferences, values, needs, and standards and can explain why behavior persists without being immediately externally supported.

> **Lessons Learned**
> We always react based on something preceding our behavior (a specific situation). Beyond that we can be influenced by something following our behavior (a consequence). How much a consequence or a situation affects our behavior is influenced by our own individual conditions (mindset, learning history, etc.). We strive for positive consequences (they lead to a reinforcement of a certain behavior) and try to avoid negative consequences (they decrease the probability of a certain behavior). Positive reinforcement should always be preferred to punishment—we're talking about building a healthy and stimulating organizational culture, right?

Therefore, talking about digitalization, we would like to suggest a couple of personal traits that might facilitate thriving in situations of change—or in other words: digitalization's success is highly dependent on a change in people's behavior and their reaction to changing situations. These traits are mainly connected to having a growth mindset and can help leaders set priorities for which strengths should be encouraged within their employees:

- **Responsible:** Feeling responsible and passionate about a task will strongly motivate a person to give their best in working on a task;
- **Independent:** Transparent expectations will lead to independence to fulfill a task;
- **Adaptable:** Staying motivated in case of mistakes, trying again instead of getting stuck and learning from failure instead of fearing to fail; it's not about making more mistakes but about organizing work to be as sensitive toward mistakes as possible to detect them and deal with the consequences in good time (supported by technological and human factors).
- Therefore, being **future-oriented**, visionary and **open** toward new ideas will reinforce the resilience needed to thrive within changing circumstances (Officevibe 2017).

A framework to support these values at an organizational level that is quite popular and might sound familiar to you is SCRUM. Commitment, courage, focus, openness, and respect as values of SCRUM shape the mindset of each team working within this framework. If you are interested in the method of SCRUM, please see the section *Inspiring Material* at the end of this article.

2.3 Show Me How to Do It

For some scientists, Skinner's radical *behaviorism* clearly wasn't enough. It took until the 60s for our cognitions to be included in this behavioral equation as parameters preceding our behavior (Kanfer and Saslow 1969). In addition to observable behavior or elements of the situation, cognitive factors in learning as a characteristic of our individual condition completed the behavioral chain. These give less observable but more deducible information about our mental events. They are all summed up within the *Organism* variable. Also, previous experiences and basically everything you have ever thought about fits in this variable to fully explain the learning process in humans—and animals.

Thus, the model that is used to analyze a certain behavior (R) combines external stimuli (S), internal mechanisms such as cognitions, feelings, etc., (O), and consequences (C) into a behavioral chain as described in the following picture (Fig. 4).

But we do not exclusively learn through personal experience, a.k.a. operant conditioning. An important contribution to developing new attitudes and skills is made by observing other people. In addition to the reinforcement of our behaviors, we also learn through imitating others. This is what Bandura called *Social Learning Theory* (Bandura 1977). People quickly reproduce emotional responses, actions, and attitudes they have observed. In addition, learning also occurs through observing the reinforcing or punishing outcomes of other people's behavior (Davis and Luthans 1980). This implies that people at work learn by observing their colleagues rather than by following rules or policies they were only told or that solely exist on paper. Therefore, we will

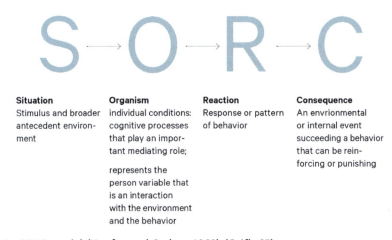

Fig. 4 SORC model (Kanfer and Saslow 1969) (© ifb SE)

look at what should characterize a team's atmosphere and how leaders play an important role in setting an example next.

2.4 We're All in This Together—The Team Level

Change doesn't only happen at an individual level. Let's take a closer look at the organizational context and focus on how to support a culture of growth and transition on our way to a digi-cultural mindset. If you remember the external factors mentioned within the SORC chain, we will now be talking about the **s**ituational factors that influence a person's behavior within an organization or group. The two main factors we will be focusing on are perceived team climate and leadership behavior.

What characteristics are necessary for a company to be a place for change toward digitalization? And how do we make change happen within our teams based on the knowledge gained about how we learn and maintain behavior?

First, what exactly is team climate? It can be described as:

> the shared perceptions of and the meaning attached to the policies, practices and procedures employees experience and the behaviors they observe getting rewarded and that are supported and expected. (Schneider et al. 2013)

This might sound familiar to you as it is the same mechanism that shapes an individual's behavior but at a group level. The hard thing about investigating characteristics of strong teams is that we are talking about characteristics like trust, cohesion or team confidence—so-called emergent states. They are intrinsic team processes, mediators between team input and output, and they indicate how a team feels, its members' relationship toward each other and shared motivational characteristics. They are the important factors that should be fostered to ensure positive team outcomes. But how to foster something we can't really see?

For quite a long time, diversity was seen as the key to efficient teams. Just put people of a different age, ethnicity, background, etc., together and you will see wonderful results—a focus more on each member's superficial individual traits. But that's only the tip of the iceberg. In line with Google's researchers who conducted a study called *project Aristotle* (Duhigg 2016), we will now talk about five key characteristics of successful teamwork, emphasizing the interaction between team members and their collaboration climate that will build strong positive team output:

- **Psychological safety:** Does everyone feel confident that the team will not embarrass, reject or punish someone for speaking up (e.g., when there is a problem or when sharing creative ideas with each other, do we have a playful attitude toward trying new things)?
- **Reliability**: Can we count on each other to complete our tasks? Do we collaborate and share our ideas?
- **Structure and clarity:** Do we know about our team's goals, positions, and strategy?
- **Valuable work:** Are our activities valuable to everyone in the team? Do we feel passionate to be engaged in the process?
- **Meaningful work:** Do we perceive our work as meaningful?

Team climate shows how cultural traits can manifest themselves simultaneously in the common experiences of a group of people with different experiences and in unique experiences as well. Therefore, you can say that team climate provides behavioral evidence for a company's culture.

Culture as a source of collective identity and commitment is defined as *"the shared values and assumptions that explain why organizations do what they do and focus on what they focus on"* (Schneider et al. 2017).

Hence, culture is connected to the strategic focal points an organization has set. This means: a company's culture becomes visible when observing the actions taken to reach the strategic goals and objectives. Let's have a look at certain actions supporting the efficacy of team and leadership behavior.

Frederick Laloux, the author of *Reinventing Organizations,* proposes that, due to the complexity of networks and fast development of new technologies, companies should move away from a centralistic, hierarchical decision-making process and move toward a decentralized system (Laloux 2017).

One example given by Laloux is that of a complex ecosystem like the forest: when winter arrives early, the tallest tree does not say "let me make a plan and then we will all abide by it." The opposite is the case, every part of the ecosystem adapts to its own needs to survive. This independency makes an ecosystem resilient to change.

What does this mean in terms of leadership? Decisions are made based on a transparent consultation process by those who are impacted by the decision (employees, managers, etc.). This leads to much shorter decision-making processes (lean) and employees are much more engaged. A side effect is that employees are more motivated. Why do you think that this is the case? Imagine a machine or a software needs to be replaced. The users know exactly which requirements the machine/software needs to fulfill. In the proposed decentralized system, one of the users is responsible for the replacement. Meaning he/she will ask colleagues also from other parts of the company who are experts, responsible for budgets, or also have a stake for their opinions and take these into account in the decision-making process. This will also happen vice versa. No decisions are made top-down, but by those affected by the decision or change. All of a sudden everyone can create and be a changemaker.

However, in this set-up, team leaders are not the experts for making decisions anymore, as they do not exclusively possess all the knowledge or skills. Therefore, focusing on getting a good fit of employees into a team is necessary. Assessing the skills and motivations of your current team members to identify necessary additions is key to building complementary team structures. As a result, combining complementary skills facilitates teams accomplishing their goals (Griffin and Moorhead 2012).

Moreover, new processes and technologies require people to work in new team set-ups. One aspect of new team set-ups could be building flexible structures that allow teams to focus on tackling a problem and to foster communication. Using elements like *retrospectives* in which a team can openly speak about their current situation provides an opportunity for constant improvement in tackling problems. By exchanging positive and negative experiences, employees build trust in each other, which also provides room to improve and define their own team culture.

One underlying concept here regarding leadership is also leading by example (we learn from watching the behavior of others: see Sect. 2.3, SORC model). By creating an environment at a team and organizational level where mistakes can be made and people can show a vulnerable side. "You can't have courage without being vulnerable" (Brown 2018).

To sum up, the leadership style described above is characterized by facilitating self-organized behaviors. A leader's responsibility is to build structures in which individual employees can react flexibly, as they are considered the experts in fulfilling their tasks. Positive feedback to foster engagement and motivation are key to creating room for independent and self-driven organizational behavior.

> **Toolbox 1**
> A company's climate is shaped, among other things, by group norms, which have a key influence on everyone's behavior. These could be possible practices to foster a strong team atmosphere:
>
> 1. Being sensitive toward each other's moods and individual differences creates **interpersonal trust**. This can be fostered by a high level of social

interaction and strong communication between the team members. Digitalization offers a variety of possibilities: introduction of a social network to bond through similar hobbies or inspirational differences or introduction of digital coffee meetings or lunch breaks, possibly with someone randomly chosen to expand personal networks.
2. Also, **psychological safety** generates more creativity and trust in own ideas. Trial and error are preferred to being stuck at the existing status quo as a result of fearing mistakes: a positive attitude toward mistakes enhances employees' participation and a project's progress. As a result, stronger innovational power is beneficial to everyone. Therefore, an assigned regular meeting to exchange experiences from failed projects or tasks can be very helpful to integrate a culture of learning from mistakes and not the need for hiding mistakes.
3. Research has shown that inconsistent procedures and policies can result in a weak climate and therefore suggest that **transparency and consistency** in processes and practices should be fostered (Zohar and Luria 2005). The more consistent employees' experiences are, the more they relate to the group. Hence, there should be more positive outcomes.
4. Building **resilient** teams: People who build strong resources can conquer change much easier as they see an opportunity in every difficulty. Failure is not seen as damaging their self-confidence (see "growth mindset" further above). "Build what's strong" instead of "fix what's wrong" (Seligman 2011): in other words, focus on strengthening resources instead of fixing problems.
5. Certain leadership behaviors such as strong communication and sharing a clear strategic vision for the work can positively influence the strength of a group's cohesive atmosphere.

Lessons Learned

The extent to which learning new behaviors happens depends on a company's culture and climate (Kortsch, Paulsen und Naegele, et al. 2016). Therefore, leaders can foster this development by being aware of the importance of learning and beyond that by building awareness for the necessity of learning within their company, ideally a learning culture. The first step in shaping an organization's learning culture is to embody learning in a company's strategy and values. Consequently, organizational and individual learning can become a matter of course and are seen as connected factors. Climate emerges through social collaboration. Learning a new skill mostly happens while performing

> the new task, which means that employees can acquire new skills most suitably during their working hours (not after work) and by collaborating with each other. Every individual's participative actions as a result of a strong team atmosphere will add up to a successful organizational cultural change.
>
> People are characterized by different capabilities, needs, and attitudes that lead to different behaviors depending on the context. Therefore, it is important to start looking precisely at individuals within your organization and how to unlock their full potential by building favorable conditions at work. By actively living a culture of learning, the company can progress and the employee's need for personal development is met (Kortsch et al., Lernkultur in Unternehmen—Wie man sie messen und gestalten kann 2019).

2.5 Target Vision: A Digi-Cultural Mindset

This general theory of perception based on the interdependency of thoughts, feelings and behavior and the underlying process of learning is where our digi-cultural mindset idea grew from. Using the analogy of a gardener, nurturing a digi-cultural mindset within a company could be translated into preparing the soil that makes flowers blossom or, in our case, digitalization achievable. We want to suggest a holistic people-centered framework to enable companies to thrive within a change process:

> The term *digi-cultural mindset (DCM)* describes the characteristics of a fundamental attitude at all people-related levels of an organization (leadership, team, and individual person) to lay the necessary cultural foundations for successful digitalization. In other words, it is a necessary requirement for any organizational change. The *DCM* contributes to a company's capability to grow and to master the transformation to a new normal working mode—in this case our goal is digital maturity. A *DCM* can therefore be described as certain cultural traits incorporated by everyone. *DCM* underlines how culture manifests itself at different levels of organizations. It describes a dynamic state of iterative learning to thrive in changing circumstances (Fig. 5).
>
> This attitude can be fostered within three different, but connected, contexts:
>
> 1. Fundamental **organizational** structures regarding leadership, working mode, strategy, processes: we propose a leadership style that focuses on fostering a culture of learning, transparent and lean processes, communicating a clear vision and being aware of a leader's role model position. It

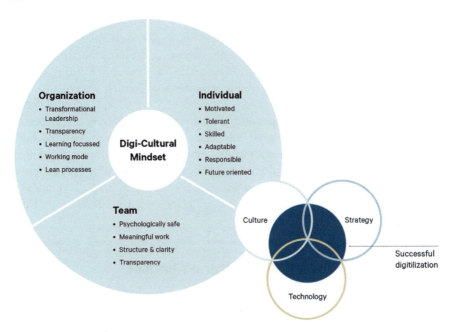

Fig. 5 Definition of a digi-cultural mindset (© ifb SE)

> is about building the conditions for a successful internal working mode in changing external circumstances.
> 2. Norms and collective behavior: Defined qualities of **teamwork** to foster innovation, cohesion and creativity as a representation of the collective culture. We propose a climate based on psychological safety and work that is perceived as meaningful and valuable to foster motivation and innovation. It is also about a culture of trial and error building a natural climate of trust and transparency.
> 3. **Individual** perception and behavior: Being aware of underlying enabling and blocking influences on everyone's behaviors and certain individual traits that we see connected to having a growth mindset. Here, the focus is on identifying the right set of skills to allow for complementary perspectives and skills.

3 Maturity Model

As mentioned earlier, there are external and internal drivers of an individual's organizational behavior. External factors such as work environment and leadership behavior, team atmosphere, and culture in general externally influence a person's behavior. Internally, there will always be individual conditions that, no matter what strategic decision is taken, will individually influence a person's reaction. Therefore, we propose **a target vision that takes into consideration that there is not one right thing to do for everyone, but common ground that can be built for everyone to thrive within changing circumstances: a DCM.** Next, you will gain an overview of how to assess your company's status regarding the journey toward a DCM.

Stage 1 in our Maturity Model describes a state where there is no awareness of the necessity for a DCM within the organization (Fig. 6). Hence, in stage 5 of our Maturity Model, all three organizational levels are thriving as they developed a DCM. Stage 5 builds the preconditions for successful digitalization, whereas in stage 1 the organization wasn't even aware of the lack of a common attitude. In stage 3 and 4, a company gains the understanding of its status quo and defines its cultural target vision. The company can focus on what steps need to be taken toward a common mindset. This awareness of its own culture is the basis for any effort to change and leverage organizational change. A company's culture is the main supportive framework for a successfully executed strategy. You might have heard the popular saying in this context "**Culture eats strategy for breakfast.**"

After reading this article, we hope you can find yourself in stage 2. A few pages earlier, you probably weren't aware of how much a mindset can influence everyone's behavior and how important culture is at all organizational levels. We tried to give you a target vision for a desirable state of mind with our digi-cultural mindset. Now we will give you an idea about how to assess the cultural profile of your organization: this can give you insights into the strategic part of organizational change and therefore how to identify the broader direction you are heading in. You are already deeply tied into a change process and it is up to you to what extent you are going to put these insights into practice.

Stage 1	Stage 2	Stage 3	Stage 4	Stage 5
No awareness of the necessity for a DCM	Awareness of the necessity for a DCM	Assessment of the status quo of the current cultural mindset	Definition of a DCM target vision with defined cultural traits on all organizational levels	Thriving DCM

Fig. 6 Digi-cultural mindset Maturity Model (© ifb SE)

4 The Whole Is More Than the Sum of Its Parts

In the following section we will propose a target vision of what your cultural focus could look like. It is based on characteristics of strategic orientation, organizational structure, and team climate. To end this chapter, we will offer you some questions to discover the focus within your team.

4.1 Target Culture

Firstly, we defined that a target culture of learning, flexibility, and a focus on people is necessary to cope with the demanding market situation and changing processes caused by digitalization. This is quite a complex target vision that encounters different drivers. Therefore, there is not one exclusive focus to be chosen, rather a balanced profile is aimed for. This cultural profile can be assessed using the *Organizational Culture Assessment Instrument* (OCAI) by Kim Cameron (Cameron and Quinn 1999) *and* (Quinn 1988) developed against the background of the *Competing Values Framework* (Cameron and Quinn 2006). These competing values are internal vs. external focus and stability vs. flexibility in structure. There are four culture types revealed by this model:

- *Clan:* Internal focus and flexible structure with a focus on people
- *Adhocracy:* External focus and flexible structure with a focus on growth
- *Market*: External focus and stable structure with a focus on competition
- *Hierarchy*: Internal focus and stable structure with a focus on organizational structure

This proposes that the focus (employee well-being vs. increased market share) of assumptions, beliefs, values, and behavior within an organization shapes the likelihood of its success. The four profiles are not mutually exclusive but can coexist within one organization. They can complement each other with usually one culture being dominant and taken as an organization's specific identity.

If digitalization as an external driver is taken into account for a company's strategy, it leads to an external market orientation: looking at the market to assess what possibilities emerge based on the latest technology and comparing one's own behavior to those of competitors and customers to probably diversify one's own activities. A company in a more stable environment would allow a dominant internal focus. But, as mentioned earlier, we nowadays find ourselves in a volatile, uncertain, complex, and ambiguous environment. Regarding the dimension of flexible vs. stable focus, a transformation would clearly mean that a culture values flexibility: striving to adapt quickly to changing circumstances, focusing on people and activities instead of structures, procedures, and plans.

4.2 Cultural Profile

As a result, the cultural profile we suggest for a company would be dominantly characterized by flexible structures with a focus on people and growth. There, work would be characterized by a dynamic, entrepreneurial and creative spirit. Every member of this environment would be committed to innovation, experimentation, growth, creating new resources, and risk taking. Also, leaders are seen partially as mentors, and they see their success in caring for people and addressing their needs. Participation and teamwork are highly valued. Aggressive competition (like within the Market profile) and uniformity and predictability (Hierarchy profile) would be less important (Fig. 7).

Hereby you can see how the cultural profile is built by asking how and why a company behaves: reacting to external or internal triggers and valuing

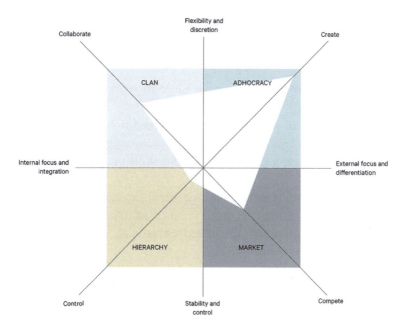

Fig. 7 Digi-cultural mindset mapped to Competing Values Framework (© ifb SE)

flexibility or stability within their structures. Typical examples of sectors for the Market profile would be consultancy, accountancy, sales, and marketing. Typical examples of the dominant Hierarchy culture would be sectors like medicine, government, banking, and insurance. Depending on what the company is striving for, the best fit should be chosen, but remember: it doesn't have to be only one profile, it can be one dominant with aspects of the others.

4.3 Deep Dive—DCM Maturity Assessment

We propose a few characteristics that enable teams to work more efficiently: feeling safe to discover and openly talk about ideas, collaboration, meaningful work, structure, clarity, and transparency. Whether your team's climate and working mode heads in the same direction can be assessed by asking the following questions that focus on observable experiences people have in their work setting:

1. Does the job allow one's own decision-making on how to schedule and plan work?
2. Does the job give a chance to use personal initiative or judgment in carrying out the work?
3. Does the job offer considerable opportunity for independence and freedom in how to do the work?
4. Does the job involve performing a variety of tasks?
5. Do the results of the job have a significant effect on the lives of other people?
6. Does the job involve completing a piece of work that has an obvious beginning and end?
7. Does the job itself provide information about an employee's performance?
8. Does the job require a variety of different skills in order to complete the work?
9. Do people working together take a personal interest in each other?
10. Do other people in the organization, such as managers and colleagues, provide information about the effectiveness (e.g., quality and quantity) of each other's job performance?

You can ask yourself: How many of these questions can I answer with yes? We are not going to set a cut-off number of "yes" answers you need to give to be successful. They are meant to be stimuli to inspire you to have a look at important characteristics during your transformation journey on a more daily and tangible basis than assessing a holistic cultural profile, taking every level of your company into account. These questions are inspired by the *Work Design Questionnaire* that can be used to inspect the current nature of work or redesign work in organizations (Morgeson and Humphrey 2006).

5   Outlook

5.1   Summary

Working on an awareness of your mindset is not only important within the context of digitalization but in the context of change in general. There are multiple drivers of change, many of them in quickly changing markets following new technologies, politics, or climate change to name only a few external drivers that will prospectively keep on influencing a company's strategic orientation. Modifications take time to settle in until they become a new normal and from time to time it can be difficult to keep on pushing forward during a transformation journey over a longer period. Therefore, it is important to incorporate a mindset that helps you to constantly question your status quo and stay passionate to be engaged in the process. The important question should be: are you still moving in the desired direction? That's alright then!

Leading through uncertainty and installing structures to actively shape the future are key challenges for company leaders nowadays. But besides these strategic decisions, communication and collaboration at all levels are necessary to stay in touch with what happens within a company and the surrounding environment to harmonize both sides. Probably, the new normal will not be a stable state of your organization that you can reach within a certain number of years, but it could be the ability to take action and thrive within consistently changing circumstances. The process to build this ability is iterative and takes many circles, which, every time you go through the process, will bring you upwards toward an inherent growth mentality (Fig. 8).

You have done a lot of mental work reading this article. The next step is putting everything into practice. This article does not aim to provide a handbook with step-by-step instructions on how to transform a business within five days, but aims to give you a feeling of what it takes to achieve sustainable change: willingness to learn and to rethink patterns of behavior and thoughts, some creativity to think about situations that haven't happened yet but that can give you hints about what challenges you might encounter in the future,

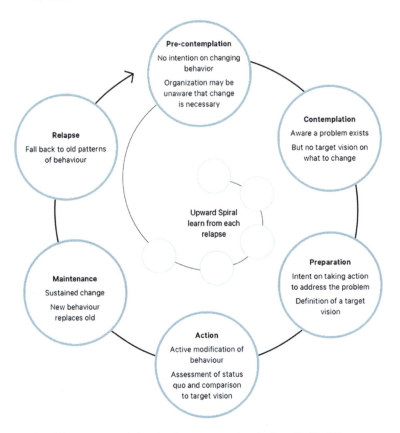

Fig. 8 Cycle of learning and developing a growth mindset (© ifb SE)

some time, lots of curiosity, and enjoying the journey instead of working toward a fixed result.

The authors would like to thank Gerhard Lucian Neubauer and Anne Hüsgen for fruitful discussions and helpful comments. Furthermore, they appreciate Marie Wocher's support in creating the images used in this article. Thank you!

5.2 Further Reading

5.2.1 # Mind Experiment 2

Are you aware of any personal experiences that influenced you so much that now they shape your reactions? Maybe you have noticed some patterns when working with your colleagues? Can you think of any circumstances that shape your behavior at work? Any role models that have ever inspired you? By being mindful of these mechanisms, multiple options arise to support healthy organizational behavior.

> **There are two basic learning mechanisms that shape everyone's behavior: reward or punishment of own behavior (consequences) or characteristics of situations (stimuli) provoking a certain behavior, as well as observing and imitating other people's behavior and observing them being rewarded or punished for a certain behavior.**
>
> Observational learning + positive consequences for defined behaviors:
>
> 1. Leadership has a major impact on the organizational culture of learning: everything a leader does, says and the way they make decisions influences how culture is perceived by employees. Leaders play a decisive role in shaping a positive learning culture by being a role model. It is on them to create room to learn—either directly by assigning time to learn, by expressing curiosity themselves or by rewarding behavior that is characterized by teamwork, communication, and learning orientation.
>
> Positive Consequences:
>
> 2. Money is one of the most famous reinforcement methods. As it is important to everyone and necessary for our survival it can reinforce certain behaviors. But, as they say, it's not all about the money. Most incentive plans work through this mechanism.
> 3. Your team is praised after a successful project. This will motivate you to give your best in the next project, if you felt like the praise was earned by your efforts.
>
> Internal Conditions + positive Consequences:
>
> 4. Money doesn't always work for everything. But personal motivation does. This could be striving for knowledge growth, which makes you use your weekend to read scientific papers even though no one asked you to. But being inspired by a researcher's results inspires you to optimize your team's workflows. This is a positive consequence for you and rewards you for investing time in reading articles. If a leader knows this fact, it can be used to give you some time during working hours to focus on reading articles—or an e-learning course with resources that can be put into practice. People with internal motivation will use their time to enlarge their competencies.
>
> Observational Learning:
>
> 5. You are the innovator of your team. As you read an interesting article last weekend, you propose integrating the main resolution into your team's workflow. One of your colleagues, who is also a friend of yours—you regularly play tennis together—also started to read books about how to

> improve his baking skills. Now he regularly provides cake at your team meetings. He observed you enriching the team climate and thus wanted to bring something positive to the team as well.
>
> These examples aim to give you a better understanding of why people behave the way they do. This can help to change conflictual behavior, either by understanding that a certain situation leads to the problematic behavior or that consequences are blocking a person from behaving differently. Here are some questions on how to assess factors that shape the observable behaviors:
>
> | Observable behavior increases or remains static | Observable behavior decreases or remains static |
> | --- | --- |
> | What are leaders saying or doing that enables these behaviors? | What are leaders saying or doing that blocks these behaviors? |
> | How are people rewarded for their behavior? | How are people punished for their behavior? |
> | What needs are being met by these behaviors? | What needs are not being met by these behaviors? |

5.3 Inspiring Material

Growth Mindset:

1. Carol Dweck: Selbstbild—Wie unser Denken Erfolge oder Niederlagen bewirkt
2. https://angelikaneumann.de/growth-mindset-interview-mit-frank-rohde/

Leadership and Change:

Herbert Diess (VW) interviews Satya Nadella: https://youtu.be/BJPbXbqal6Q

Digital Transformation at Companies:
https://www.iao.fraunhofer.de/lang-de/presse-und-medien/aktuelles/2313-digitalisierung-in-unternehmen-mut-zum-ausprobieren.html
   https://hbr.org/2020/11/how-apple-is-organized-for-innovation

New Forms of Leadership:
https://www.amazon.de/New-Work-needs-Inner-Selbstorganisation/dp/1094947709

Workplace:
https://hbr.org/2015/12/ideos-employee-engagement-formula

SCRUM Method:
(Akhgarnush et al. 2021).
www.scrum.org

Literature

Akhgarnush, Eljar, Fabian Bruse, and Ben Hofer. 2021. "New Project Structure." In *The Digital Journey of Banking and Insurance, Volume I—Disruption and DNA*, edited by Volker Liermann and Claus Stegmann. New York: Palgrave Macmillan.

Bandura, A. 1977. *Social Learning Theory.* Englewood Cliffs, NJ: Prentice Hall.

Beck, A. T. 1967. *Depression: Causes and Treatment.* Philadelphia: University of Pennsylvania Press.

Berson, Y. O. 2008. "CEO Values, Organizational culture and Firm Outcomes." *Journal of Organizational Behavior* 29: 615–633.

Brown, B. 2018. *Dare to Lead.* Vermilion.

ameron, K. S., and R. E. Quinn. 1999. *Diagnosing and Changing Organizational Culture.* Addison Wesley.

———. 2006. *Diagnosing and Changing Organizational Culture Based on the Competing Values Model.* Addison Wesley.

Davis, T. R. V., and F. Luthans. 1980. "A Social Learning Approach to Organizational Behavior." *Academy of Management Review* 2: 281–290.

Duhigg, C. 2016. *What Google Learned From Its Quest to Build the Perfect Team.* https://www.nytimes.com/2016/02/28/magazine/what-google-learned-from-its-quest-to-build-the-perfect-team.html.

Dweck, C. S. 2007. *Mindset: The New Psychology of Success.* Ballantine Books.

Ellis, A. 1957. "Rational Psychotherapy and Individual Psychology." *Journal of Individual Psychology* 13: 38–44.

Griffin, R.W., and G. Moorhead. 2012. *Managing People and Organization.* Cengage Learning.

Haggbloom, S. J., R. Warnick, J. E. Warnick, and V. K. Jones. 2002. "The 100 most eminent psychologists of the 20th century." *Review of General Psychology*, 139–152.

Kanfer, F. H., and G. Saslow. 1969. "Behavioral Diagnosis." In *Behavior Therapy: Appraisal and Status*, by C.M. Franks. McGraw-Hill.

Kortsch, T., H. Paulsen, and S. Kauffeld. 2019. "Lernkultur in Unternehmen - Wie man sie messen und gestalten kann." *Wirtschaftspsychologie aktuell* 26: 27–32.

Kortsch, T., H. Paulsen, L. Naegele, F. Frerichs, and S. Kauffeld. 2016. "Branchentrends und Betriebskultur als Basis strategischer Kompetenzentwicklung." *PERSONALquarterly*, 16–21.

Laloux, F. 2017. *Reinventing Organizations.* Verlag Franz Vahlen GmbH.
McLeod, S. A. 2018. "Skinner—Operant Conditioning." *Simply Pschology.* https://www.simplypsychology.org/operant-conditioning.html.
Meacham, M. 2017. "Why the Brain Is Still a Black Box and What to Do About It." https://www.td.org/insights/why-the-brain-is-still-a-black-box-and-what-to-do-about-it.
Morgeson, F. P., and S. E. Humphrey. 2006. "The Work Design Questionnaire (WDQ): Developing and Validating a Comprehensive Measure for Assessing Job Design and the Nature of Work." *Journal of Applied Psychology* 91: 1321–1339.
Officevibe. 2017. "Passion for Work Is More Important Than Engagement." *Officevibe.* https://officevibe.com/blog/passion-work-important-engagement.
Quinn, R. E. 1988. *Beyond Rational Management: Mastering the Paradoxes and Competing Demands of High Performance.* Jossey-Bass.
Schneider, B., V. González-Romá, C. Ostroff, and M. A. West. 2017. "Organizational Climate and Culture: Reflections on the History of the Constructs in the Journal of Applied Psychology." *Journal of Applied Psychology* 102: 468–482.
Schneider, B., M. G. Ehrhart, and W. H. Macey. 2013. "Organizational Climate and Culture." *Annual Review of Psychology* 64: 361–388.
Seligman, M. E. P. 2011. *Flourish: A Visionary New Understanding of Happiness and Well-being.* Free Press.
Zohar, D., and G. Luria. 2005. "A Multi-Level Model of Safety Climate: Cross-Level Relationships between Organization and Group-Level Climates." *Journal of Applied Psychology* 91: 616–628.

New Project Structure—Agile & Scrum

Eljar Akhgarnush, Fabian Bruse, and Ben Hofer

1 Need for a New Project Structure

1.1 Cultural Change

This buzzword echoes throughout the literature and media, as it affects an increasing number of companies regardless of industry and size. Even more so, cultural change fuses into a crucial aspect of project management since it accounts for the success or failure of the outcome. Establishing the facilitating atmosphere, where the strengths of a company's culture are embraced, while weaknesses are mitigated, requires a project management approach which is prone to change. This, in turn, enables the teams involved to be adaptable to the business environment.

One of these methods—and the one that is most applied within the agile project management terminology—is Scrum (Petrova 2019). It breaks down rigid structures like conservative hierarchies, re-prioritizes from stability to functionality and agility, moves away from top-down to bottom-up and hybrid decision-making, emphasizes the market or customer to deal with rapid changes of the environment and introduces iterative processes as well as dynamism and scaling flexibility. The implementation of the latter three

---

E. Akhgarnush · F. Bruse (✉) · B. Hofer
ifb SE, Grünwald, Germany
e-mail: Fabian.Bruse@ifb-group.com

factors in particular ensures learning constantly and therefore deducing insights to optimize processes and, in the end, the outcome.

1.2 The Guiding Framework

Scrum consists of more than just trivial rules that supposedly lead the teams through projects. It is a framework consisting of work culture and ethics accompanied by tools and additional methodologies (Wijetunge 2019) that are meant as complementary additions to give Scrum a specific structure, enabling the realization of principles and values even, or rather especially, within highly complex projects. One of the main reasons why complex projects can be simplified within Scrum is the provision of a potentially shippable increment, a partitioning of the work packages, so to speak. Since Scrum is supposedly the most used agile methodology in projects (Lamelas 2018), this article takes a closer look at its content, describing how it works and providing practical experience.

2 Agile Principles and Values

The following section deals with principles and values included in the work culture and ethics of the Scrum methodology. They consist of the Core Scrum Values, the Agile Manifesto and the Scrum Pillars. The former represent the overall Scrum foundation and have been deduced from the Agile Manifesto. Therefore, it makes sense to introduce the latter first, then address the derived Core Values and afterwards briefly explain the link to the Scrum Pillars, which wrap up the other two.

2.1 The Agile Manifesto

Starting off with one of the most recent essential milestones of the agile movement, the Agile Manifesto from 2001: It lays out priorities upon which the Scrum Team should act (Beck et al. 2001) and refers to deductions taken from practical experience. They therefore represent best-practice maxims, so to speak. The following figure (Fig. 1) sums up these four maxims throughout the project development. It is worth noting that, in Fig. 1, all the aspects of each maxim mentioned are of significance, but the ones mentioned first (in blue) are considered more crucial for the success of the project.

Fig. 1 The Agile Manifesto (© ifb SE)

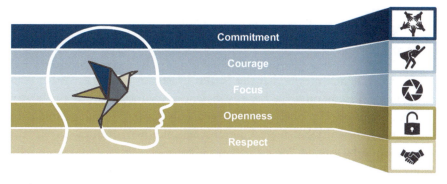

Fig. 2 The five Core Scrum Values (© ifb SE)

2.2 Scrum Values

Probably the most important part of the Scrum methodology, though, are its five Core Values (Schwaber and Sutherland 2017), without which it would be robbed of the foundation on which all the other ideas are based. The following figure (Fig. 2) illustrates the values mentioned enabling the Scrum participants to excel.

The Scrum Values of commitment, courage, focus, openness, and respect are mutually interdependent, with some weighing more than others. Furthermore, when the values are embraced and implemented by the Scrum Teams, the Scrum Pillars of transparency, inspection and adaptation take effect, ensuring trust within the teams. The Scrum Pillars, in this respect, represent the framework of the methodology.

While the realization of all the Scrum Values relies on the responsibility of each team member themselves, there are varying degrees of design, or rather influence, that some Scrum roles can exert more than others, facilitating the successful implementation of values. So, what do each of these five terms represent exactly? Why do they exist? And how are they linked with each other?

- **Commitment**: True to the mantra that nothing beats diligence and grit, the methodology requires each team member to be highly engaged in the sense of being inherently motivated and showing unity as well as solidarity. This condition cannot be achieved by external force, for example by command or order. Instead, it is crucial to provide and establish the parameters under which all team members feel comfortable and the necessity to act self-directed. One way to maintain these framework conditions is to have regular conversations and listen carefully. But, of course, commitment does not stand alone here.
- **Courage**: Whenever individuals work closely together, courage needs to be their constant companion, as it is the beginning of the action, which leads to contentment in the end. It is often a fine line between courage and high spirits, which means that the Scrum Master as well as the other team members must maintain a healthy balance. Courage within the Scrum methodology—and probably beyond—means not only speaking the truth, but also risking mistakes and taking unsafe, unknown, or unpleasant paths, for example by saying "no" when necessary. The term courage enriches the value commitment with resilience, increasing the chances for success. However, commitment and courage are just a portion of the complete Scrum picture.
- **Focus**: As distraction can lead to the destruction of productivity, there is an overwhelmingly strong argument to include the value "focus" on the list. This term contains the inherent self-discipline of each team member as it does the external consideration to refrain from disturbing the team. Maintaining or enabling a maintaining of the focus within the team is one of the most significant factors the Scrum Master can control by, for example, keeping away any occurring impediments. Nevertheless, the values listed so far are barely enforceable without the next two.
- **Openness**: Smart solutions to complex challenges can be tapped with an open culture prevailing within teams. To delve deeper, establishing welcoming communication for topics like criticism, opinions, etc., enables all team members to be committed, have courage and stay focused. Openness is, in a sense, a tool for introducing honesty, fairness and information as well as knowledge exchange and that way improving the productivity of the team. After all, this term is closely related to—or rather a precondition

Fig. 3 The interplay between the Scrum layers (© ifb SE)

for—the success of every collaboration project and hence one of the most important values within Scrum, right after respect.

- **Respect**: Everything within the agile methodology comes down to respect. Being open, committed, focused, and courageous are in essence an act of respect toward the team members and oneself. Respect, in turn, stems from taking responsibility for one's own actions. In that sense, addressing and agreeing on guidelines or considering potential personal values of mutual respect in the very beginning of a new Scrum Team can facilitate later problem-solving considerably and prevent possible conflict situations from arising.

Now that the five Core Values of Scrum have been addressed, it is worth mentioning that the various principles and values are laid out as an interplay between each other without a rigid and self-containing structure. Therefore, in the following figure (Fig. 3), the Scrum architecture is summed up as a circulating and open illustration emphasizing the iterative and reciprocal interdependence of each Scrum layer.

In the next section, the theoretical foundation of the Scrum framework is introduced including different roles, events and tools encountered when using this method.

3 The Scrum Framework

3.1 Scrum Teams and Roles

Within the Scrum Team, only three roles are defined (where "Scrum Team" refers to everyone internal to the project team): the Product Owner, the

Scrum Master, and the Development Team. To stay in line with the philosophy of Scrum, one should not define any roles other than these three. A team member usually has exactly one of the three roles, even though there might be good reasons to fulfill more: a common example is a Scrum Master who also supports the Developers. All other people involved in the project, such as stakeholders or management, do not belong to the Scrum Team, as they are not considered internal to the project and only appear for certain events.

In order to be flexible, creative, and productive, i.e., to create an agile environment, Scrum Teams are supposed to have two key characteristics: self-organization and cross-functionality. This means that the team manages itself in terms of priorities, how things are done, who is doing what, etc. Additionally, it has all the expertise to finish tasks without help from outside the team (see Dräther et al. 2013; Rubin 2013; Stellman and Greene 2013).

3.1.1 Scrum Master

The Scrum Master is a servant leader and protector for the Scrum Team who fully understands the Scrum framework and helps the team to perform at their highest level. This role is in charge of the Scrum processes, coaches the team through them, and makes sure that they are implemented and understood correctly within the team and the company. The Scrum Master therefore ensures that important Scrum events take place (within their timebox) and tries to facilitate these events. Scrum Masters usually have a big toolbox of communication and planning techniques, as well as mediation experience to support and coach the Product Owner, if requested, or to remove impediments to the Development Team.

The Scrum Master is not limited to his own team. If a project does not require 100% of the role's attention, it is possible for the Scrum Master to work for several teams, or to help others in the organization to understand Scrum and how to interact with Scrum Teams.

3.1.2 Product Owner

As the name suggests, the Product Owner "owns" the product and is therefore responsible for the output of the project. Sometimes this role is described as the project manager because it is the most business-oriented, but in fact in Scrum there is no role like a traditional manager. However, the Product Owner's goal is to maximize the value of the work the rest of the team does.

Therefore, he is in close contact with the product's customers and stakeholders rather than having hands-on application or development knowledge. While in contact with customers, the Product Owner identifies items (so-called User Stories) that have to be implemented to satisfy their requirements. These are prioritized in a Product Backlog, one of the main artifacts and planning tools of Scrum. The Product Owner creates and maintains this Product Backlog but does not manage the daily activities of the team. His decisions for the project and the Product Backlog must be respected by the entire organization. This also means that not even the CEO should approach the Development Team directly to tell them what to deliver but rather discuss issues with the Product Owner.

3.1.3 Development Team

The Development Team (usually three to nine people) is responsible for delivering the Backlog Items entirely and for organizing itself to accomplish this task. The team therefore should consist of experts capable of doing everything from, for example, analyzing and programming in different systems to testing and documentation. This is called a cross-functional team. During the Sprint, specific team members might work on a task—a team decision, not a management order—but it is the team as a whole that will always be accountable and responsible for the task.

In order to plan and prioritize tasks, the team relies on Sprint Goals that have been discussed with the Product Owner. During that Sprint (a two- to four-week project period), the Development Team will focus on creating a potentially shippable increment piece of the product. That way, the new functionality becomes transparent to the customers quickly.

What about more specific roles? It might surprise you, but there are no other roles in Scrum. One should not try to tag team members with titles like tester or team leader. Everyone is just a Development Team member. This highlights the fact that the team needs to have a united and profound understanding of the tasks. This ensures that the Sprint Goal stays in everyone's focus, rather than specific roles or jobs.

3.1.4 Where Is the Management?

As you might have noticed, the tasks of this traditional role have been distributed among the three Scrum roles. Short-term planning and implementation is carried out by the Scrum Team, creating a product vision and

Table 1 Scrum Artefacts explained (© ifb SE)

Artefact	Description
Product Backlog	Ordered wish list of everything needed to finish the project. This list should be written in a non-technical way and always be up to date. The Product Backlog is "owned" by the Product Owner and can change dynamically. Backlog Items should also have a work estimate, e.g., Story Points, for comparative reasons
Sprint Backlog	Recreated in every Sprint Planning. This contains the Sprint Goal, selected stories from the Product Backlog for this Sprint and a plan for how to deliver them
Increment	The sum of all completed Product Backlog Items of the Sprint, plus the Increments of all previous Sprints. The Increment should be potentially shippable, but it is up to the Product Owner to release it. The very first increment is often the MVP (minimal viable product)
Definition of done	The company and the Scrum Team should have a common and transparent understanding of when a Story can be declared "done." What kind of tests have to be performed (integration testing, positive/negative test), the kind of documentation, update of specific charts and tables, etc.

taking decisions about the product, as well as communication with customers are carried out by the Product Owner, while coaching and dealing with problems is carried out by the Scrum Master.

However, managers do exist, but outside of the Scrum Team. They can help to energize people and promote the values of Scrum. They define the team's boundaries and are still responsible for the personal development of the team members (Table 1).

3.2 Scrum Events

We talked about a Scrum Team that has to self-organize and know a lot about the product, but how can this work if no customers or stakeholders are part of the team? And how can the team benefit from the key pillars mentioned: transparency, inspection, and adaptation? For this we must have a closer look at the Scrum lifecycle and the related events.

3.2.1 Sprint

The work, from the first project kick-off to the final product, is done in small increments in order to break down a complex product idea into manageable

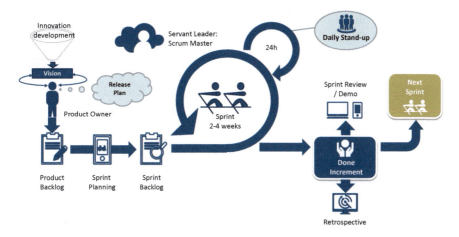

Fig. 4 A visualization of the Scrum process (© ifb SE)

chunks. This is one of the reasons why Scrum is said to be particularly useful for chaotic and complex projects, where either the "how should it be done?" or the "what should be done?" is unclear. Each Sprint (i.e., every two to four weeks), an increment of functionality should be potentially releasable and add value to the previously done increments for the customer. All desired functionalities are transparent in a Product Backlog that the Product Owner maintains and that evolves with the product. The increment of a Sprint will be the sum of completed Backlog Items plus all the increments of previous Sprints (for the whole process, see Fig. 4).

After the Sprint period has started and tasks have been selected for the Sprint (see Sect. 3.2.2 Planning), they should not be changed anymore, so that the team can focus. If questions arise while working on the topics they can of course be addressed and clarified. However, within the scope discussed, the story has to be 100% done at the end of the Sprint. It cannot become a part of the current increment if it is "almost" done.

If it should turn out that the Sprint Goal cannot be reached or has become obsolete, the Product Owner has the authority to cancel the Sprint entirely and restart. Otherwise, the Sprint is a frozen period where the Scrum Team focuses on reaching its Sprint Goal.

3.2.2 Planning

How do Backlog Items become part of the current Sprint and how does the Scrum Team know what to do? For this, Scrum has an event fittingly called

Planning. In this meeting, which all three Scrum roles attend, the Development Team first estimates the work capacity for the next Sprint period and then selects an appropriate number of Product Backlog Items into their Sprint Backlog. The Product Owner should have made sure beforehand that the Product Backlog is ordered by the value of the User Stories, so that the Development Team will work on the most important topics first. With the stories in mind, the Scrum Team should think about a Sprint Goal that allows the Development Team to plan their work within the Sprint and guide them on what they are building and why.

After the Backlog Items are selected, the team plans how to turn them into a done increment of the product in accordance with the Sprint Goal. The amount of detail discussed here should be enough to get the Development Team started for the first couple of days and longer; the rest can be prepared later.

3.2.3 Daily Scrum

During the Sprint, the Development Team meets every day for 15 minutes to inspect their work and to plan the day. This is called the "Daily Scrum." The Scrum Master should make sure that, firstly, the meeting will take place, and, secondly, it can be held at the same place and time to reduce complexity. During the meeting, it is suggested that each Development Team member answer "the three questions": What has been done since the last meeting? What will be done before the next meeting? Are there any obstacles blocking me proceeding toward the Sprint Goal? A lot of teams combine this with some kind of planning board, like a Kanban board, to make the current status of all User Stories transparent to everybody.

Please note that this should not be a traditional status meeting with stakeholders and customers. The Daily Scrum's purpose is to synchronize the work of the Development Team.

3.2.4 Sprint Review

At the end of a Sprint, it is time to inspect its outcome, the increment of done functionalities. Everyone—the team, stakeholders, and customers—meet for a maximum of four hours where the Scrum Team demonstrates its work. The idea is not to waste time preparing a labor-intensive presentation. For example, if you work with software, the increment is commonly shown live in the system.

The Review is the main event to gather feedback, adjust the strategy and update the Product Backlog with new requirements. The customer gets the chance to see real new product value early and to check it regularly. It is important to mention that only completely done User Stories that fulfill all the requirements from the Product Backlog, as well as general organizational requirements ("definition of done") can be presented and approved.

After the Sprint Review, everyone should have a common overview of the project status.

3.2.5 Sprint Retrospective

While the Sprint Review is an inspection and adaptation event for the product, the Retrospective is one for the Development Team. Directly after the Review, the team will hold another meeting to talk about things that went well or badly during the last Sprint. Think of it as a regular "lessons learned" workshop. This is the time to inspect the team's processes, tools and relationships and think about how to improve them. This meeting of up to three hours can become quite emotional and stressful, so remember the most important value of Scrum: respect. It is also the Scrum Master's time to shine, with the role's ability to mediate and a large toolbox of feedback and brainstorming techniques.

The output of the Retrospective should be at least one thing that the team will try to improve in the next Sprint, no matter how small the improvement might be ("kaizen").

4 Scrum—The Holy Grail of Agile Project Management?

Like with medicine, Scrum can cause a great improvement—if applied correctly—but can worsen things just as easily in some cases. So how can we know when to use Scrum? First of all, experience with different projects and methods will help. Luckily, a lot of people have thought about this matter already. Consider the (Ralph Douglas) Stacey Matrix (Fig. 5) and answer the two questions: "How clear is it what has to be done in the project?" and "How clear is it how it should be done?" (Stacey 1996). If the answers are "it's all very clear," a traditional approach, or even no project management at all, probably suits you better. In that case we are in a simple project situation and can work with a straight plan. This can be the case for routine work, or another iteration of a project that has been done already.

If the situation is more complicated, one can differentiate: if the goal of the project (the what) is unclear, we are in the area of political decision-making. It is important to compromise and stay in close contact with the stakeholders. If we are unsure about how problems can be solved, we are in the area of judgmental decision-making and it is all about discussions with technical experts to find alternatives and best solutions. In these situations, traditional or agile methods can be equally beneficial.

If either the "how" or the "what" become completely unclear and—worse—requirements are constantly changing, we find ourselves in a complex situation. It becomes practically impossible to estimate the time and cost of the project. This is when one should not try to order the chaos; planning anything too far into the future here is a waste of time. This is the perfect

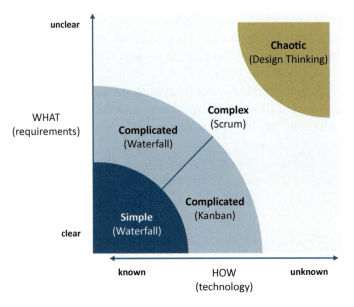

Fig. 5 The adapted Stacey matrix (© ifb SE)

environment for an iterative approach where small pieces of functionality can be inspected and adapted regularly. It is the perfect setting for using Scrum.

If nothing at all is clear, the situation is chaotic: a very risky endeavor to start a project. Try to clarify the goals of the project to order the chaos, for example with the Design Thinking method.

Apart from this theoretical analysis, there are other things to consider as well while choosing your project approach. The (potential) Scrum Team itself is key and needs to have a certain set of skills to support Scrum. A certain level of seniority is required for being able to self-manage and self-organize. With an inexperienced team, therefore, the correct implementation of Scrum might become more complex. Also, the Product Owner's availability for the project is an important factor. He creates the Product Backlog and prioritizes the User Stories, while needing to spend a lot of time communicating due to meetings with stakeholders and the developers. The Product Owner will decide how to "cut" the stories and therefore play a major role in how the increments are created. If the Product Owner is not available for the project, it is difficult to be successful and to keep the big picture in mind.

On the other hand, Scrum also needs to match the client's culture. Do they have experience with Scrum or are open to innovation and change? With Scrum, it will be difficult to plan the exact scope (or cost) of the project given the agile nature of the methodology. Trust is key so that everyone understands that the team will do its best to achieve its goals.

In some cases, it might be beneficial to use a hybrid method to mitigate some of the issues mentioned (see Beister and Zeljkovic 2021).

5   Common Mistakes and How to Avoid Them

With the introduction and use of any new method, misunderstandings and mistakes can never be avoided completely. For this reason, we would like to give you an understanding and some examples of the most common mistakes and challenges to deal with from our experience.

Most importantly, Scrum must not be mistaken as a universal remedy. An existing project or even an entire organization cannot simply be converted into an agile approach overnight. Why? Long-established processes, outdated structures, and thought patterns need to be broken up first and a rethinking process must be initiated. This process takes several weeks to months—possibly years—and requires a willingness for a change in attitude and mindset for the change to be successful.

One of the main challenges in introducing agile methods is creating a common sense for both principles and necessary changes. Only if everyone is willing to leave old habits behind and allow new things to happen will the introduction be successful. For this, efficient change management and training for both management and employees are essential. This importance becomes particularly clear when we compare the priority with those in aviation: of course, all passengers expect above all to reach their destination safely. Self-realization, creativity, and long-term commitment are not important for a single flight. To prioritize safety, the pilot should always first aviate, then navigate, then communicate—simple as that. To make a change successful, the sequence must be different: today, employees not only attach importance to a secure job and salary payments, but also to the working atmosphere, integration, and motivation. Hence communication is key. Only if everyone is well informed can a change or project manager safely navigate and lead the people involved, and then ask for their support to make it a success. We recommend paying special attention to the introduction of the framework, in particular the Scrum process, values, and roles behind it, in order to make the introduction of Scrum or other methods successful and sustainable.

You can find some other aspects and common mistakes in Table 2.

6 Methods and Tools of Effective Scrum Teams

6.1 Agile Metrics

Agile project management is often criticized for not allowing a clear schedule and budget. Agile Metrics can help solve this discrepancy. In particular, three Agile Metrics will be highlighted here that have proven themselves in practice for planning, controlling, and reporting.

6.1.1 Story Points

With constantly changing requirements and a high level of uncertainty, it is almost impossible to create a reliable and absolute estimate based on time expenditure only. For this reason, a second dimension—complexity—should always been considered.

In classic approaches, complexity is often added to an absolute estimate as a risk surcharge. With agile approaches, both dimensions are united in a so-called Story Point estimation. Story Points are always considered relatively,

Table 2 Common mistakes with prevention and improvement options (© ifb SE)

Aspect	Problem/common mistake	Prevention/improvement options
Agile Manifesto and values	Agile principles and values are not understood by all team members	Let the team take the Scrum Values as a basis for setting up their own rules. Next, make these visible to the Scrum Board and verify their compliance in the Retrospective
Meetings and sequencing	Meetings follow each other directly, without any breaks or set-up times. The team rates meetings as more disruptive than profitable and preparation suffers	Arrange 10–15 minutes' break time between meetings to ensure a clear separation of content and allow for set-up times and short preparation
Timeboxing	The set duration of meetings is regularly exceeded in order to achieve supposedly determined content goals	Ensure that the timebox is consistently adhered to, e.g., with a clock/countdown, and refer to follow-up meetings in which only affected stakeholders can participate
Moderation and coaching	The team repeatedly loses focus in meetings and drifts off into detailed discussions	The Scrum Master should act as a servant leader, identify such situations and help the team to regain its focus
Impediments	Impediments are either not documented or at least not tracked visibly. Measures are not taken consistently	Create an impediment backlog and make it accessible to everyone. Prioritize the impediments by degree of disability or severity of impact and log the date of first occurrence and progress

comparing two or more tasks to each other. In order to not fall back into sole estimation of time expenditure, Story Points are deliberately not assigned linearly, but along the Fibonacci number series (0, 1, 2, 3, 5, 8, 13, …). The more iterations the team runs through, the more precise the "gut feeling" for allocating Story Points will get—and thus the estimation itself.

Important: Story Point estimations are only valid for the team that carried out the estimation since each team establishes a unique estimation culture.

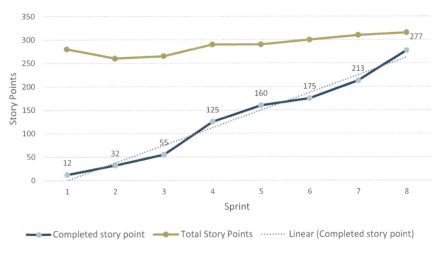

Fig. 6 Burnup Chart (© ifb SE)

Fun fact: Some teams have completely dropped estimation with numbers to get rid of the temptation to make absolute estimates. Instead, they estimate using animal sizes from ants and mice to dogs and elephants to blue whales—just to focus on the relativeness.

6.1.2 Burndown/Burnup

A Burndown Chart is a great tool to show progress during a Sprint. It shows the completion of work, usually measured in Story Points. The x-axis shows the time and the y-axis shows the work that still needs to be completed, measured in Story Points or hours. With this report, deviations can be identified immediately and measures can be taken to restore effectiveness to not endanger the Sprint target. The same is true for a Burnup Chart (Fig. 6), where the progress of the whole Product Backlog is shown in an inverted Burndown Chart. Deviations from the usual velocity can be detected, both positive, if the curve rises steeper, and negative, if the curve flattens.

6.1.3 Velocity

Velocity is defined as the average amount of work a Scrum Team completed during a Sprint, measured in Story Points or hours. This metric is very useful for forecasting. The Product Owner can use the velocity to predict how quickly a team can process upcoming work in the backlog, which has been estimated by the team beforehand. The more iterations, the more accurate the estimations and the more accurate the forecast will be.

Say the Product Owner wants to complete 450 Story Points in the backlog. We know that the Development Team typically handles 45 Story Points per iteration. So, the Product Owner can pretty much safely assume that the team needs approximately 10 iterations to complete the required work.

It is important to monitor how the velocity develops over time. In new teams, an increase in velocity can be expected as long as the team establishes and optimizes both relationships and processes. Existing teams can track their velocity to ensure consistent performance over time. They can also use the velocity to identify whether or not a particular process change has brought improvements. A decrease in average velocity is usually a sign that part of the team's development process has become inefficient and should be discussed at the next Retrospective.

Be aware, the velocity of each team is unique. A difference in velocity between teams does not mean that the throughput in a specific team is higher. Therefore, a comparison of velocities is not possible. Effort and output of tasks should be measured based on the interpretation of Story Points unique to each team.

6.2   Additional Artefacts

6.2.1   Impediment Backlog

In addition to Product and Sprint Backlog it is advisable to also establish an Impediment Backlog. This backlog lists every impediment that negatively affects a Scrum Team but cannot be solved by the Scrum Team itself. The Scrum Master manages this list, tries to solve the issues or enables the team to solve them. Besides a description of the problem, the date of its first occurrence, a responsible person, and a status should be tracked.

6.2.2   Scrum Board

This auxiliary component serves as a clear display of current task statuses during a Sprint. The legitimate question about the difference between a Scrum Board and a Kanban Board is quickly answered by a look at the two methodologies: while Kanban focuses on continuous product improvement, Scrum is best suited to iterative product developments with defined

Fig. 7 Simple Scrum Board variation (© ifb SE)

durations. The figure (Fig. 7) depicts a simple Scrum Board variation with differently colored post-its (e.g., for different kinds of task).

6.3 Daily Routines

In order to make the Daily Meeting and team collaboration more efficient, agile teams have developed multiple routines. We recommend establishing these routines in your daily work to increase effectiveness:

- In the Daily Meeting, all team members stand up and use an object (pen, ball, etc.) to pass the word around. This helps to prevent talking at the same time.
- The central questions for the Daily Meeting are pinned somewhere visible for the whole team, so everybody can focus on answering them:
  - What did I do yesterday?
  - What will you do today?
  - Are there any impediments in your way?
- Colors are used on the Scrum Board to help categorize User Stories and tasks.
- The team establishes rituals like joint coffee breaks or leisure activities to strengthen team spirit and enable an informal exchange of information.

6.4 Estimation Methods

Could you estimate the exact length of the room you are currently in? Or the weight of a whale? Probably not. As it turns out, it is much easier if you have something to compare it to. Like how many tables could fit into your office? Or how many times bigger is the blue whale than the orca swimming right next to it? Similar (relative) estimation approaches are used in agile methods to determine the complexity (not duration!) of a User Story.

6.4.1 Planning Poker

Every team member is given a special deck of Planning Poker cards with numbers that represent the complexity of a story (Story Points), plus additional cards to represent "no idea," "infinity," and "I need a break." The values used are the beginning of the Fibonacci series (as mentioned in Sect. 6.1.1) to indicate that it does not make sense to make an estimate in too much detail for high-complexity stories, as there will be a high amount of uncertainty involved. When it is time to estimate Product Backlog Items, all team members pick a card, depending on how complex they think the item could be. This evaluation is based on their personal experience with previous User Stories. The team members' choices are then disclosed simultaneously. If the values are too different, the person with the highest and the lowest number should share their opinion on the complexity level of the User Story. This is a playful way of detecting hidden stumbling blocks and ambiguities in a Backlog Item. The estimation is repeated until the team comes to a common understanding of the User Story.

6.4.2 T-Shirt Sizing

T-Shirt Sizing is another estimation technique to categorize User Stories. Rather than using numbers like in Planning Poker, items are classified into T-shirt sizes (XS, S, M, L, XL). This less numeric approach can help some teams to think in a more dynamic manner and avoid confusion between Story Points and story duration or effort. It is a great introduction to relative estimation for new teams.

6.5 Retrospective Methods

A good Scrum Master has a big toolbox of methods and games for Retrospectives that he can apply, depending on the project situation. Since a Retrospective is a key event for inspection and adaptation, the goal is to bring to light unspoken issues that are on the team's mind and to identify what worked well or didn't work well in the last Sprint. Instead of directly asking questions like "what do we have to do differently in the future?", it is more goal-oriented to split the Retrospective into five phases. Each phase

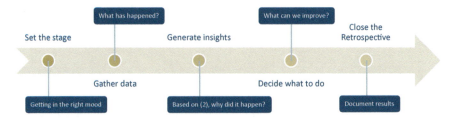

Fig. 8 Retrospective—five phases (© ifb SE)

consists of a task or a game to eventually reach a common understanding of potential improvement. Let's have a look at these phases (Fig. 8) and give one example of how this phase could be executed in your Retrospective.

- Setting the stage to enable the participants to mentally adjust to this event and to highlight that something other than their regular work is about to happen. Game idea "Weather Report": Prepare a flip chart with a drawing of storm, rain, clouds, and sunshine. Each participant marks their mood on the sheet.
- Gather data to remind people what has been done in the Sprint and to find out what they would like to talk about. Game idea "Tweet my Sprint": Ask participants to write three Tweets on sticky notes about the iteration they have just completed. Tweets could be about individual stories, a rant, or shameless self-promotion. Hashtags and emoticons are all welcome. Arrange the Tweets in a timeline and discuss themes, trends, etc. Now invite participants to mark their favorites, retweet, and write replies to the Tweets.
- Generate insights based on the gathered data to find the root cause of an issue. Game idea "Election": Split into political parties with two or three members. Work on a manifesto for change. What isn't working? How would they improve things? Present the manifestos to the group and summarize them with sticky notes, one color per party. What do the parties agree on? Which promises are unrealistic and which can you achieve?
- Decide what to do based on the generated insights. What is the top priority, what would you like to try? Game idea "Low Hanging Fruit": Draw a tree on the whiteboard and write the ideas and actions of the last game on cards. Read the shuffled cards one by one and place each "fruit" according to the assessment of how easy it is to achieve (lower placement) and how beneficial it would be (place it more to the left). The straightforward choice is to pick the bottom left fruit as action items. If there is no consensus, you can take a quick vote.

- Close the Retrospective. Like every good meeting, the Retrospective needs a closing. Document the results and what you would like to try in the next Sprint. Try the game "Retro Darts": Draw a dartboard on a flip chart. Write a statement next to each dartboard, e.g., "We talked about what's important to me," "I'm confident we'll improve next iteration." Participants mark their opinion with a sticky note.

Many more interesting games can be found on retromat.org (Baldauf, n.d.), a great and continuously expanding source of ideas in different languages.

6.6 Timeboxing

Timeboxing is the pre-allocation of a limited period of time that Scrum events may last at the most. This includes the following timeboxed events within the methodology: The Daily, Sprint Review, Sprint Retrospective, Sprint Planning, and the Sprint itself. Implementing a timebox aims to use resources—in this case "time"—efficiently and simultaneously motivates the team and increases their focus. Like in all project management frameworks, "time" is crucial within Scrum, too.

7 Other Agile Approaches

Besides the Scrum Framework, other agile approaches have become popular in recent years. Projects are increasingly aligned to these new approaches, with the goal of becoming faster and more flexible.

7.1 DevOps

The aim of DevOps is to combine software development (Dev) and operations (Ops) to shorten the development lifecycle and provide continuous delivery and integration but also to raise software quality. A toolset, also referred to as toolchain, consists of different categories from Coding, Building, and Testing to Packaging, Releasing, Configuring, and Monitoring. As neither academics nor practitioners have developed a unique definition of the term and method, it tends to be referred to as a set of practices (Loukides 2012).

7.2 Extreme Programming (XP)

Extreme Programming (XP) is a method of software development in which the development of the solution is given priority over the observance of formal rules (Beck, Extreme Programming Explained: Embrace Change 2000). Extreme Programming runs in recurring cycles, follows a structured approach and emphasizes teamwork, openness and constant communication between all participants. Communication is a basic pillar.

The main goal of Extreme Programming is faster provisioning, higher software quality, and customer satisfaction. The customer receives a ready-to-use product in the development of which he has actively participated. New functionalities are permanently developed, integrated, and tested. For each of the functionalities to be developed, the steps risk analysis, benefit analysis, the provision of a first executable version (prototyping), and an acceptance test are performed.

7.3 Feature-Driven Development (FDD)

FDD defines a process model and a role model that harmonizes well with existing project structures. For this reason, some companies prefer implementing FDD over XP or Scrum. In addition, FDD is very compact in terms of agile methods. It can be completely described on 10 pages.

The feature concept is crucial for the FDD process, where each defined feature represents added value for the customer.

Five steps have to be carried out in FDD (Palmer and Felsing 2002):

1. Develop overall model
2. Build feature list
3. Plan by feature
4. Design by feature
5. Build by feature.

The Chief Architect constantly monitors the overall architecture, keeps track of the functional core models and coordinates the Feature Plan. For larger teams, individual development teams are led by Chief Developers.

7.4 Kanban

Kanban is all about workflow visualization, limitation of current work, and meaningful feedback loops.

Kanban does not require any specific configuration and can be placed over an existing workflow or process to detect problems. Thus, Kanban can be easily introduced in every company because no comprehensive changes are necessary to get started. The method has been developed to contribute to continuous, incremental, and evolutionary changes in the current process with minimal resistance (Brechner 2015).

The only tool Kanban introduces is the Kanban Board, which is quite similar to the board often used in Scrum Teams. There are different vertical lanes (minimum: To Do, Doing, Done) and tasks cards can be placed in these lanes to transparently show the status (see Sect. 6.2.2).

Kanban also considers the potential value of existing processes, roles, responsibilities and titles, as well as their possible retention. The method does not prohibit changes, but it does not prescribe them either.

7.5 Lean Software Development

Lean software development is a translation of lean manufacturing principles and practices to the software development domain. Adapted from the Toyota Production System, it is emerging with the support of a pro-lean subculture within the agile community. Lean offers a solid conceptual framework, values, and principles, as well as good practices, derived from experience, that support agile organizations (Lean Software Development 2020).

Lean development can be summarized by seven principles, very close in concept to lean manufacturing principles (Poppendieck and Poppendieck 2003):

1. Eliminate waste
2. Amplify learning
3. Decide as late as possible
4. Deliver as fast as possible
5. Empower the team
6. Build integrity in
7. Optimize the whole.

8 Summary and Outlook

It becomes more and more apparent after reading this chapter about agile methods that each methodology has its perks and flaws depending on the situation and the project to which it is applied. The presented status quo is open to change and will do so continuously. In that sense, it is essential to assess each project and company individually, when considering which methodology to use and in what manner or rather in which combination. The next chapter will give more insights into this and illustrate how to mitigate disadvantages of agile methods by using such combinations with the help of "hybrid project management methods." Still, whatever method you choose, it is of utmost importance to keep the company structure, including its employees, open to change and flexible to quickly adapt to new models yet to come.

Literature

Baldauf, Corinna. n.d. *Retromat.* Accessed September 01, 2021. https://retromat.org.

Beck, Kent. 2000. *Extreme Programming Explained: Embrace Change.* Boston: Addison-Wesley.

Beck, Kent, Mike Beedle, Arie van Bennekum, Alistair Cockburn, Ward Cunningham, Martin Fowler, James Grenning, et al. 2001. *Manifesto for Agile Software Development.* https://agilemanifesto.org.

Beister, Uwe, and Milica Zeljkovic. 2021. "Hybrid Project Management." In *The Digital Journey of Banking and Insurance, Volume I—Disruption and DNA*, edited by Volker Liermann and Claus Stegmann. New York: Palgrave Macmillan.

Brechner, Eric. 2015. *Agile Project Management with Kanban (Developer Best Practices).* US: Microsoft Press.

Dräther, Rolf, Holger Koschek, and Carsten Sahling. 2013. *Scrum - kurz & gut.* Köln: O'Reilly Verlag.

Lamelas, Ana. 2018. *Top 5 Main Agile Methodologies: Advantages and Disadvantages.* November 10. Accessed September 01, 2021. https://www.xpand-it.com/2018/10/11/top-5-agile-methodologies/#:~:text=Scrum,time%20for%20a%20software%20product.

Lean Software Development. 2020. *Lean Software Development.* October 5. Accessed September 01, 2021. https://en.wikipedia.org/wiki/Lean_software_development.

Loukides, Mike. 2012. *What Is DevOps?* June 7. http://radar.oreilly.com/2012/06/what-is-devops.html.

Palmer, S. R., and J. M. Felsing. 2002. *A Practical Guide to Feature-Driven Development.* São Paulo: Prentice Hall.

Petrova, Sandra. 2019. *Adopting Agile: The Latest Reports About the Popular Mindset.* January 18. https://adevait.com/blog/remote-work/adopting-agile-the-latest-reports-about-the-popular-mindset.

Poppendieck, Mary, and Tom Poppendieck. 2003. *Lean Software Development: An Agile Toolkit*, 13–15. Boston: Addison-Wesley.

Rubin, Kenneth S. 2013. *Essential Scrum—A Practical Guide to the Most Popular Agile Process.* Boston: Addison-Wesley.

Schwaber, Ken, and Jeff Sutherland. 2017. *The Scrum Guide™.* November. https://www.scrumguides.org/scrum-guide.html#values.

Stacey, Ralph. 1996. *Complexity and Creativity in Organizations.* San Francisco: Berrett-Koehler Publishers.

Stellman, Andrew, and Jennifer Greene. 2013. *Learning Agile: Understanding Scrum, XP, Lean, and Kanban.* Sebastopol: O'Reilly Media.

Wijetunge, Rumesh. 2019. *Scrum: As a Culture Rather Than a Process.* August 27. https://www.knowledgehut.com/blog/agile/scrum-as-a-culture-rather-than-a-process.

Hybrid Project Management

Uwe Beister and Milica Zeljkovic

1 Introduction

The right project management method is of crucial importance to companies since it determines how a project is planned and executed and therefore should be well chosen. Depending on the complexity of the project and the corporate culture, this should be carefully thought through. In the banking and insurance industry, purely traditional project management methods are outdated, since banks and insurers need to become more flexible and faster due to further development of the regulatory system, the increasing dependency on IT systems and, in particular, the market development regarding fintech companies.

One of the top reasons why projects fail besides insufficient communication, poor planning, and the lack of expertise is the use of inadequate project management methods (Grushka-Cockayne Yael et al. 2015).

As described in the previous chapter, Scrum is an agile method that may adapt to the needs of the project outcome. Nevertheless, some typical limitations in using the method and deficiencies of the approach have been

---

U. Beister (✉) · M. Zeljkovic
ifb SE, Grünwald, Germany
e-mail: Uwe.Beister@ifb-group.com

M. Zeljkovic
e-mail: milica.zeljkovic@ifb-group.com

outlined. The hybrid project management approach tries to combine the best of agile and traditional project management approaches. Surveys show that this kind of approach is on the rise since projects varying in size and scope may adapt their project management needs to changing framework conditions, ensuring the best project outcome.

The flexibility within the planned project content dictates whether a project should be planned according to agile or traditional project management methods. The question is therefore how to set the scope. In a traditional project, the scope is fixed and changes may be made, but mostly involve either a prolongation of the project or an extension of the budget. Some situations require changes to the scope though, e.g., regulatory changes, which need to be considered. If the scope is fixed by external constraints, rules, or a client who has a very specific idea of the future product, the agile approach does not fit. Whereas traditional project management generally tries to avoid changes, Scrum supports changes within the scope.

Within ifb, we apply hybrid project management methods to almost all of our current projects. All projects following the hybrid methodology have received positive feedback from customers, as well as within the project, becoming "best practice" examples. We therefore think, it is important not to overlook or underestimate hybrid project management when looking for the right project management method.

The following sections will portray the differences between traditional and agile project management. We will focus on the term "hybrid project management," give a precise definition and present the different variations of hybrid project management. In addition, best practices will be outlined and an empirical study will be presented.

As already mentioned in the previous chapter, which deals with Scrum and other agile methods in detail, this chapter is about taking the previously mentioned common mistakes into consideration and showing an opportunity to avoid these by following the hybrid project management approach.

Why hybrid project management should not only be seen as a substitute or workaround to Scrum will be explained in this chapter.

1.1 Traditional Project Management

In traditional project management, the entire project is planned in advance. Therefore, all information needed, all requirements and work packages must be provided and defined upfront. The project is divided into subsequent phases, covering different elements of stages in the process.

In a traditional project, the focus is on achieving the previously planned goals. Changes in most cases trigger a need for additional time and/or budget (*Visual Paradigm* 2020). Furthermore, a potential need for changes may only be discovered late in the project (e.g., during the testing phase), resulting in significant additional work.

The waterfall method is one of the most well-known traditional management approaches. The waterfall approach was the go-to approach for a long time because it has many advantages.

It focuses on delivering a finished product of high quality, instead of speed. It is well suited to projects that are not urgent and for clients who know exactly what they want to achieve with their project results. The traditional project testing period is extensive, if not cut short due to the rest taking too long, which may lead to fewer bugs once the project is complete.

In terms of disadvantages, the waterfall approach may result in increased cost and time, since some deviations to the plan set at the beginning of the project may still occur. Clients are not involved at every step, therefore the approach works best when clients have clear ideas about, for example, what new software, once finished, needs to do. If users have only an unclear idea, or the project takes longer than anticipated, the finished software may fail to meet the user's requirements. When waterfall projects come to the testing phase, making changes to the software is very complicated. If changes need to be made at this stage of the project, the customer will need to pay more money and to wait longer for the software to be delivered (*Solus Informatics* 2018).

1.2 Agile Project Management

Agile approaches such as Scrum assume that IT projects are so complex and fast-changing that they cannot be captured in a linear manner on the day of the project start. Constantly new requirements, which often become visible during the project, require dynamic action and short-term planning corrections. Significantly smaller deliverables are being developed and processed (Stens, n.d.).

While, in the traditional approach, factors like scope, cost, and time play the most important role, agile project management focuses on teamwork, customer collaboration, and flexibility. Agile methods aim to constantly incorporate user feedback. The work structures and the team are designed for creating things that are of immediate use for the customer or client since every task output is also a product sold to stakeholders (*Visual Paradigm* 2020).

When it comes to agile there are many advantages, as well as some disadvantages, which may become clear. The main advantage is that agile projects are more likely to finish on time, since the users provide constant feedback on how the software operates, and clients' change requests can easily be considered during the implementation. This also implies involvement of the client and close collaboration (*Solus Informatics* 2018).

1.3 Hybrid Approach

In order to overcome the disadvantages of both methods, traditional and agile, hybrid project management is the way forward. The following Fig. 1 visualizes the development of project management methods. Nowadays, many companies do not choose between traditional or agile, they combine both methods to find the best fit for their individual project. This happens either out of full conviction for the advantages of a hybrid approach or because agile approaches have not brought the desired success or have failed.

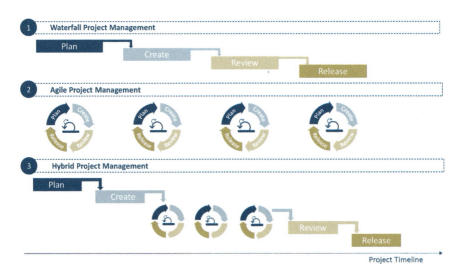

Fig. 1 The evolution of project management (© ifb SE)

2 Hybrid Project Management

This section will explain the term "hybrid project management" in detail and give reasons why project leads should gain deeper knowledge of this project management approach. On the basis of an empirical study, the positive aspects of hybrid project management will be discussed in detail below.

2.1 Definition of Hybrid Project Management

The term "hybrid" means the combination, mixing or crossing of "something" (*t2Informatik* 2020). Transferred to project management, a hybrid approach describes the integration of: "*two or more separate methodologies on a project, commonly a blend of agile and waterfall project management methods, though sometimes incorporating Kanban, lean or other methodologies of project management. Employing hybrid methodology enables teams to apply what works best where and when it is most needed, or to suit different teams within an organization. For example, for software development teams, agile is suitable for the phase of a project near launch to push development in 'sprints,' often 2 weeks in duration. This supports how software is often bundled and packaged for release. For longer-term software development projects, however, the beginning phases might be more waterfall in nature, demonstrating multiple dependencies as different teams need to produce different components prior to the implementation phase*" (Westland 2015).

The combination of traditional methods with elements of the agile methodology gives organizations the chance to take advantage of the best of these two worlds to find the solutions that best suit their individual needs. This can lead to better results compared to projects managed in either a purely traditional or purely agile way, minimizing expenses or achieving the goals faster. Overall, the project's benefits may be enhanced (*Teodesk* 2020). In the banking and insurance industry in particular, where the traditional project management approach is the "one size fits all approach," hybrid project management can take over the role traditional project management once played.

2.2 Success Model Hybrid—An Empirical Study by PMI on the Success of Hybrid Project Management

The Project Management Institute has released a study, "The Drivers of Agility," which comes to the conclusion that companies who operate with a high degree of agility bring more projects to a successful outcome than companies that do not use agility. Among the companies that used a high level of agility, it was notable that 72% used hybrid methodology, followed by 71% who used predictive and 68% who used purely agile methods. Among the companies that exhibited a rather low degree of agility, 51% used hybrid methods, 45% predictive methods and 41% agile methods (Strasser, n.d). This shows that among companies who consider themselves as having a low degree of agility, the hybrid approach is the most prominent one as a compromise between purely traditional and purely agile approaches, since the organizational structures in companies are usually too rigid to be able to implement purely agile approaches. This clearly portrays the increasing use of hybrid project management methods in companies who are actively trying to incorporate agile methods, as well as in companies that do not force themselves into using agility.

Some factors such as the following have contributed to the rising popularity of hybrid management approaches:

- Complexity and uncertainty: The percentage of projects with high complexity is on the rise, as the PMI's 2018 "Pulse of the Profession" survey stated. It rose from 35% in 2013 to 41% in 2018 (Pradeep 2018).
- Competitive markets: Due to today's market, you need to anticipate competitive influences and guarantee proactivity in order to be ahead of the competition.
- High client expectations: Even within large-scale projects, speed, personalization and ease are expected from most clients (*Teodesk* 2020).

It has become clear to the large majority of banking and insurance institutions in recent years that they can only prevail against the new challenges presented by fintech companies if they become at least as innovative, fast and flexible as their new competitors. The banking and insurance industry also realized that the key success factor is fundamentally renewing their structures and processes. As the "Banking Study Agile Organization" showed, over 90% of the institutions surveyed assume that their bank will only be able to take this necessary step by transforming itself into an agile organization. A first step toward a more agile organization could be the move to hybrid project management. Evolutionary implementation of agile methods in combination with traditional process models could be the better step to soften entrenched structures and processes.

In summary, the question "why should companies use hybrid project management?" can be answered as follows:

1. Enhancement of efficiency compared to innovative financial service providers like fintech companies.
2. Smoothing transformation towards agility while maintaining proven structures and processes.
3. Avoiding the weaknesses of Traditional Project Management and Agile Project Management by using the best of two worlds.

3 Criteria for the Introduction of Hybrid Procedure Models

Various criteria must be considered when setting up a hybrid model. Depending on the weighting, this should lead to different distributions of agile and traditional elements in the project approach. Criteria to be considered include the corporate culture and analysis of the general conditions of the project, project complexity, documentation requirements, transparency in the project, sprints and meetings, roles and project procedure, as well as knowledge and training on project management methods (Fig. 2).

3.1 Corporate Culture and Analysis of the General Conditions

It must be considered whether projects have already been carried out according to a hybrid approach within the company. If no experience exists, the client and the project participants must agree to a new hybrid approach. The project lead and the framework conditions should be able to change if necessary.

Furthermore, the communication culture of the company should be considered. For the success of the project there should not be a strong division between internal and external employees. Everyone should operate on one project approach.

Fig. 2 Criteria to be considered for hybrid management methods (© ifb SE)

This means that the respective model should be set up individually according to the circumstances after a thorough analysis of the specific situation. In addition, relevant criteria and goals for the introduction of hybrid project management should be developed.

3.2 Project Complexity

Experience shows that with increasing complexity, more changes can be expected. In this case, it is recommended to integrate agile elements in the respective project phases. Especially in long-running, complex software development projects, changes in the general conditions often occur, be it regulatory or due to the client's requirements changing. A purely traditional approach is no longer recommended. The waterfall model is suitable in projects for rough planning and should be amended with agile elements.

Which elements should be integrated into which process is explained in more detail in the section Hybrid Project management models—Variants.

3.3 Documentation Requirements

Before the start of a particular phase, the requirements for documentation should be defined, implemented and accepted by the project members. For the commencement of the implementation phase, for example, the technical concept should be available, and before the start of the test phase the test concept should exist.

All functions to be implemented are listed in a product backlog. By means of a Kanban board, the work packages to be processed are listed for a defined period. In addition, this is laid down in a sprint backlog. Furthermore, the product backlog could be merged with the requirements specification so that a new document is created, which represents a pool of requirements (Kanbanize, n.d.).

3.4 Transparency in the Project

In order to be able to understand decisions that have been made, who does what and which roles are responsible for what, they must be documented. Information is distributed centrally across all levels so that everyone is informed about the current status and all project participants can understand why and how things were done.

In addition, terms that are used in agile and/or traditional project management should be mentioned explicitly. If the client does not want to use terms from agile and/or traditional project management for various reasons, an ubiquitous language should be established for a common understanding.

Furthermore, it should be transparent at all times what stage the project is at. In addition, it should be traceable how many work packages still need to be processed in order to reach the milestone. In projects with predominantly static requirements, a complete overview of the current status of the project should be guaranteed.

3.5 Sprints and Meetings

Elements from agile approaches should be integrated into the project. For example, sprints from Scrum should be used so that individual increments can be developed at frequent and equal intervals and presented to the customer.

In addition, Scrum dailies, planning, reviews and retrospectives should be included in the project process in order to ensure a continuous exchange between the team members and to harness optimization potential. The reviews are particularly important so that the customer can take part in the process and can find out whether their specifications are being followed. The Kaizen culture of Kanban should be pursued in order to increase effectiveness and efficiency.

Due to the different meeting cultures in the traditional and agile approach, it should be determined in advance what kind of meeting should take place, for example whether jour fixes should be held in addition to the agile meetings.

3.6 Roles and Procedures

Depending on the complexity of the project, the roles of the respective project members can vary.

Agile teams should be structured according to Scrum, for example, since the Scrum approach prescribes these roles. In addition, the development team should be able to assign tasks to itself so that team members are given more responsibility and autonomous work is encouraged. Across projects, there should be a project manager for planning and coordination.

In addition, the project manager can operate between the management and the project team and thus form the link between a hierarchical organization and agile teams.

There should be a clear assignment of roles and this should be laid down in a document. Every project participant should know who has which function and who is responsible for which tasks.

Furthermore, key roles (e.g., product owner, project manager) should not be occupied only by an external employee and might be occupied twice if individual roles (e.g., project manager) are overloaded.

In addition, the project manager should analyze the skills and abilities of the employees who will later be involved in the process. Role assignment should be on the basis of these characteristics. These factors should also be taken into account for employees who are to take on roles in the project other than those intended. If there are comprehensive role changes, these should be carried out successively and not in one go. If necessary, this could save time for changes or improvements.

3.7 Knowledge and Training

When creating a hybrid model, project managers must have a high level of expertise in project management methods. They must have knowledge of various agile and traditional models so that a suitable hybrid model can be established for the project at hand. For this reason, training courses on various project management methods would have to be attended in order to build up knowledge. Furthermore, the project manager should have a certain creativity in order to combine elements of agile and traditional project management.

Training is considered necessary so that the structures and functions of the corresponding roles can be internalized.

Training should be attended by all project members. It may be the case that individual team members have only worked according to the traditional or agile approach before. The change could lead to problems, for example if a development is to move from a traditional to an agile approach. In addition, team members may have knowledge of the hybrid approach, but this knowledge may vary. The training courses could (largely) harmonize the knowledge of the members.

It is highly recommended that a kick-off event is held before the project starts, in which all relevant project members are informed about the hybrid approach. A clear form of the hybrid approach or hybrid model must be presented to the project participants. There should be a certain degree of employee involvement.

Hybrid working methods could be practiced in advance through training. For example, if the push principle has always been used and the pull principle is to be used in the future, experienced experts could provide training in this.

4 Hybrid Project Management Models—Variants

Based on the above criteria for the use of hybrid project management models, this section deals with the classification of hybrid project management models, showing four different variations. The variations differ in content regarding the portion of agile elements in the respective phases.

These models have been developed according to our personal understanding and experience. The names of the models have been chosen in such a way that the amount of agile elements used becomes clear to the reader (Fig. 3).

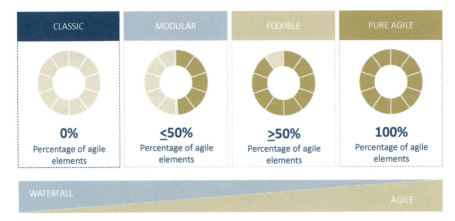

Fig. 3 Hybrid variants (© ifb SE)

4.1 Variant A—Traditional

The general conditions for the project are absolutely fixed. No changes are expected during the project, or changes in the project environment have no relevant influence on the project. The project is traditionally implemented according to the waterfall model in all phases of the project.

4.2 Variant B—Modular (Packaged Solutions)

The framework for the project is expected to be largely stable for the entire project duration. Most phases are based more on traditional approaches, but during the project agile approaches are used, especially in the implementation phase, in order to catch up with possible sprint's delays in development or to accommodate (individual customer) changes in requirements in the short term. We use this approach very successfully for medium-sized companies, which, on the one hand, are dependent on implementing regulatory requirements, but for cost reasons must rely primarily on standardized components (modules) that have already been developed. We call this procedure "Packaged Solution."

4.3 Variant C—Flexible

The regulatory environment or customer requirements are not final or are subject to major changes, which must be responded to in all phases of the project. The consideration of agile elements in several phases of the project is therefore helpful to be able to react to the regularly expected changes/adjustments. This is especially useful for projects where the regulatory requirements and/or the software for the implementation of the regulatory requirements are not yet fully developed. For example, this was a successful approach in the implementation of IFRS 17 and the use of SAP FPSL with traditional planning and agile elements during the developing and testing phases.

4.4 Variant D—Pure Agile

The development of new software or a new product must be very creative and very dynamic. Continuous changes in all phases of the project are desired. The highest possible flexibility in all phases of the project is therefore required. Even the planning of the project is done in an agile way, i.e., rolling and regularly adapted to the changes in the respective phases. This variant is mostly used in the software or gaming industry.

5 Agile and Traditional Elements During the Project Flow

The following section will outline how hybrid elements should be considered, from planning to testing.

5.1 Definition of the Project Phases

Agile or traditional? Or both? And how much "agile" do we need? Often, companies are of the opinion that they have already implemented an agile organizational structure. However, it is not enough to only occasionally develop software with an agile approach like Scrum. Agile means much more in this context, but many organizational structures quickly reach the limits of their flexibility to implement and apply agile processes.

So how can companies resolve this contradiction of being faster and more efficient, while at the same time gradually expanding the limits of resilience in the organization, processes and employees in a more evolutionary way?

An alternative approach is the use of traditional and agile methods combined within an organization or within a project. The use of two methods offers the possibility to skillfully combine the best of both worlds and to only burden the organization with proportionate evolutionary changes.

While agile methods in software development bring many advantages and have been used for approximately 20 years with increasing success, agile methods are less known in the other phases of a project.

The following project phases will be considered in this section:

- Planning phase
- Specification phase
- Implementation phase
- Test phase
- Project completion and roll-out.

5.2 Hybrid Planning Phase—Agile Versus Traditional Planning

"Failing to plan is planning to fail" means if there is no reasonable and sustainable planning, the project plans its failure. This statement from time management expert Alan Lakein perfectly hits the point of the importance of planning in project management (Goodreads, Inc. n.d.).

But what kind of planning is the right one? The onion model shows on which levels planning can or should take place, depending on the project approach used. An agile company should also have agile product management, agile portfolio management and an agile strategy (external three levels). It is absolutely not sufficient to apply planning only to (Scrum) team level around day, iteration and release (Fig. 4).

From our point of view, agility is the most important and decisive element of a general dynamic approach of companies. If teams are trained in agile methods, but no changes have been made to the management of goals and strategic initiatives, the company is by no means agile! The hybrid method is especially important if the company is not agile in itself (organization/framework/structure).

Agile planning is iterative. This means that the plans must be developed and adapted several times, as needed. The goal is to invest time in planning regularly (after a phase) or as needed and to adapt to changes that occur during project implementation.

Regardless of the level at which you are active, our agile plan has similar characteristics. Let's take a closer look at them.

- Goal from the customer perspective (manage expectations!)
- Gradually increase granularity (commit as late as possible)
- Regular deliveries (deliver increments on a monthly basis)

Fig. 4 Onion model of agile planning (© ifb SE)

- Time periods instead of fixed dates (probability vs. determinism)
- Focus on work results, not on the worker (the team is jointly responsible for the product)
- Quality assurance is integrated in each phase
- Two-level plans (timelines for initiatives, tasks without start/end date)
- Consideration of process mining, i.e., recording and evaluation of IT processes is data-driven (based on historical data and current processes and simulations).

If agility has not yet been established within the portfolio and strategy level, purely agile planning can also be difficult at the project (product) level. In highly hierarchical companies, where projects have so far only focused on a traditional approach, agility often meets resistance.

A compromise for an evolutionary introduction of agile methods can be the combination of traditional and agile elements:

For example:

- Planning of the project on the basis of annual slices until the end of the project
- Structuring of the project in phases, with integrated quality assurance
- Defining milestones, monthly milestones also possible for sprints
- Granular planning for the first three months, then rolling planning for the coming phases
- Delivery of increments after each sprint and phase
- Regular feedback sessions with the team and clients
- Lessons learned at least twice a year
- Meeting structure with dailies within the project team and with the customers
- Regular meetings with the customers.

5.3 Hybrid Specification Phase

Hundreds of business and IT concepts have been the core of every project in recent decades and the core requirement for a project manager before the requirements of the customer could be implemented. The creation and maintenance of these traditional concepts is very time-consuming; sometimes it takes several years until such concepts have been completed and approved in a time-consuming review process. After completion, it is usually the case that parts of the technical concept are outdated again. Changes can only be implemented through extensive and time-consuming change processes.

This can be remedied by creating so-called user stories or use cases. What exactly is meant by this?

A use case comprises all possible scenarios that can occur when a user tries to achieve a certain business objective with the help of the system under consideration. It describes what can happen when trying to reach the goal and abstracts from concrete technical solutions. The result of the use case can be success or failure/termination.

The philosophy of agile programming is therefore: "A use case should be understandable to customers, developer-testable, valuable to the customer and small enough that the programmers can build half a dozen in an iteration" (Beck 2005).

Characteristics of use cases:

- Use cases are written in the client's specialist departments
- Use cases contain one or a few clear processes or functions
- The scope is small compared to a traditional technical concept
- The effort for the implementation can be estimated very easily

- The addition of the technical requirements is carried out by the developers
- A use case usually takes one to two weeks at the most to implement. More extensive use cases are possible, but are the exception
- The use case is tested immediately after completion and released to the customer immediately after successful testing
- Test data is available (synthetic or near-production)
- Errors and problems are discussed on a daily basis, and there is always transparency about the status of the use case throughout the project
- The process steps, from creation to the sign-off by the customer, and from the backlog to the functional test by the contractor, are always known and transparent via a Kanban board.

5.4 Hybrid Implementation

In the waterfall approach, for example, a new development phase can only begin once the previous one has been completely finalized. It can take years to complete a project. In addition, a waterfall project cannot guarantee that the solution will provide everything that users need at the end of the development process, since many errors or missing components usually only become apparent at the end of the project.

The traditional implementation with a long implementation phase, in which all customer requirements are fully implemented, is therefore now a thing of the past in most software development projects, one would think. A combination of the traditional and agile approach with an accompanying separation of development lines does not seem to make sense either. So which solution is optimal, especially for long-running projects?

In our view, agility in software development avoids long development cycles. The weaknesses of a pure approach, e.g., Scrum, have already been examined in the previous sections. Only how do we enable agility in projects without the disadvantages of agility?

One possibility is the combination of two or more agile methods, in which the strengths of the respective approach are applied during implementation. The two agile methods Scrum and Kanban offer a good example.

The hybrid process model uses the roles, events, and artifacts from Scrum and the practices and principles from Kanban with the following characteristics:

- Use of Kanban board
- No time limits for the tasks
- Limitation of work per process area/team area

Fig. 5 Kanban board (© ifb SE)

- Daily meetings
- Role model according to Scrum
- Artifacts after Scrum
- Setup of product backlog and sprint backlog (Fig. 5).

5.5 Hybrid Test Management

In traditional test management, the so-called V-model, also known as the waterfall model, is used. This starts with the requirements definition, followed by the functional system design, then the technical system design, the component specification and finally the programming. This is the left side of the V-model. In order to test the system in the individual phases or stages, the right side of the model is now drawn, the so-called test stages:

- Component test (also unit test, module test or class test): Functionality of individual components is tested.
- Integration test: Interaction of the individual components is tested.
- System test: The entire system is tested internally against requirements.
- Acceptance test: Entire system is tested against requirements by customers.

All test levels run one after the other. The focus in the traditional approach is on the control and steering of test management. For this purpose, a large number of documents, such as test concepts, test plans or test protocols, are set up.

Agile testing links development with testing. Instead of scheduling a test activity at the end of the project, testing is already carried out within the iterations.

All tasks run in parallel in one iteration and not in successive activities as in traditional test management. In addition, agile testing takes into account the traditional test levels. This is because these levels define different types of tests, which simultaneously entail certain test methods and tools. Both traditional and agile projects use these methods and tools.

6 Best Practices IFB Model

Our best practice model is called Water-ScrumBan-Fall and will be explained in detail further on.

6.1 Water-ScrumBan-Fall

The suggestions and procedures described in the previous sections have already been reflected in our projects of all sizes. Due to the consideration of the corporate culture and the expectations of the customer, projects are often planned within the framework of the well-known waterfall method on an annual basis and additionally until the end of the project.

Traditional planning with phases and milestones divides the project into meaningful sections. The initialization and specific action phases are carried out according to the waterfall method, the implementation is carried out according to Scrum with monthly sprints, supplemented with the functions of the Kanban approach to increase transparency about the status of the work packages and about bottlenecks. Testing is very agile for the functional testing of the use cases; system and integration testing follow a traditional approach. In the end, the product launch is again based on a traditional, i.e., waterfall, approach.

It is important that at each end of a phase or milestone there is always a delivery of products, results or increments. These results are secured by continuous quality assurance across all work streams.

From our point of view, this is the most successful method for implementing projects sustainably and with high customer satisfaction (Fig. 6).

The overview below illustrates the most important elements from the traditional and agile project management approaches combined in a best practice approach, a hybrid approach (Fig. 7).

Fig. 6 Hybrid model: Water-ScrumBan-Fall (© ifb SE)

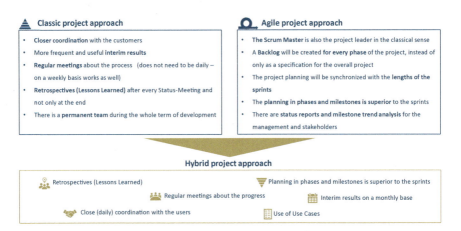

Fig. 7 Summary of advantages for traditional, agile and best practices (© ifb SE)

6.2 Eliminating Project Fatigue with a Hybrid Approach

Projects, especially software implementation projects, may take up several years until the software is implemented in such a way that the customer can use it totally independently. Project fatigue is a term commonly used to describe a situation where the focus switches from the project goals to the tasks (*Imaginative Thinking* 2014).

When following a traditional project management approach, such as waterfall, all the plans are made and objectives set at the start of the project. The objective is, for example, to deliver a product with some specific features by a set date. If the project is planned to take 24 months to finish, it is likely that individuals will lose focus, or get distracted since the delivery seems very far away (*Imaginative Thinking* 2014).

If the project is managed by agile principles, the focus is on producing working software. Even if the overall project is planned to take 24 months, the project team will be kept on track at the end of every interval. Project fatigue may still find its way in, but can be weakened if, during an interval, it is explained how the intervals are in line with the overall objectives of the project (*Imaginative Thinking* 2014).

A very good way to fight project fatigue is to follow a hybrid project management approach. Our experience in various projects underlines how a hybrid approach eliminates project fatigue: simply adding agile elements to the traditional approach can keep the project team's spirits high. Planning according to the traditional, creating according to the agile and releasing according to the traditional approach again is so versatile that fatigue is not likely to occur.

A way to fight project fatigue is to set SMART goals, in order to maintain the focus and to enhance the team's motivation to ensure a successful project outcome (*Imaginative Thinking* 2014).

SMART goals must be the following (Mind Tools, n.d.):

- Specific
- Measurable
- Achievable
- Relevant
- Time-bound.

In addition to setting SMART goals, there are some useful tips that can be followed to avoid project fatigue. The team should be reminded on a regular basis what the implementation is about and which role they play individually in achieving the common goal. Time should be invested upfront in order to provide a road map, which functions as a powerful tool in keeping the project members engaged and motivated. Introducing new members every once in a while keeps the spirit of the team fresh and motivated. To keep motivation high, the benefits of the project need to be understood by everyone. Success should be celebrated and rewarded accordingly, to acknowledge the team's efforts (Quay Consulting, n.d.).

Despite all these tips, a certain amount of project fatigue during a lengthy transformation may still occur. By being aware of the possible consequences of project fatigue and by following some of the above tips, you can get the best out of your project team and ensure that they stay engaged and motivated (Quay Consulting, n.d.).

7   Summary and Outlook

In summary, it is important to say that there is no "one size fits all" approach that suits every type of project or industry sector perfectly. For our company, since we operate in the banking and insurance sector, hybrid project management has proven itself successful. In such an environment, where regulatory affairs play an important role and cannot be ignored, hybrid project management successfully manages the need for flexible and fast implementation.

Before the Covid crisis, only 8% of people in regular employment worked from home. This is because Germany has a very strong "presence culture." People who regularly worked from home were considered not very career focused. Companies used various excuses for not allowing their staff to work from home, such as costs to supply their workers with the necessary equipment. Since Covid, the amount of people working from home has risen to 35%, showing that this is possible. The German Employment Minister, Hubertus Heil (SPD), even wants to make working from home a legal right and wants every employee to be able to work from home, if desired—even when the pandemic is over (Magill 2020).

Europe's largest software company, SAP, is one of the pioneers when it comes to remote work. Before the pandemic, its roughly 25,000 employees were working from anywhere for an average of 2.6 days a week. Once the virus spread, almost the entire company stayed at home. SAP has not noted any difference in productivity when it comes to reaching software development targets (Miller 2020).

Hybrid project management models are perfectly suited to adapt to the general conditions. Whether on-site or remote working time models are predominant or whether these working time models have to be varied during the course of the project is of secondary importance for flexible hybrid project management. Compared to other project management models, such as "traditional" or "purely agile," it is possible to react more flexibly to changes at any time. The advantages of going remote with agile or hybrid project management will be described in the following chapter.

Literature

Beck, Kurt. 2005. "The XP Geography: Mapping Your Next Step, a Guide to Planning Your Journey." International Conference on Extreme Programming and Agile Processes in Software Engineering. Berlin, Heidelberg: Springer. 287.

Goodreads, Inc. n.d. Alan Lakein > Quotes. Accessed September 23. https://www.goodreads.com/author/quotes/104977.Alan_Lakein.

Grushka-Cockayne Yael, Holzmann Vered, Weisz Hamutal, Zitter Daniel. 2015. "A New Hybrid Approach for Selecting a Project Management Methodology." London: PMI Global Congress.

Imaginative Thinking. 2014. August 8. Accessed September 17. http://imaginativethinking.ca/what-the-heck-is-project-fatigue/.

Kanbanize. n.d. Accessed September 22. https://kanbanize.com/kanban-resources/getting-started/what-is-kanban-board.

Magill, Sarah. 2020. *The Local*, June 12. Accessed September 22. https://www.thelocal.de/20200612/homeoffice.

Miller, Joe. 2020. *Financial Times*, July 23. Accessed September 22. https://www.ft.com/content/338b1d6d-8b46-4c75-8c2b-d9518477b8e1.

Mind Tools. n.d. Accessed September 17. https://www.mindtools.com/pages/article/smart-goals.htm.

Pradeep, Drew. 2018. *Project Management Institute*, February 15. Accessed October 10, 2020. https://www.pmi.org/about/press-media/press-releases/2018-pulse-of-the-profession-survey.

Quay Consulting. n.d. Accessed September 17. https://www.quayconsulting.com.au/news/managing-project-fatigue-during-transition-programs/.

Solus Informatics. 2018. November 7. Accessed September 17. https://www.solusinformatics.com/agile-vs-traditional-project-management-waterfall/.

Stens, Michael. n.d. *Karrieretutor*. Accessed September 17. https://www.karrieretutor.de/blog/weiterbildung/klassisches-vs-agiles-projektmanagement/.

Strasser, Johann. n.d. *The Project Group*. Accessed September 17. https://www.theprojectgroup.com/blog/en/hybrid-project-management/.

t2Informatik. 2020. Accessed September 17. https://t2informatik.de/wissen-kompakt/hybrides-projektmanagement/.

Teodesk. 2020. Accessed September 17. https://www.teodesk.com/blog/all-you-need-to-know-about-the-hybrid-methodology/.

Visual Paradigm. 2020. Accessed September 17. https://www.visual-paradigm.com/scrum/classical-vs-agile-project-management/.

Westland, Jason. 2015. *Project Manager*, November 2. Accessed October 10, 2020. https://www.projectmanager.com/blog/glossary-of-project-management-terms.

Remote Projects

Eljar Akhgarnush, Fabian Bruse, and Daniel Pott

1 Introduction

The term "remote work" (ILO 2020) gained a lot of traction due to the pandemic the world had to face at the time we wrote this article which has hopefully disappeared by the time you are reading it. We are certain that everything we have learned in 2020 will change the way many people work in offices for years to come. But this is in no way the only reason to carry out remote projects and is not the main driver nor the first one.

We, the authors, as well as the companies we have worked for, have carried out remote projects for most of the past 20 years, and we have collected our experience and knowledge to write this article and start sharing our experience over the following pages.

In the next subsection of Sect. 1, we will talk about how to identify remote projects, what they have to do with remote work and "shoring," why you should consider them and the main challenges.

In Sects. 2–4, we will talk about culture, methodologies, and technologies to consider and use for successful remote projects. The great thing about these

---

E. Akhgarnush · F. Bruse (✉) · D. Pott
ifb SE, Gruenwald, Germany
e-mail: Fabian.Bruse@ifb-group.com

D. Pott
e-mail: Daniel.Pott@ifb-group.com

are: they are generally relevant for any other projects or even helpful for just remote work—so please keep reading even if remote projects are not for you or your organization.

1.1 Remote or Distributed, Near-Shore or Virtual? All the Same?

First, let's define a "remote project".

With our definition, we are focusing on projects and not on any other activities in your lines of business. A project has some very distinctive properties. The most important ones are a "fixed start and end (or fixed budget)", "defined scope (or vision)" and they are a collaboration of different skills and/or departments (ergo: no easy tasks). Many projects incorporate external help, simply because they are by definition something you don't do every day and might need extra expertise.

Let us have a closer look at what defines the "remote" part of it.

Do your employees have a day working from home (pre-pandemic) but are on site for the rest of the time? Or did you get external and remote help with a certain problem in your project for a few days (e.g., a performance expert, legal advice, etc.)? That does not necessarily make your project remote! A little bit of remote work does not automatically convert your project into a remote project. But if you completely outsource a large chunk of a project (e.g., development), then you have a remote project. Let us look at specific examples.

The first real remote projects were the outsourcing (offshoring) development projects in the 90s (Fig. 1).

Many projects and companies failed in this endeavor, but in the end this model did succeed and is still a very viable way of carrying out projects. The

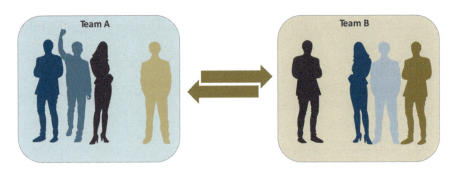

Fig. 1 Two distinct teams with one connection (© ifb SE)

key success factors included developing better requirements engineering (the invention of the modern business analysis) and emphasizing the importance of testing. Both have made their way back to traditional on-site projects as well and should be considered the state-of-the-art when doing any kind of project.

Some of the methods in Sects. 2–4 have also been developed in these offshore models, but in the end the number of connections between the on-site project team and the off-site team is very limited to the point of only having a single line of communication that transmits requirements and test results (i.e., defects). Also, in most cases, both parts of the project are ultimately not remote because both teams are (for themselves) physically close.

These offshoring projects paved the way for the modern remote project. First of all, they developed many methods and tools we use in all projects today, but, secondly, the high chance of failure of these projects and the high costs of labor in the countries where the ordering companies resided fueled the creation of the modern agile project management methods that help highly experienced and expensive employees to still be competitive with these offshore projects.

Basically, you either had to be flexible in your approach or be strict or carry out outsourcing when it came to certain project deliveries. Therefore, the next question is: why not combine these two ideas? Shouldn't being flexible and remote be even better?

This directly leads to the idea of the new remote projects. If we take it to the extreme, this might actually look like Fig. 2.

As you can see, the main difference is not someone being off site or being somewhere else, but the number of relevant connections increases exponentially.

In your remote project, you might find something in between these two examples, with more than just a few connections between teams that might be together locally and some experts working completely remotely (Wikipedia 2020). All of the above need more than what an offshore team needs and that is what this article is all about.

1.2 Reasons for Remote Projects and Why Pandemics Have Little to Do With Them

Normally, we would start with many other reasons to go remote, but since this book was written during the first global pandemic in the lifetimes of all the authors, we should address the elephant in the room.

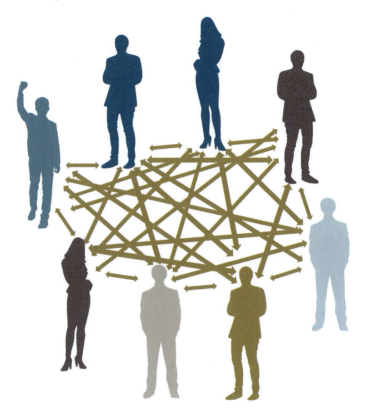

Fig. 2 Connections between remote project team members (© ifb SE)

Yes, pandemics are a good reason to go remote. More precisely, *disaster planning* has always been a reason to not rely on being able to work from an office. Depending on where you are, *snow storms, tornados, floods, civil unrest, man-made catastrophes*, or *extreme weather* can surprise you, but "[…]it is safe to assume that office closures and public transit disruptions will happen at some point[…]" (O'Duinn 2018, 34).

When going back to our normal list/priority of reasons to go remote, number one will always be "the real cost of an office" (O'Duinn 2018, 7), which consists of far more than just the rent. If you take into account the extra employees who are only there to take care of your building, empty spaces in offices that are too big, not enough space in offices that are too small, costs of architects, builders, desks, chairs, coffee machines, security doors, alarm systems, internet access, time to make floor plans, etc., you end up with much higher costs than expected. But if you then also take a look at hiring costs (how much do you have to pay someone to move to your office location) or diversity costs (the extremely skilled Mongolian JAVA developer who will never move to your office location—or is not allowed to, see also Kissflow 2020; Gale 2019) or the costs of higher salaries because you have an office in an extremely fast-developing area of Silicon Valley—you have a lot of reasons to think about going "remote" (O'Duinn 2018, 7–19).

While these reasons are all also valid for remote work they apply even more to remote projects.

Commute times impact the health and well-being of employees (and indirectly also part of their salary) greatly. For remote projects, with experts who have never decided to live somewhere close to YOUR office, this becomes even worse because we are not talking about commuting anymore but travel. This travel can take a day or more and will cost more than just an add-on to their salary, and you will have to pay their expenses as well as the travel times if they are excessive.

Thinking this through, people will spend more time traveling and less time working. In all the projects that we experienced, project managers were more concerned with travel expenses, but the real costs are opportunity costs. Employees are working fewer productive hours than they could, since they are on the road, in airplanes or trains.

If you run a consultancy firm, these travel costs will affect you even more, because until today travel times and being away from home are still the number one reason to look for another job and also a major factor in salaries for consulting.

What is even worse are inefficiencies due to being on site. We expect employees (internal or external) who are being paid to work on a project to work efficiently when they are on site. In a project office or an on-site location, they will always pretend to do just that and will certainly also bill you as much as they are on site. Does that necessarily mean they are working or are even productive? Most project managers know that skills are only needed at certain times. A developer is needed when a specification must be written or when defects occur but, if everyone is on site, all these people will bill you even though they should be working on something completely different. If there is a day without defects and new specifications, another customer (and you) would be better off if your developer worked for them. Instead, you put them in an office where they probably cannot do anything else for you at that time but will pretend to do so. That is not productive at all.

The situation above also relates to the main reason why (project) managers like having employees on site—it is neither the easier communication nor collaboration but control over what they are doing. This control is an expression of mistrust but also insecurity about the real status of the project and about the output of your employees. And it isn't completely unfounded!

Who doesn't have or know a colleague or co-worker who is notorious for not answering e-mails and calls on the day they work from home? Is control the solution? Yes, it can be. But not by putting them in an office, because then they will do something even worse: appearing to be busy but not productive, bestowing you with an unfounded feeling of security. The better response to the situation is: more knowledge about your actual project status and the productivity of your project members, not by checking how they work but by what they produce. Read more about how to do this in Sect. 2.

When looking at human resources in projects (and not day-to-day business), we tend to pretend that assigning three people with 100% of their time to the project makes sense even though everyone knows that the real work can range from 0% to several hundred percent of a single person's output. We still plan like we can always build a productive workload of tasks to do but that is not true for most projects and is also contradictory to the nature of projects.

What we would really need for a lot of tasks is "on-demand" resources, at least for the excess workload of a project. What should be obvious is that this "on demand" cannot happen on site if travel arrangements are costly and need planning ahead. Therefore, any part that can be worked on remotely is much more feasible. If I put my best experts on two to three projects at the same time from their homes instead of having them at one project one week and on another project the next, we end up with much better efficiency for all projects. This could only be mitigated if all these parallel projects were at the same office location but for external consultants or bigger companies that scenario is not very likely.

Imagine letting people only work for your project if they really had something important to contribute, they would work and bill far fewer hours for nearly the same progress in a project.

If these reasons are still not enough, consider the following question if you aren't already remote anyway. Do you have different office locations across the globe/country/town and people rarely see each other and/or you have certain parts of the projects in India/Eastern Europe/or elsewhere already? Then you work remotely (in parts) and could easily go the next step towards creating a fully remote working environment. We are confident that this will help you save money and achieve your project goals much more efficiently and reliably.

1.3 When Should You Not Carry Out a Remote Project?

There are pitfalls for remote projects, and it is good to know them. There are even some situations where remote projects can be damaging or are not feasible.

An obvious example would be that you cannot build a bridge remotely. That might sound like common sense and is also true at the same time, but is that the full story? In fact, the larger value gain in construction work is not on site. Most of the planning before and during construction work (or a construction project) is already done remotely and even those working in and with the planning team are instructed remotely by very clear specifications. But nonetheless, the building part is carried out on site by the construction team. The same can be true for any project. There might always be tasks that can only be done on site.

Another situation where a remote project is not a good option is when you are a small organization with everyone located in the same office on the same floor. In these kinds of project, a lot of overhead-producing project management tools can be left out and you are usually much more productive without these tools than with them.

But what if you still have all the resources in one location yet your organization has grown beyond the point where everyone can fit in one room and still work? In their 2009 article "How to manage virtual teams" (Siebdrat et al. 2009), show that the increased productivity of collocation only works for really small teams and really small distances. Even different floors are already enough to create all the disadvantages of a remote project and if you don't consistently apply the appropriate management methods to these projects, they will end up producing worse results than real distant project teams. The effect of being dispersed but not feeling it makes it worse, because project members are not aware of their situation and don't act appropriately.

If you are looking for signs that your whole team has gone remote already (even though they work in the same office), take a look at the following two interesting questions:

- Does your project team frequently use e-mail, telephone and other meeting tools to communicate? Do they argue and have intense discussions via these media?
- In a development project: has someone on the team worked hard to improve a function while others have worked on replacing it?

All these are signs that you should already treat your team and the project they run with the same tools you would use to run a "remote project." Even more so, you could go "fully" remote quite easily after applying the methods described below and be much more efficient than you are today. We, the authors, also believe that you should always consider "remote project" methodologies because "[…] carefully organized work procedures outperform all-in-one location teams" (O'Duinn 2018, 59).

2 Are There Methods to Be Considered? Can I Jumpstart from on Site to Remote?

You cannot keep on working like before but just from home, it is not as simple as that. Some people tend to have problems focusing, so they have to do their work in smaller chunks, and they need an area in their apartment dedicated to work. Others struggle to stay up to date or are even prone to get depressed due to the lack of social contact, which is why dedicated face-to-face time and regular meetings are required. If you are managing projects and usually like to micro-manage your team, this will not work well in a virtual environment. So it makes sense to invest some time upfront to plan and in particular communicate a project properly. To not get caught on the wrong foot when moving to "virtual", we have handpicked four areas of typical business interactions and compiled a collection of best practices and suggestions to help you lead your virtual team to success.

2.1 Being Prepared Is Everything—Set Up Your Tech Correctly

If you are planning to spend a lot of time in your home office and talk a lot to your colleagues virtually, this might be a good time to rethink your office setup and to recall basic rules on how to use your tech.

Since everyone has different ideas about how a perfect office should look, it is certainly a good idea to install your office yourself instead of relying on your IT department. Employees know best what they will need to work effectively from home. Hence, why not give them a budget to update their desk, to buy the latest tech, a nice lamp, or inspirational room decorations? Certain furniture purchases, like ergonomic desks for better health, can be encouraged. Make sure you avoid "forced budgets" by setting budgets that must be spent.

While designing your office, keep in mind how your colleagues' work experience can be improved with visuals and audio. Muting your microphone when you are not talking should be a matter of course. Disturbing noise and a wrong video stream can be easily avoided like this (a lot of conferencing tools will show the video of the person talking). Also, when setting up your webcam, place it close to your chat window. This will create the illusion of eye contact with the colleague you are talking to. And, speaking of webcams, learn from professional YouTube streamers: the picture is always too dark! If you want to look good in your video, invest in a small USB LED floodlight to illuminate your face, and always keep the background in mind as well. People are curious and socializing will be easier if your counterpart is able to see your real office space rather than a green screen background replacement. For a great summary of video etiquette and technical advice, also see (O'Duinn 2018, 73ff.).

2.2 Plan Ahead and Use Your Time Wisely

When working remotely, communication certainly is key. You cannot quickly walk over to the other office to get the latest news or ask a colleague to demonstrate something on his computer. Coordination gets unreasonably complicated if you try to transfer all of your old habits from on-site to off-site working. As a result, a lot of people develop the habit of setting up a huge amount of calls and web sessions when isolated in their home office. You have probably experienced the consequences yourself: complaints about the lack of time to actually get any work done.

Here are a few tips and tweaks to enhance your time management in remote teams. To avoid constant interruptions and to increase your productivity, define a block of time each hour that is reserved for team communication. For example, the first ten minutes of every hour. This time window can be used to coordinate during calls and chats and should naturally be identical for the whole team. When the time is up, switch your messaging tool to "do not disturb" mode. Additionally, it can be beneficial to agree emergency guidelines with your team for if something unforeseeable and important happens that cannot wait until the next time window.

But even this practice might not give you enough time to focus on complicated topics. Instead, you could try to establish a "no meeting day." Select a day of the week that works best for the whole team and make sure that there won't be any meetings that day. You can try to block that day as "busy" in your calendar to remind meeting schedulers of your focus day. Don't forget to regularly assess whether you and your team have picked the right day for this practice.

If, in spite of everything, you are still thrown off by an unjustified amount of meetings, try to rework your calendar. Sometimes, recurring meetings lose their purpose, but nobody dares to cancel them. Discuss the practice of removing every meeting once a quarter and re-adding what is necessary afterwards. Like this, you can ensure that only meetings that add value to your goal or are required for coordination will accompany you through the next quarter. When adding back a meeting, ensure that only the required people are invited. Use this chance to clean up and minimize the group of participants.

Planning gets even more complicated if your team is scattered across multiple time zones. Not only will it get increasingly improbable to find common time slots, the colleagues in the "minority time zone" will also feel more and more disconnected from what is going on in the project. Keep the following in mind to facilitate communication (Mahn 2020):

- Know the time zones: nothing can be more discouraging than if your counterpart does not even know what time it is in your location, or does not care whether you have to get up at 5 a.m. for a meeting. The same is true for local holidays. Add a second time zone and holiday calendars into your tools.
- Speaking of getting up early: make sure virtual meetings—if really necessary—are well prepared. It can be very frustrating to work at unusual times just to find out there are no productive results.
- Keep in mind that people who just started the day might not be up to date with the information flow yet. Give at least one hour of overlap before starting a meeting.
- Try to change your way of working to asynchronous communication. If you have a public Scrum Board, or tools like Slack, OneNote, Google Docs, etc., every employee (no matter in which time zone) can catch up at their pace. This is a good idea for every remote project anyway (also see 2.4).

2.3 Communicate Effectively, but How?

Be it in scheduled meetings or in direct one-to-one calls, at the end of the day communication will be a crucial stepping stone to the success of your project (see 2.2). If you do not see the reaction of your counterpart, especially, make sure everything has been understood (by overcommunicating or giving more time for feedback). Hold virtual meetings to reduce social isolation and to build trust. Suggest video chat to your team to see body language and each other's reactions. Video will also be an important part of team-building, you are not just a voice on the phone anymore (Powers 2018). Try to join video chats early so you can have a casual chat and set the right mood. Share a funny story or a picture of your desk. Also, similar to real-life meetings but even more important now, plan the meeting in advance and send an informative agenda (a great list of ideas for ideal meetings can be found here [Foroni 2020]). In this way, your colleagues can already think ahead and thus ensure a productive meeting leaving more time for other things. In the meeting, try to address people by name. You cannot look at somebody and expect an answer. If not addressed directly, open questions will usually remain unanswered. This technique can also be used to encourage silent participants. While talking, the moderator should make sure that nobody is interrupted. Instead, announce the rule of using the "raise hand" feature several tools have, or just raise your hand on the video. If, on the other hand, nobody is talking, don't underestimate the power of the "pause." This needs to be much longer than in non-virtual conversations. But, after 10 seconds at the latest, one meeting participant will probably start to take the initiative. Once the meeting is over—and we have come full circle here—summarize the outcome of the meeting and make it available to everyone to enable asynchronous communication.

The importance of small talk was already briefly mentioned. However, this small period of time certainly does not suffice for getting up to date with the latest technical skills or to really share (non-project-relevant) knowledge with your colleagues. Continuous learning is such an essential part of being a good developer, so block some time for learning when everyone is available: Pizza Day. Everyone loves pizza. Use a lunch or dinner to present a new topic to a group of interested colleagues regularly over food and beverages (locally consumed at each location) (Keith and Shonkwiler 2020). The topic can be chosen by interest and doesn't have to be related to the current project directly.

Another communication idea we would like to share, even if it appears outdated at first, is newsletters. Everyone used to have one until mailboxes got flooded and either spam filters started deleting or users started ignoring these messages. But in times of virtual work, newsletters might experience a second boom. If the whole company or a complete team is working remotely, it is difficult to spread information that is of interest to everyone. The office grapevine does not work as fast anymore, if at all. Of course, newsletters could be much more modern than they used to be. Ask your managers and team leads to write a short summary of their week, introduce new employees, highlight technically interesting features or present the results of Pizza Day. Also, this update does not have to be sent by e-mail. Whatever tools suit your company best will work (e.g. MS Teams, hashtag #News).

2.4 Requirements, Agreements, and Status—Managing Remotely with a Single Source of Truth

Of course, communication is a crucial factor for managing projects. You will, for instance, easily get an impression of the status when others talk about their progress in calls. Or will you? How is your counterpart evaluating the communicated progress? Maybe they relate to the kick-off meeting at the beginning of the project, or requirements from a stakeholder, or what you discussed in e-mails with them? They might have gotten their information in private channels back when they needed it or made verbal agreements in face-to-face meetings. Which version of information in which communication channel is the correct one?

This example highlights the importance of a single source of truth (SSOT, also single version of truth) available to everyone (Dykes 2018). A platform used to store all information is needed to make a project a success: requirements, open issue lists, documentation, meeting minutes (yes you need them) and test artifacts. Making this work is not rocket science. Most project management tools will already enable you to work in an SSOT kind of way. You can also create the SSOT manually using Excel spreadsheets or other files and clean and merge data yourself. The greater challenge is the change in culture to accept the advantages of having up-to-date information centralized in one place. Of course, it is easy to quickly store files locally in your notebook or calendar, but if it comes to sharing the documents or to communicating the progress, the increased time to coordinate destroys that time saved. Publicly accessible information will at the same time reduce the need for continuous meetings where, according to a Harvard Business Review study, 15% of an organization's collective time is spent. In the large company examined, just one weekly ExCom meeting accounted for 7000 hours a year (Mankins 2014).

On the other hand, a single source of truth, where everyone sees who's working on what task, will make everyone stay accountable. No excuses like "I thought you took care of that." This transparency will automatically reduce the need for lengthy status meetings and align the team (see The Teamwork Team 2019). Productivity is increased by eliminating dependencies and preventing the toggling between sources of information, also fostering data-driven decision-making based on that one source (Kim 2020).

2.5 Onboarding the Right Way—Some Hands-on Tips

Even a well-coordinated remote team with effective best practices does have a weak spot: integrating new members into that team because they don't know the rules nor the people yet. To make it worse, it is the new employees in particular who are often reluctant and shy to ask for help. So how can onboarding be facilitated in an off-site team?

First of all, create a well-defined process to provide tools like laptop, phone, and access rights. Make the good impression that you have been getting ready for the new colleague, rather than too busy to focus on onboarding. Consider adding a personal message and company merchandise to the laptop parcel. These goodies will be useful and create a common company spirit. Instead of being completely remote, you may want to grant a small budget for real-life meetings in the first few weeks. This provides a chance to get to know each other better on a personal level and also shows the new team members how important they are to the company. This on-site meeting could also be combined with onboarding training or coaching, enabling the new colleagues to get up to speed quickly.

However, just one training session will usually not be enough. Therefore, one way of coping with the long-term onboarding process for new joiners is to establish a "buddy system" (Walker 2020). A more senior member of the team who understands its culture will block up to 50% of their time to be their "buddy." That time is used for helping and mentoring the new member, as well as explaining the team's processes and practices. This effectively fosters a sense of belonging quickly. Certainly, being a buddy is challenging. The chosen mentor needs to be able to cope with the additional responsibility and have a good attitude to their job. The new joiner should pair with the buddy as much as possible. Screen-sharing is a great way to learn during that time and, while being in contact, an uncomplicated chance to ask questions. While the new joiner is working, the mentor can offer suggestions. Every couple of hours, the roles should be swapped, and the mentor has time to work on something, while the new joiner observes.

Try to break up tasks into small chunks, as is naturally done in some working environments, like Scrum, and set clear short-term goals to reduce confusion and misunderstanding. Making the goals achievable and hitting them will be very satisfying for new colleagues, while clear communication minimizes interruptions in the workflow and fosters focus. Don't forget to check regularly how the new hires are doing independently from the buddy program (e.g. in lunch calls or regular check-ins). Starting a new job can feel overwhelming and they might be hesitant to approach you as they want to seem competent. Also, this chance can be used to survey the level of happiness of your employees to find out if they have regrets working for you.

Keeping these strategies in mind within the first 90 days will ideally prepare your new employees for becoming part of a highly productive team where they feel welcomed and accepted.

2.6 Team Spirit—The Most Difficult Challenge

Working remotely can be isolating, so good team spirit becomes even more important than it already is. You have to ensure that everyone in the team is connected and foster a common team spirit. Even though it seems reasonable to assume your team members perfectly understand their role and function within the team, being off site needs overcommunication. Building trust takes a lot of interactions and will not happen overnight. Therefore, make sure you talk to your teammates daily. If a family member walks into the video, introduce them (coming back to using video as often as possible). Do not underestimate the value of explaining to everyone the manner in which they contribute to the project goal and what you expect from them. Ask for their opinion on topics and value accomplishments. Highlight how a milestone or increment could not have been possible without everyone's contribution. With these practices, it becomes evident quicker if team members cannot connect with their work anymore or don't agree on "putative" common values.

To build a stronger commitment and better relationships, getting together is in our human nature. We have discussed the importance of real-life meetings in 2.5 already, but the same holds true for more senior teams. If possible, get your team together at least twice a year to improve the morale. But try to get away from boring, old-school seminars or scary outdoor adventures that reveal anxieties. Ideally, let the team choose what they would like to try (Some ideas: cooking classes, escape room, city scavenger hunt, team laser tag). You might even consider inviting family members along as well.

But social interaction is also important in the rest of daily working life. Find a way for employees, including the boardroom, to socialize virtually if the office kitchen is not available. You can probably use the tools you already have: chat groups about hobbies, interests, favorite holiday locations, and other random things (see [Bariso 2020] and [Embry 2016] for more ideas and methods). Anything where people are able to post pictures and comment on posts is feasible.

3   Do We Have Any Tools at Hand for Remote Projects?

The obvious answer to the question above is: yes, there are plenty of tools. Aside from soft-skill tools like leadership styles, coaching techniques (driver, enabler, director, and supporter), conflict resolution styles (collaborative, competitive, compromising, etc.) and guidelines (ethical standards, collaboration codes of conduct, etc.), remote project teams can choose from an array of software tools. But before breaking down some of these in the subsequent sections, it is equally important to clarify the structure of the virtual teamwork, i.e., whether a rather dispersed or more centralized convergence comes into play: while a centralized project structure improves knowledge management, a more dispersed makeup promotes remote accessibility as well as remote updatability. They are both compatible with each other and can co-exist, facilitating each of their advantages.

3.1   Tools to Be Considered for Project Planning and Conduct

There are different types of tasks arising during a remote project, for which corresponding technologies exist. While some tasks are of a creative nature, including idea generation, or negotiations, others are of a structural nature, including routine actions or planning. The corresponding technologies can be divided into basically two categories (Rouse 2005):

- **Synchronous groupware** covers all tools enabling the virtual team members to communicate in real time: shared file editing, file transfers, audio, video and web conferences, electronic chats.

- **Asynchronous groupware** includes all tools facilitating collaboration between multiple participants at different times.

Groupware aims at the supportive control of a group process, i.e., the cooperative or collaborative leadership of the team when working out a result or the transformation of information from an initial to an end state. With that function in mind, the two illustrations Figs. 3 and 4 indicate some of the main characteristics of each tool. On the one hand, these characteristics should be balanced with the personal as well as project intentions and goals, avoiding miscommunication and any sort of surprises due to misleading tool applications. On the other hand, including the aspect of "tasks to be carried out" in the tool selection processes further reduces the degree of miscommunication and misleading tool applications. Considering these previous thoughts increases the overall chances of efficient communication within the remote teams resulting in a highly successful project outcome.

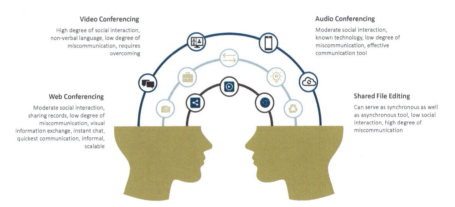

Fig. 3 Illustration of synchronous groupware and some of its characteristics (© ifb SE)

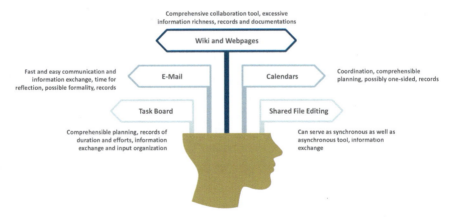

Fig. 4 Illustration of asynchronous groupware and some of its characteristics (© ifb SE)

3.2 When Is Best to Use Which Tools?

Now that light has been shed on the two categories of technology useful for remote projects, the question of when to use which tool during remote project tasks still needs to be addressed. There is no doubt that in the end communication and collaboration choices are strongly dependent on the teams per se, e.g., preferences, personalities, teamwork, and so forth. However, general statements can be made on the usual suitability of most communication and collaboration tools within a remote project. These statements ought to be understood as mere guidelines and should be altered according to each project and especially each team.

Table 1 is a summarization of appropriate tool use, while considering the relevant tasks and the characteristics of the various displayed tools. The classifications are "less suitable," "moderately suitable" and "suitable." For each classification in each cell there are keywords provided explaining the labeling as such. Nevertheless, as mentioned before, in the end it depends on the individual team members, the team as a whole and the project itself with their preferences, notions, goals, and many more things, requiring the remote teams to conduct extensive mutual exchanges in these topics and extraordinary prior planning as well as organizing.

3.3 Let's Scale Up Our Remote Project!

Many factors that are also relevant for scaling remote projects have already been addressed in the previous subsections. What is meant are factors such as transparency, trust, communication, hiring, and onboarding as well as tool selection. However, when it comes down to scaling, new challenges come along with the topics mentioned and new ones occur.

As for communication, it is far from a secret that an increasing number of team members or teams results in an increasing number of communication channels. In that sense, well-established, stable, and appropriate communication channels are required. One aspect among others linked to the factors of communication, transparency, and tool selection alike, is real-time arrangements, i.e., continuous merging and delivery of work packages within a scaled virtual team demands exceptional coordination skills and the corresponding tool (Asproni 2019). The same thoughts apply to further aspects, e.g., finding mutual agreements or taking hold of structured feedback loops.

Apart from thorough planning, preparations, tech setups, goal setting, trust and availability, which all apply to scaled remote projects as much as to unscaled ones, but simply in more extensive ways, there is one factor requiring

Table 1 Communication tool allocation to purposes (© ifb SE)

	Brainstorming and research	Routine execution	Complex execution	Conflict management
Video conferencing	**Moderately suitable:** Face-to-face compensation, lack of overview, lack of documentation, lack of idea illustration possibilities	**Suitable:** (Group) discussion, distribution of tasks, interviews, input request	**Suitable:** Face-to-face compensation, discussions, finding options, debates, task distribution, interviews, input request	**Suitable:** Face-to-face compensation, one-on-one possibility, expressing opinions, discussions, negotiations, agreements
Audio conferencing	**Less suitable:** Lack of overview, lack of documentation, lack of idea illustration possibilities	**Suitable:** (Group) discussion, interviews, task distribution, input request	**Suitable:** Simple discussions, finding options, debates, interviews, task distribution, input request	**Suitable:** One-on-one possibility, expressing opinions, discussions, negotiations, agreements
Web conferencing	**Suitable:** Overview, in-depth research, documentation, idea illustration	**Suitable:** (Group) discussion, quick conduct, task distribution, consultation	**Moderately suitable:** Lack of interpersonal exchange, (group) discussion, debates	**Less suitable:** Lack of interpersonal exchange, high degree of miscommunication
Shared file editing	**Moderately suitable:** Idea collection, information and knowledge exchange, insufficient communication	**Moderately suitable:** Quick conduct, insufficient communication, task distribution	**Less suitable:** Insufficient communication, lack of interpersonal exchange	**Less suitable:** Insufficient communication, lack of interpersonal exchange

	Brainstorming and research	Routine execution	Complex execution	Conflict management
Wiki and webpages	**Moderately suitable:** Idea collection, information and knowledge exchange, insufficient communication	**Moderately suitable:** Documentation, structured approach, insufficient communication	**Less suitable:** Insufficient communication, lack of interpersonal exchange, high degree of miscommunication	**Less suitable:** Insufficient communication, lack of interpersonal exchange, high degree of miscommunication
E-Mail	**Moderately suitable:** Elaborate feedbacks, information and knowledge exchange, insufficient communication, slow	**Moderately suitable:** Elaborate input, information and knowledge exchange, insufficient communication, slow	**Less suitable:** Insufficient communication, lack of interpersonal exchange, slow, miscommunication possible	**Less suitable:** Insufficient communication, lack of interpersonal exchange, slow, miscommunication possible

more attention here: measurability. In a small team, whether remote or on-site, the ease of measuring results lies simply in the outcome and interim meetings. In a scaled remote project, however, it is rather easy to lose track and fail as a result. Measurability with the right selections of metrics and indicators is imperative for the success of these kinds of virtual endeavor. What needs to be measured is not just the outcome, but many more aspects influencing the outcome: utilization, workload, quality assurance, team member satisfaction, etc. Appropriate measurability enables optimization processes and, hence, increases the success rate.

Another important factor is knowing the limits of scaling, which prevents avoidable project failures (Asproni 2019). For one thing, this factor applies to the number of people within a team as well as the overall number of teams and the right timing of enlarging these numbers in remote projects. That means there is a threshold in every team and project where additional manpower results in a productivity decrease instead of increase. This is also strongly dependent on the timing in which the team expansion takes place, since an already advanced project is likely to be inhibited and an early stage endeavor is more likely to benefit. Therefore, at a certain point, it is advisable to allocate more time instead of adding more workers. Then again, the factor of knowing the limits of scaling also applies to the capacity of tools. This means there is most likely a threshold here, too, above which either the tool hits its limits—resulting in system crashes and lags—or communication via tools becomes inefficient, or both. There are many more aspects of the limit factor to consider, varying from project to project and hence requiring an analysis in each project prior to scaling.

In summary, prior to scaling a remote project, examining how much it makes sense to do so for one's own projects by considering what additional efforts and challenges are going to be faced in existing factors, what new factors will have to be included, what are the limits of scaling in each project, how can I measure the effectiveness and many more questions is strongly advised.

4 On-Site Culture and Virtual Culture: Is It a Thing?

If we try to wrap up everything that has been said about best practice and how remote teams work, the result could arguably also be labeled "virtual culture." Fostering that culture within the project team will help your endeavor to succeed. However, there are not many literary sources offering a general framework for remote projects with a focus on culture. One could mistakenly come to the conclusion that there is no noteworthy difference in project culture between on-site and remote projects. The following subsection will critically discuss this observation by outlining key points of a virtual culture and illustrating successful approaches to setting up such a framework accordingly.

4.1 I See no Changes... Do I? A Shift in Mindset

When addressing culture in an on-site project, it looks like a relatively simple matter due to, for example, rather similar individual cultures (in the strict sense) working together, direct communication and absence of factors like different time zones. However, there is more to culture than solely geographically conditioned differences: there is also a "project culture," even though it will naturally be influenced and co-determined by the former.

In virtual teams in particular, this project culture has to contain a shift in the mindset of each team member to cope with the complexity that remote project work entails, requiring a higher degree of transparency and trust at the same time (Panagoulias 2019). What appears to be a contradiction can be broken down as follows: trust toward team members is required to give them the leeway on how to tackle, conduct and complete their work, while at the same time maintaining transparency by involving every employee engaged in the project in the decision-making process. More ideas on promoting this trust are investigated by Paul Zak's key management behaviors (Zak 2017). He introduces essential actions (see Fig. 5) to be conducted by management specifically with the purpose of endorsing strong mutual trust within a team or even an organization.

Fig. 5 Illustration of Paul Zak's key management behaviors leveraging trust (© ifb SE)

With an awareness of project culture, it will eventually become much easier to work remotely and, consequently, to hire people for your project from all over the world. This facilitates another shift in mindset, an embracing attitude of the strengths that diversity, e.g., the cultures involved, brings. With the change from on-site to remote, each (new) team member may also gradually work at different locations, embedded not only in the local culture and, thus, background but also differing more in nationality, disability, generation, way of life, personal experience and so forth.

For issues on culture (in the strict sense and in contrast to project culture), geography, habits, etc.—which are especially relevant to international projects now—different applicable models, dealing with the values of each region and offering context, do exist and can be consulted. To mention two, Trompenaars' model of national culture differences (Trompenaar and Hampden-Turner 1997) or Erin Meyer's eight scales (Meyer 2014) are recommended to the interested reader. However, for points such as differing personal experiences, clash of generations, etc., a substantial amount of emotional intelligence is still required to get the best out of these diverse teams. Therefore, communication within a remote project framework will always be of extreme importance and strongly linked to the established culture in a team (Coon 2017). Besides providing trust plus transparency, therefore, establishing a working communication culture is another aspect to focus on more thoroughly in remote projects than in on-site assignments, and will be addressed in the following subsection.

4.2 The Right Culture for Communicating Over Distance

Where else does culture play a role in projects? You might have heard the term "feedback culture," but in general we could also call it "communication culture." When we generalize what is known about effective communication from Sects. 2.3 and 4.1, specific factors influencing the way we communicate in remote projects can be found. Trust, choice of tools, leadership style, coaching competencies, conflict resolution management, planning scope, feedback culture, and group dynamics come to mind. The Project Management Institute (Project Management Institute 2013) offers five of these factors and an approach on how to improve the related communication culture in Fig. 6. It is one way out of many to tackle a communication improvement process.

Also, appropriate leadership as well as coaching styles should be considered as part of your remote project communication culture, see (Bonnie 2017).

Fig. 6 Illustration of PMI's five-point communication model (© ifb SE)

When managing remote projects within an international scope especially, team members can have very different (cultural) backgrounds and personalities. In some cases, a diplomatic leadership approach with sophisticated communication and caring feedback may be far more suitable than being a straight-shooting coach giving direct feedback. In other cases, it can be advantageous to seek consensus in the whole team rather than acting as the sole decision-maker. A certain sensitivity, the ability to read the room and the right interpretation become more important (contextual intelligence). However, if things get out of control, the team needs a plan for conflict management over distance as part of the team's communication (Twist 2019). One way to achieve this could be using techniques from Retrospective meetings (known from the Scrum framework) virtually and on a regular basis.

Being strongly related to culture, (team) identity remains a fundamental factor in a virtual context as well. Due to the abstract nature of working from home, the leadership should therefore not tire of communicating the vision and mission of the project on a regular basis, enhancing the identification of team members with the remote project. Once these foundations for trust and transparency are in place, combined with a conflict management plan covering various scenarios, a remote team culture will slowly start to emerge, increasing the acceptance and feasibility of the best practice mentioned.

5 Conclusion

In this article, we roughly introduced the topic remote projects, including differentiations from other forms of projects, best practice and scaling considerations. It should be stressed once again that changes in the way business works (and beyond) are not only driven by pandemics or costs, but also by ecological considerations, a change in lifestyle and better ways to handle remote work in general. Companies that adapt to these developments technically and culturally on time will be better prepared for upcoming challenges. Hence, once again, adaptation is the key to success.

Literature

Asproni, Giovanni. 2019. *The Hard Truth About Scalability: What to Know Before Scaling Up*, April 9. Accessed October 15, 2020. https://thedigitalprojectmanager.com/scalability-scaling-up/.

Bariso, Justin. 2020. "Inc." *Inc*, August 3. Accessed August 25, 2020. https://www.inc.com/justin-bariso/googles-remote-work-policy-has-9-great-tips-you-should-definitely-steal-today.html.

Bonnie, Emily. 2017. *Long Distance Leadership: Successfully Scaling a Remote Team to 50+ Employees*, February 7. Accessed September 24, 2020. https://www.wrike.com/blog/long-distance-leadership-successfully-scaling-remote-team-50-employees/.

Coon, Spencer. 2017. *The Tricks to Building a Scalable Remote Team*, October 18. Accessed September 11, 2020. https://www.hibox.co/de/blog/tricks-zum-aufbauen-eines-skalierbaren-remote-teams/.

Dykes, Brent. 2018. *Forbes.com*, January 10. Accessed October 19, 2020. https://www.forbes.com/sites/brentdykes/2018/01/10/single-version-of-truth-why-your-company-must-speak-the-same-data-language/#160045b31ab3.

Embry, Patrice. 2016. *dpm*, November 14. Accessed August 25, 2020. https://thedigitalprojectmanager.com/remote-project-management-strategies/.

Foroni, Lucile. 2020. *doist.com*. Accessed August 25, 2020. https://doist.com/blog/how-we-manage-projects-on-a-fully-remote-team/.

Gale, Gren. 2019. *The Remote Project Manager*. Independently published.

ILO, technical note. 2020. *International Labour Organization*, June 5. Accessed July 7, 2020. https://www.ilo.org/global/statistics-and-databases/publications/WCMS_747075/lang--en/index.htm.

Keith, Clinton, and Grant Shonkwiler. 2020. *Remote Teamwork Tools*. Independently published.

Kim, Farah. 2020. *Agile Zone*, April 21. Accessed October 19, 2020. https://dzone.com/articles/why-your-remote-team-needs-a-single-source-of-truth.

Kissflow. 2020. *Remote Project Management—Tips to Manage Successful Remote Project Teams*, September 3. Accessed October 15, 2020. https://kissflow.com/project/remote-project-management/.

Mahn, Jan. 2020. "Wenn Remote, dann Full Remote." *c't*, July 3: 132. https://www.heise.de/select/ct/2020/15/2015013545453707528.

Mankins, Michael. 2014. *This Weekly Meeting Took Up 300,000 Hours a Year*, April 29. Accessed October 19, 2020. https://hbr.org/2014/04/how-a-weekly-meeting-took-up-300000-hours-a-year.

Meyer, Erin. 2014. *Harvard Business Review*, May. Accessed January 21, 2020. https://hbr.org/2014/05/navigating-the-cultural-minefield.

O'Duinn, John. 2018. *Distributed Teams: The Art and Practice of Working Together While Physically Apart*. Release Mechanix, LLC.

Panagoulias, Kosta. 2019. *Challenges of Scaling Remotely*. Accessed September 11, 2020. https://www.founderviews.com/challenges-of-scaling-remotely/.

Powers, Tara. 2018. *Virtual Teams for Dummies (For Dummies Business and Personal Finance)*. For Dummies.

Project Management Institute. 2013. "Communication: The Message Is Clear." *pmi.org*, December. Accessed September 18, 2020. https://www.pmi.org/-/media/pmi/documents/public/pdf/white-papers/communications.pdf.

Rouse, Margaret. 2005. *Synchronous Groupware*, September. Accessed October 2, 2020. https://whatis.techtarget.com/definition/synchronous-groupware.

Siebdrat, Frank, Martin Hoegl, and Holger Ernst. 2009. "How to Manage Virtual Teams." *MIT Sloan Management Review*, July 1.

The Teamwork Team. 2019. *teamwork.com*, September 18. Accessed October 19, 2020. https://www.teamwork.com/blog/why-you-need-a-single-source-of-truth-in-project-management/.

Trompenaar, Fons, and Chales Hampden-Turner. 1997. *Riding the Wave of Culture*. London: Nicholas Brealey Publishing. https://en.wikipedia.org/wiki/Trompenaars%27s_model_of_national_culture_differences.

Twist. 2019. *Remote Projects 101: The Remote Guide to Project Management*. Accessed September 16, 2020. https://twist.com/remote-work-guides/remote-project-management#solving-common-problems-with-remote-projects.

Walker, Tat Bellamy. 2020. *Business Insider*, April 24. Accessed October 9, 2020. https://www.businessinsider.com/buffer-how-to-use-virtual-buddies-to-onboard-remote-employees-2020-4?r=DE&IR=T.

Wikipedia. 2020. *Wikipedia—Virtual Team*, June 8. Accessed July 7, 2020. https://en.wikipedia.org/wiki/Virtual_team.

Zak, Paul J. 2017. "Organizational Culture: The Neuroscience of Trust." *hbr.org*, February. Accessed September 18, 2020. https://hbr.org/2017/01/the-neuroscience-of-trust.

Project Management and RPA

Sefa Soybir and Christopher Schmidt

1 Introduction to Project Management Methods for RPA Projects

Robotic Process Automation (RPA) is accepted as a technology with rapidly rising potential in business processes. The technology offers promising potential to automate mundane, routine tasks that provide little motivation to employees while driving process costs since they are prone to mistakes and rework. Meanwhile, they provide little value to the organization's actual business.

RPA promises a fast and scalable solution to automate and therefore lower the process costs in these environments. Yet a lot of initiatives utilizing the technology are failing. While utilizing complementary technologies, such as Process Mining in order to identify processes suitable for automation with RPA, a key aspect of a successful RPA implementation is the right project setup as well as proper project management.

Therefore, project management is an essential part of automation projects. It shall be noted that there is no one-size-fits-all approach. Therefore, this

---

S. Soybir (✉) · C. Schmidt
ifb SE, Grünwald, Germany
e-mail: Sefa.Soybir@ifb-group.com

C. Schmidt
e-mail: Christopher.Schmidt@ifb-group.com

Fig. 1 The four phases of an RPA project (© ifb SE)

article does not represent the "one correct way." Still, based on our experience, we identify four phases in which an RPA project is to be set up. These are: process identification, process analysis, RPA implementation and the go-live of the solution. In the following, the four phases named will be discussed in detail (Fig. 1).

2 The Four Phases of an RPA Project

2.1 Process Identification

A systematic approach is essential for the identification and management of requirements. Process requirements are important in RPA projects in order to evaluate the process below. This procedure for RPA projects provides important process details and outlines data as a basis for decision-making for the project start in the process identification phase. A pipeline is helpful in consolidating this information from potential processes. Basically, two models are used to fill the pipeline with potential processes for RPA.

In conventional RPA project management methods, process identification is controlled top-down. In order to achieve the business goals, processes are registered by departments. The content, budget and dates are set by the client without any further details. A quick implementation is achieved with this approach, but not with the highest possible potential or the right technology. The technology should be selected independently of an overall decision made under the process conditions. Central control is important for deciding to choose the right technology. In order to bundle the knowledge for technologies and to make the right choice, companies have established innovation centers. The process employee is the best specialist for the process. For a successful process identification, information from the process employee is the decisive factor. In the bottom-up method, potential is reported directly by the employee. The basic parameter for this approach is the employee's acceptance and willingness for innovations. The core task of the innovation center is to create awareness for process registrations throughout the company.

With this procedure, process identification is divided into five sub-phases (Fig. 2).

Fig. 2 Five sub-phases of RPA process identification (© ifb SE)

As already described, technologies are made known throughout the company in the innovation center. The first phase of process identification is formed with the technology awareness and the key RPA information in the innovation center. With the questions about process repeatability, standardized process steps, order volume and the input for the process start, the employee can make the decision to register for an RPA initiative. The Continuous Improvement Process (CIP) is the second phase and is completed with the decision to register. The third phase is the delivery of the processes. The following information is filled in by the registrant:

- Volume
- Handle time
- Standardization
- Frequency
- Stability of UI
- Speed of the affected systems.

With these assessments from the employees, it is possible to design workshops with the first assessment by the RPA specialists in order to carry out initial periodization and fill the project pipeline. In this pre-analysis workshop, the process is demonstrated by an expert. In order to build a pipeline with potential processes, the pre-analysis is crucial.

The following is a brief checklist of parameters for assessing RPA suitability (Fig. 3):

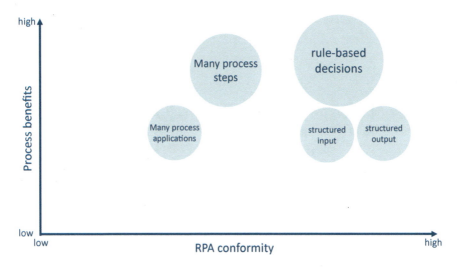

Fig. 3 Parameters for assessing RPA suitability (© ifb SE)

- Number of process steps
- Number of applications
- Process decisions
- Process input for the process beginning
- Process output for the process result.

The pipeline is periodized with the evaluation of the processes. The appropriate selection of processes, the project method and planning are crucial for a project's success. These phases are supervised by the process analyst as an expert. The analyst operates as a sub-project manager for the RPA initiatives and accompanies the automation from the process identification to go-live.

As a result of the process identification, the evaluated and prioritized processes are expected in the pipeline. A detailed initial analysis of the processes is important for the start and success of the project. Process Mining analyzes the entire process in the desired period and reproduces all eventualities, process steps and sequences. This technology shows the steps that are already running automatically and analyzes the slightly automated steps in more detail. With this focus we can quickly identify process steps for Robotic Process Automation. With Process Mining in the pre-analysis workshop, prioritizing according to potential, savings and effort in the pipeline is possible. There is also a significant advantage in the analysis phase with the results already available.

2.2 Process Analysis

As a rule, the automation of business processes is part of the digitalization strategy. The RPA technology is thus anchored in the strategy. In order to achieve the goals related to automation, the strategic planning and implementation of initiatives is necessary. Consolidating, controlling, and measuring these automation projects is the basic structure of a center of excellence (CoE) for RPA projects. RPA projects are carried out by specialists in the CoE as a department and internal service provider in the company, where the ideal project orientation, organizational structure, and the entire RPA lifecycle are controlled. A separate consideration of the RPA initiatives by the IT department makes sense through the special focus in the projects. With the knowledge and resources in a CoE, fast, effective, and sustainable implementation of the solutions in the teams is possible.

The goal is fast implementation with the highest possible savings for RPA solutions. Mentoring in the form of process support alongside the employee is usually used for the analysis in the project management method for RPA implementations. For large insurance companies and banks with complex organizational and responsibility structures for processes, regulations, and applications, there are often gaps such as actual process dissemination, acceptance of the target process, application changes or abolition, and the entire development environment in the project management context. In most RPA projects, the analysis and implementation phases in the RPA tool are strictly separated. Based on the acceptance of the Process Design Document (PDD), the analysis is completed and the second phase can start with the configuration. The concept for success is the combination of the phases to reduce the project duration and avoid gaps. The analysis of the actual processes for the target RPA process design is data-based and can be carried out quickly with Process Mining technology. By connecting the technology to the processes, it is possible to represent and display all process steps and decisions up to the click level. With this basis in the analysis phase, process recording is full and detailed. Mistakes and missing findings such as rare process steps, process exceptions, application reactions, and missing information for future processing are eliminated by data-based Process Mining analysis, in contrast to conventional process analysis.

The process analysis is understood as preparation for the actual implementation in the RPA tool. The evaluation of the process steps according to number and complexity is important for planning the implementation phase. With this basis in the analysis, implementation times and distributions in applications or process modules are decided.

The analysis by Process Mining prior to the start of the project offers a high degree of precision for the recording, evaluation and periodization of the process and in the pipeline. This pre-analysis of the technology enables consolidating the first two phases to be effective. The identification and analysis of the process is more efficient with data-based analysis by Process Mining experts than in the classic procedure. Based on technical know-how, the results are already prepared for a fast and qualitative bot development in the RPA tool. The bots and their machines are provided by the support team in the center of excellence.

In large insurance companies and banks, responsibilities for the processes are usually divided into three types:

- Technical process responsibility
- Application responsibility
- Operational process responsibility.

With technical process responsibility, a product owner accepts the actual and target RPA process and is the direct customer. In order to provide the bots with authorizations and store application data such as usage times, reboot time and workloads in the project, the application managers are invited to the project kick-off. In conventional RPA projects without Process Mining, this instance is the supplying unit for the development. The operational team in agile RPA projects is involved for operational support as process experts.

The automation of an incorrect or incomplete process also leads to errors and negative project results. Accordingly, it is imperative to check optimization prior to automation. RPA is not an end-to-end automation technology. In most cases, it is a sub-process automated with RPA. The interaction between people and bots is essential for further editing in the employee process. Manual process steps by the employee should be excellent. Suitable interaction, such as providing the input and further processing the output, is also a new process step that must be optimally designed. Process optimization is crucial even prior to automation. Through Process Mining, steps that are not within the automation scope can be identified quickly and precisely. With these results and the optimization, effects can be raised even prior to Robotic Process Automation. An optimized and excellent process after an RPA initiative can ensure better results and a higher automation rate.

2.3 RPA Implementation

The implementation of the processes is carried out by the developers. Nevertheless, the process analysts are the first point of contact and coordinators of the phase. If necessary, the experts in the operational teams are also involved in any questions. RPA stands out as a low-code application. However, it is important to follow guidelines and best practice. In addition to the descriptions, as in all programming languages, reusability is a basic principle in the RPA development environment. The use of applications is also associated with a login. It therefore makes sense to develop reusable bundles as modules for the respective applications. Component libraries are also suitable for standard steps such as triggering a printout, saving a file or reading out documents. With these reusable workflow components, a library has also been created for the processes to follow. In addition to standardized development, a compilation of information about applications, workings in the process and general best practice is helpful. The speed and quality of the developments is increased by firm anchoring in the projects to follow.

The development of processes in the RPA tool is divided into two variants of agile teams. In the first variant, the teams are formed in sprints for each application. By dividing the process steps into the respective applications, a fast and parallel development is possible. The core process and bringing together the individual parts is designed by a master developer. For a flexible implementation and documentation, the sprint time is usually set at between two and three weeks. In the second variant, the process steps are divided into logical modules, which are developed independently from the applications. These process components are also developed in sprints by several developers. To test the bot, the process in the test environment is initialized by an independent tester who has not configured the process. The test environment of the applications is used for development and testing. Companies with self-developments have a test environment where the applications are located. Test environments are provided for purchased web applications. These test versions are a mirror image of the production environment (Fig. 4).

Project planning with agile instruments also offers advantages. The dailies and the project board with tasks and responsibilities ensure that overall project communication and continuous exchange are maintained. The structuring and prioritization mean that both project planning and project implementation are documented and can be viewed by the project leader at any time.

To provide added value in the agile project structure and the division of the development effort, testing for the process parts can be carried out through

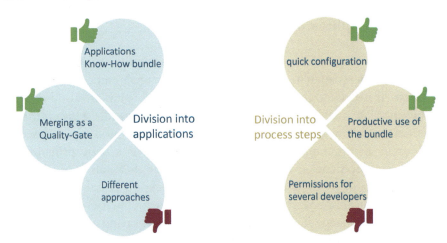

Fig. 4 Advantages and disadvantages of application and process-driven development approaches (© ifb SE)

interim completions. This procedure shortens the duration of the test and, based on tangible results, it also increases customer satisfaction. After the iterative tests, the implementation phase is completed with the User Acceptance Test (UAT). The UAT is the final acceptance of the development by the customer. This test is initiated by the tester with predefined test data, test cases and made available for approval by the analyst.

2.4 Go-Live

The go-live phase of an automation project is the last step and is the moment of truth as the previous efforts are now transferred to the actual production system and the estimated benefits, such as cost reduction and increased process quality, are verified in day-to-day business.

In order to make the go-live a success, there are a few things to consider:

Previously it has been mentioned that the test environment should be an exact replica of the production system in order to ensure efficiency and avoid rework in configuring the bots. Yet experience shows that in many cases there are minor differences which need to be handled in order for the virtual workforce to carry out the defined process properly. A field in the production system deviating from the one in the test environment may cause a robot to not recognize it and throw an error, ultimately stopping the process. Also, in day-to-day business, there may still be some cases the robot has to deal with, but which have not been fully captured before. Then, the configuration of the bots needs to be adjusted and/or expanded in order to include these previously unknown cases and enable the bots to deal with them.

Therefore, it is crucial to establish an intensive care or hypercare phase. This usually covers a period of two weeks in which the robots are monitored very closely, and which is used for minor bug fixing and ensuring proper functionality of the automated process in the production system.

It is advised that during this phase the automated processes are scheduled in cooperation with the process SME and are also triggered manually in order to keep control over when the processes start running. This is to ensure that the process SME is present when the bots start doing their work and can get involved with the bots carrying out the process in case errors arise. When striving for efficiency it is just as crucial to have the developer available who actually configured the process taken to production. They should take care of the adjustments as they know the bot configuration inside out and can either restore functionality or expand it quickest.

Best practice for securing the feasibility of this close monitoring during the hypercare phase is sticking to the principle of agile development and utilizing an approach of fractional releases. Put into practice, a smaller number of bots carrying out a process is taken and transferred to the production system. The necessary adjustments are identified and after the bugs have been fixed another fraction of bots is transferred into production until all bots are running on the target system. This phase is referred to as the ramp-up phase (Fig. 5).

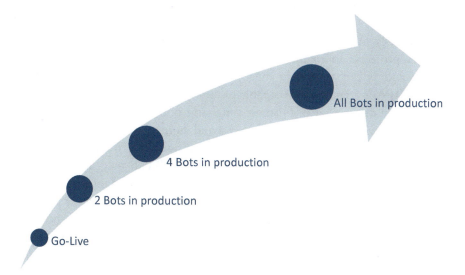

Fig. 5 Illustration ramp-up phase (© ifb SE)

After the hypercare phase is over for all bots, and bugs in the production environment have been fixed, the bots must be scheduled so that they do not have to be triggered manually—unless defined so. With the scheduling installed for all bots, a monitoring process must be set in place along with a definition of who is responsible for watching the bots' performance. Also, an incident handling process is needed in case errors arise in the future that need to be dealt with to re-establish a fully functional automated process. With that in place, the last thing to do is the out-phasing of processes that are not needed anymore in order to free up bot capacity so that they can take on new tasks.

The decision as to where the monitoring of the virtual workforce takes place is a strategic one and depends on how a company is planning to incorporate RPA into its organization. A set of different approaches will be discussed in subsection 7 of this article.

3   Challenges

Utilizing RPA technology brings a set of challenges. A selection of these and possible approaches for resolving them shall be discussed below. The challenges to be discussed include expectation management, process identification and change management.

3.1   Expectation Management

As previously mentioned, expectation management is crucial for the success of RPA projects. In many cases, RPA is confronted with expectations it cannot and is not meant to meet. As indicated at the beginning of the section, RPA is a technology capable of automating rule-based routine tasks. This already offers a lot of business value and potential in helping organizations to reduce manual workload and avoid human mistakes in day-to-day business across various departments and functions. Yet there is a tendency for companies to raise the stakes too high for RPA to meet alone, such as automating complex processes end-to-end which require data interpretation and decision-making. Because while it is possible to automate these processes as well, RPA alone cannot solve these problems. Machine learning and artificial intelligence need to be introduced as complementary technologies to the bots. And while they do harmonize together well, it creates greater project complexity, different skill set requirements and additional technologies to be implemented, thus ending up with higher project costs and duration—while RPA promises easy implementation, fast and simple scalability and cost-efficient implementation. In conclusion, realistic expectations are a key aspect before starting an RPA project. In-depth knowledge of the capabilities and the limits of the technology are required for organizations to make proper judgments on how and for what the technology is going to be used.

3.2 Process Identification

Having understood the technology's capabilities, the processes to be automated can be determined. In this context, one challenge is fully capturing the processes with every exception and variation. All too often a good process candidate is chosen for automation but the requirements for the configuration of the bots only partially reflect the actual process. Ultimately, this results in a malfunction of the process as soon as the bots are deployed to production since the bots are unable to carry out the process correctly. A reason for these shortcomings is often found in outdated process documentation (Fig. 6).

Organizations tend to document their processes in a one-time effort. As these processes evolve over time, updating the documents visualizing the processes as well as the guidelines describing them is forgotten. Therefore, relying on the documentation alone does not provide a reliable approach for identifying the steps and tasks to be performed by the robot. Most commonly, this challenge is met by conducting workshops and work shadowing with business analysts in which the business analysts are told and

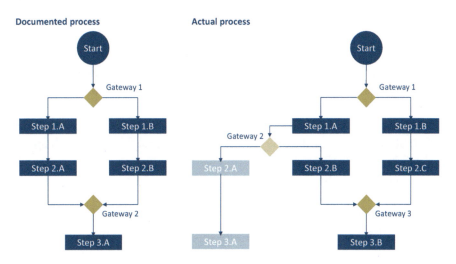

Fig. 6 Documented vs. actual process (© ifb SE)

shown the process steps in order for them to document them. Although this does provide better reliability in capturing the process, thus automating the process correctly, it is still unlikely that all variations and exceptions can be captured by this approach. In workshops, there is the risk that the participating employees forget to mention process steps and/or exceptions. In cases where the analyst is watching the employees performing the process steps and documenting what they see, it must be kept in mind that such work shadowing usually lasts only for a short period of time in which some variations just may not show up. Either way, the requirements for the bots' configuration are unlikely to be captured entirely using these qualitative approaches. A suitable measure for mitigation is the introduction of the hypercare phase to the project already mentioned in this section. During this phase, the bot configuration can be updated quickly according to needs as the development team is still present. Another approach is to utilize Process Mining as an upfront technology to RPA in order to fully capture the process objectively and based on data before the automation project itself starts. To read more about Process Mining and its capabilities, please refer to the *Process Mining* section of this book.

3.3 Change Management

Another vital element in managing RPA initiatives is proper change management. The following discusses the application of conventional change management elements with particular attention to social work/life aspects in RPA projects and how they are beneficial to the project's success.

By introducing RPA technology to a company's business, the workforce of that organization is confronted with change in their daily working lives. Previously, employees carried out tasks manually. Now that these tasks are performed by a robot, the workforce can take on new ones which may require them to develop new skills, think differently, and take on more or different responsibilities. Typically, employees see these kinds of changes and changes in general as a threat at first, as they force them out of their comfort zone. This is also reflected in the seven phases of emotional response to change by Richard K. Streich (Fig. 7).

In consequence, they oppose the new situation, which poses a major threat to the entire RPA initiative. No matter how well chosen the processes to be automated are and no matter how well the bots have been configured, eventually it is the employees who carry and implement the change. Therefore, it is crucial for companies planning to utilize the benefits of RPA technology in their organization to include a properly planned and effectively implemented

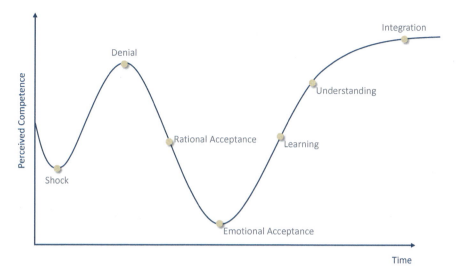

Fig. 7 Seven phases of emotional response to change (Streich 1997)

change management process throughout their RPA projects right from the beginning. The goal is to move the employees from the phases of negative emotions—shock, denial, anger, resistance and depression—to the positive emotional states as quickly as possible.

A key element in this regard is a thought-through communication plan that creates transparency with regard to the strategy and goals of the RPA initiative as well as the impact its introduction will have on the organization's people. It is advisable to give updates on the project's progress and the measures that are coming up next on a regular basis—to everyone, not just management. Their main goal is to give employees a feeling of being understood, taken into consideration and being important to the organization in order to foster their understanding for why the change is required and what it aims to achieve, and, consequently, their acceptance.

Another element to speed up the process of integrating and "embracing" the change is to find promoters within the organization itself. These are employees who are more adaptable and also willing to change with a positive or even enthusiastic response toward the usage of RPA technology. Once identified they can be recruited and instructed to promote their positive attitude to the rest of the workforce. It is important that the promoters are not only members of the management. Otherwise, their effectiveness is likely to be diminished. A further key component for making the change a lasting success is the development of training concepts for employees. This is especially important for RPA initiatives since the employees who previously carried out the tasks of the now automated processes are going to dedicate themselves to new assignments, which may require new skill sets, and these need to be trained first. In cases where the RPA projects are at first carried out with help from a third-party provider, it is also in an organization's interest to build up its own RPA competencies. Firstly, to be able to better control the third-party provider in terms of efficiency as well as effectiveness and, secondly, to be able to conduct RPA initiatives by itself in the future.

In conclusion, change management is a vital element of RPA implementation projects. Transparency is key for fostering employees' trust in the technology and for getting rid of anxious thoughts, such as fear of losing their job due to substitution by a software bot. It is important for organizations to realize that automating tasks does have a high impact on employees' day-to-day work. This change and the associated challenges need to be managed actively right from the start of the project for RPA to be fully effective.

4 Long-Term Integration of RPA

One of the main benefits of RPA lies in its easy and fast scalability (Hacıoğlu 2020). Therefore, in order to utilize the technology's full potential, RPA should not be seen as a one-time project but integrated as part of the company's digitalization strategy. There are a variety of approaches for integrating RPA within an organization of which three shall be discussed in the following.

The first approach is integration based on functions. Function-based integration provides selected functional departments, in which RPA is likely to deliver the best results, their own RPA competencies (Fig. 8).

In this scenario, each function utilizing the technology initiates RPA implementation projects individually and independently of other functions. This integration model enables companies to establish RPA in specific functions where it provides the most benefit in a highly focused manner. Due to the low dependency on other functions it also provides a high level of flexibility as well as cost efficiency caused by the lower project complexity. When comparing it to centralized integration approaches it is also more efficient in the sense that there is no need to create a new functional department specifically dedicated to RPA. On the downside, the model prevents the previously mentioned benefit of scalability across the entire organization since the different functions would work on RPA projects independently and therefore would not have to communicate and coordinate their initiatives. Typically, this leads to redundancy across the different departments in terms

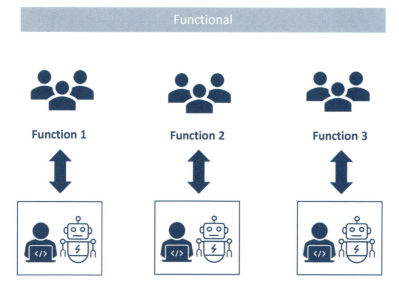

Fig. 8 Functional integration of RPA (© ifb SE)

of workflow configurations and hardware set-ups. Lastly, it aggravates the establishment of RPA implementation standards, such as development best practice and reusable component libraries.

Another approach is the centralized center of excellence (CoE). The centralized CoE acts as the central point for initiating, conducting and controlling all RPA implementations across all departments throughout the organization (Fig. 9).

The main benefit of this form of integrating RPA is the centralized ownership of the technology. All RPA initiatives are driven from a central function and are therefore coordinated. In consequence the technology becomes available for scaling throughout the organization and at the same time risks of duplication and inefficiencies are minimized.

In contrast, RPA projects tend to become more complex as the different initiatives are dependent on each other in terms of resources. In an extreme scenario, this might lead to the centralized CoE being the bottleneck for RPA implementation. In addition to this, it is time-consuming and expensive to establish a central CoE in cases where there is not already one in place, since there is a need for creating a new function within the organization. Lastly, if CoEs in general are new to the company, this approach also demands additional cultural change, since employees are not yet used to working in such cross-functional environments.

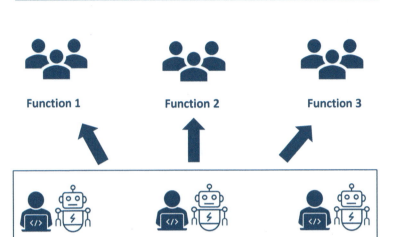

Fig. 9 Centralized center of excellence (© ifb SE)

In an effort to combine the benefits of the first two forms of integration mentioned while mitigating their disadvantages, there is a third form of integration: the hybrid approach of a federated center of excellence. In this, a centralized CoE is installed while the functional departments also receive their own RPA competencies (Fig. 10).

This approach ensures the necessary flexibility from the functional method with every functional department conducting their own RPA implementation projects and therefore avoiding bottlenecks in terms of resources, while exploiting the benefits of a centralized center of excellence in terms of scalability and standardization. It also reduces the cultural impact since the process ownership remains within the functional departments while the CoE only provides consultancy and guidance for the automation initiatives. Yet this approach is easier to implement if the company is already familiar with CoEs. It also still imposes the increased project complexity through the centralized controlling and consultancy by the CoE. Lastly, a CoE would also need to be established leading to higher investments.

In conclusion, there is no one-size-fits-all approach for integrating RPA into the organization. It is highly dependent on what the company wants to achieve by utilizing the technology and how it complements the digitalization strategy. For a first introduction, say in the form of a proof of value, the functional approach constitutes a viable option. However, as soon as the company

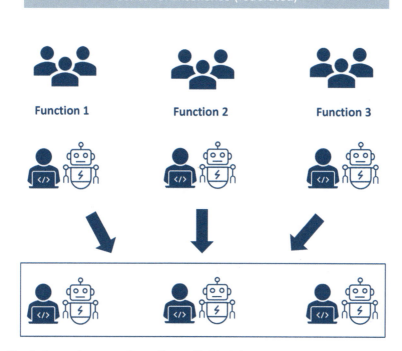

Fig. 10 Federated center of excellence (© ifb SE)

is planning to scale RPA and incorporate it as a part of its long-term strategy, the establishment of a center of excellence is recommended.

Literature

Hacıoğlu, Ümit. 2020. *Handbook of Research on Strategic Fit and Design in Business Ecosystems.* Hershey: IGI Global.

Streich, Robert K. 1997. "Veränderungsprozessmanagement." In *Change Mangement. Programme, Projekte, Prozesse*, edited by Lutz von Rosenstiel, Annete Lanz Michael Reiß, 237. Stuttgart: Schäffer-Poeschel.

Summary

Volker Liermann and Claus Stegmann

The only constant factor in our world is change. Incremental change (analogous to incremental innovation[1]) is better for adapting because we do not realize the small movements due to their continuous nature. Disruptive change makes us realize where the fundamentals start to move. The financial services industry has gone through both incremental and disruptive changes. Margin reduction due to low interest rates and rising competition put enormous pressure on the cost side. Institutes only looking at this side of the coin are on the overcrowded road walked by many automotive suppliers at the end of the last century (role of a manufacturer).

The other way for an institute to go is to take on the role of an orchestrator, trying to be as close to the client as possible. This is a challenge, because of competitors from outside the financial services sector, such as Apple, Google,

---

[1] Incremental innovations are small continuous improvements made to existing processes, methods, products, or services.

V. Liermann (✉)
ifb SE, Grünwald, Germany
e-mail: volker.liermann@ifb-group.com

C. Stegmann
ifb Americas, Inc., Charlotte, NC, USA
e-mail: claus.stegmann@ifb-group.com

and sector-specific platforms like Facebook, Amazon and comparison platforms of all kinds. An orchestrator does not have to deliver the products to solve the customer problems by themselves. The open banking idea can enable the orchestrator to compose a solution (maybe with a bouquet of white label products). Understanding and serving the customer is what makes you stand out from the competition (customer-centric).

Combining both roads (manufacturer and orchestrator) will be challenging and has the greatest prospect of success in a niche market with specialized products.

To stay competitive on the customer-centric road requires patient capital and long staying power (an advantage fintech companies and Big Tech have) as well as a culture (customer-centric and agile) that significantly differs from the existing players. Cultural change is extremely challenging, but not impossible. There are reasons why Goldman Sachs (with Marcus) and Aegon (with Knab[2]) opted for the greenfield approach.

Doing nothing or continuing as usual is the easiest approach—especially given all the challenges and insecurities—but only a very short-term survival guide. Some institutes wait and see, planning to discover from the competition the parts of digitalization that work and improve them using well-established and practically approved methods and approaches. These institutes misjudge the velocity and the extent by which an organization's culture can change.

Changes in culture and technology infrastructure are long-term by nature and need investments in limited resources (culture and skills) as well as a good instinct when choosing the technological infrastructure. Changes in the technological infrastructure are hard to achieve by an incremental approach, especially the legacy of the existing operative systems.

Use cases can support the organization in understanding the potential of the new technology and how to leverage technology. It is important to have experience in leveraging technology in the business context. This can be transferred for standard situations and non-key processes for other institutes. The core, business- and success-defining processes differ among institutions, and therefore so do the ways to improve them by leveraging technology.

The first part of Volume II of this series focuses on use cases. The use case's business context is paraphrased, and the tools are offered to leverage the new

---

[2] See Negenman (2021).

technologies. The second volume also offers insights into business demands met by technology (second and third part). The fourth part deep-dives into the world of process optimization.

Literature

Negenman, Ebbe. 2021. "The Knab Story: How We Turned the Bank Around." In *The Digital Journey of Banking and Insurance, Volume I—Disruption and DNA*, edited by Volker Liermann and Claus Stegmann. New York: Palgrave Macmillan.

Index

A

ABM. *See* Agent-based model
Accounting department 42, 69
Accuracy figures 76
Action and messaging sequence 148
Actor-model 145
Actuarial data science 120
   definition 120
Adaptable 195
Adequate prices 127
Aerobotics 132
Agent-based model 102, 137, 139, 143, 145
   actor-model 145
   agent interaction 147
   drawbacks 146
   elements 146
Agents 102
Agent specific data 151
Agile 75, 214
   manifesto 214
   metrics 226
Agile project management 184
Altman-model 141
Amazon 308

AML 36
Anomaly detection 68, 75
Apple vii, 126
Apple Pay vii
Application programming interface (API) xi, 27
Architecture viii
Architecture-Based Modularization 90
Area under the curve 77
Artificial intelligence (AI) 9, 12, 19
AUC. *See* Area under the curve
Autoencoders 75

B

Balance sheet
   dynamics 138
   dynamics simulator 137
      account data 151
      agent-specific data 151
      client and bank data 151
      matching algorithm 144
      product parameters 151
      structure 137

Index

Balance Sheet Dynamic Simulator 82
Bank Bó 26
Banking business capability domains 11
Banking industry architecure network 7
Barclays 20
Basel III
   IRB approach 142
   standard approach 142
BayernLB 29
BBVA 19
Behavioral scientists 194
Behaviorism 196
BIAN. See Banking industry architecure network
Big data 19, 55, 82, 162, 180
   non-financial risk 82, 180
Big Tech v, 1, 67
Bitcoin vii, xii
Bottom-up dynamics simulations 144
BPaaS. See Business Process as a Service
BSDS. See Balance Sheet Dynamic Simulator
Burndown chart 228
Business capabilities 5, 6
Business objects 5
Business partner(s) 92, 94
Business Process as a Service 29
Business processes 46

C

Capital/equity costs 155
CCAR. See Comprehensive capital analysis and review
Capital projections 130
Center of excellence 293
   centralized 303
Centralized center of excellence 303
CFO. See Chief Financial Officer

Challenger bank 2, 20
Change 187
Change management 300
Chief Financial Officer 41, 45
Chief risk officer 38
Claims 123
   fraud 123
Classification 68
Classification matrix 11
Classification of risk events 168
Client-first 2
Cloud 19
CoE. See Center of excellence
Collateral instrument(s) 92, 99
Collateral type 100
Commercial real estate 153
Commodity risk 167
Communication
   asynchronous 272
   over distance 284
Company
   digitally mature 188
Company culture 36
Compliance 36
Compliance risk
   example 178
Comprehensive capital analysis and review 81, 138
Comprehensive liquidity analysis and review 138
Conformity 291
Continuous improvement process 291
Control Parameter unit 107
COO 45
Correction process 70
COVID-19 vi
Credit demand 154
Credit demand/supply matching 154
Credit interest rate 155
Credit metrics 141
Credit portfolio model 141, 143
CreditRisk 141

Credit supply 153
Credit Value at Risk 95, 143
Crypto currencies ix
Cultural 183
Cultural change 213
Cultural profile 205
Culture viii, 36, 308. *See also* Virtual culture
Culture types 204
   adhocracy 204
   clan 204
   hierarchy 204
   market 204
Customer channels
   digital 28
Customer-centric 2
Customer-facing frontend 27
Customer service desk 37
Cyber risk 163
   example 163
Cycle of learning and developing a growth mindset 208

D

Daily scrum 222
Dashboard 89
Data analytics 68, 133
   framework 133
Data analytics framework 133
Data architecture 46, 73
Data-driven intelligence 44
Data flow 72
Data protection laws 126
DCM. *See* Digi-cultural mindset
DCM Maturity Assessment 206
Decision-making processes 198
   shorter 198
Deep Feed Forward network 74
Deep learning 75, 99
Deep learning models 141
Development team 219
DevOps 233
Digi-cultural mindset 183, 186, 189
   definition 188, 202
   maturity assessment 206
Digital communication channels. 28
Digital customer channels 28
Digitalization 68
   insurance 121
   outside xiv
   strategy 1
   successful 187
Digitalization landscape 8
Digitalization strategy 26
Digital landscape 36
Digitally mature company 188
Digital native 26
Digital transformation 75
Disruption v
Distributed computing 10, 14, 86
Distributed ledger technology ix, xii, 9, 12, 19
   permissioned ix
   unpermissioned ix
Distribution-free methods 127
DLT. *See* Distributed ledger technology
Dodd-Frank Act 138
Dodd-Frank Act stress test 81, 138
dplyr 73
Driver identification 63
   process 63
Duality
   key figure trees and impact graphs 177
Dutch banking 35
Dynamic dashboard 89, 140
Dynamic model 156
Dynamics simulations
   bottom-up 144
DZ BANK 29

E

EAD. *See* Exposure-at-Default
Economic capital 100, 105
Employee satisfaction 186

Enterprise architecture 5, 17
Enterprise risk management 161
ERM. *See* Enterprise risk management
ESG risk 171
   example 167
Etherium xii
Ethics 132
European Insurance and Occupational Pensions Authority's Quantitative Impact Study 124
Events
   risks and consequences 119
Everledger xii
Exogenous scenario 140
Expectation management 298
Explainability 129
Exposure-at-Default 95, 101
   development 101
Extreme programming (XP) 234

F

Facebook 308
False negative 76
False positive 76
FBI. *See* Federal Bureau of Investigation
Feature-driven development (FDD) 234
Federal Bureau of Investigation 124
Feedforward neural network 141
FFN. *See* Deep Feed Forward network
FiCuTech viii
Financial controlling 85
Financial insight and risk control 44
Financial instruments 85
Financial navigator 81, 87, 139, 140, 149
   conceptual framework 87, 88
   real-time capability 88
Financial planning process 56

Financial risk 161
Financial risk management 161
Financial statements 69
Fintech v, 1, 32
FIS 21
Fitbit 126
Fixed mindset 191, 192
Flexibility
   infrastructure 90
   infrastructure in the narrower sense 90
   infrastructure in the wider sense 90
   methodological 90
FN. *See* False negative
FNN. *See* Recurrent neural network
Forecasting 68
Forecasting horizons 58
Four phases of an RPA project 290
FP. *See* False positive
Fraud 123
Fraud detection 124
   systems 123
Fundamental organizational structures 201
Funding cost 155
Future-oriented 195

G

Garmin 126
GDP. *See* Gross domestic product
General linear models 125, 127, 129
GLM. *See* General linear models
Goldman Sachs 308
Go-live 296
Google vii
Google Pay vii
Graph
   processing 148
Graph database 10, 14
Graph processing 148
Greenfield xxiii
Green field approach 23

Gross domestic product 62, 143
Growth mindset 191, 192
    cycle of learning and developing 208

H
H2o.ai 74
Hadoop 113
    cluster 113
Hadoop cluster 113
Healthcare sector 124
    research on fraud 124
Helaba 68
Heuristic methods 127
Home office 270, 271
HSBC 20
Human Mortality
    database 130
Human Mortality Database 130
Hybrid project management models 184, 249
Hyperautomation 9, 13
Hypercare phase 297
Hyperparameters 74

I
IFRS 9 56
IFRS 17 xiii, 56
Impact graph 165
    types of Edges and Nodes 168
Impact graphs 172, 176
    example ESG 171
    loss estimation 173
Impact matrix 11
impairment accounting 42
Impairment process 75
Income statement 54
Increment 220
Independent 195
Individual perception and behavior 202
Influencing factors 54

Infrastructure flexibility 90
    in the wider sense 90
ING Bank 36
In-memory database 10, 14, 86
Insurance fraud 123
Insurer
    value chain 121
Insurtech vi, 24, 121
Integrated models 172
Integrated planning 55
Interaction
    bank-client 152
    of feelings 190
    of our behavior 190
    of thoughts 190
Interactivity 89, 109
Interdependence
    of feelings 190
    of our behavior 190
    of thoughts 190
Interest rate risk 167
Internal optimization x
Internet of Things xiii, 10, 15
Interpersonal trust 199
IRB approach 142

K
Kafka's little fable 138
Kanban 235
Key figure trees 176
Key performance indicator 53, 58, 85
Key risk indicators 163, 174, 180
    forecast 180
    trees 176
Klarna vii
Knab 2, 308
    future 38
Knab Bank 35
KRI. See Key risk indicators
KYC 36

L

Lapse rate 124
   modeling 124
Lapse rate modeling 124
Leadership 198
Leading GAAP 48
Lean 198
Lean software development 235
Lee-Carter model 129
LGD. *See* Loss-Given-Default
Life insurance 129
   capital projections 130
   mortality rates 129
Liquidity risk 167
Lloyds 20
Loan type 100
Logistic regression 99
Loss-Given-Default 95
   determination 99
Loss-Given-Default Determination 99

M

Machine learning 122, 127, 130
   algorithms 130
   environment 74
   estimator 129
   non-financial risk 181
   non-life insurance 127
   supervised learning 124
Machine learning environment 74
Macroeconomic development 143
Macroeconomic indicator 94, 96
Macroeconomic scenario data 149
Manufacturer 23, 308
Marcus 308
Market segmentation 37
Mass-individualization xiv
Matching algorithm 144
Matching Credit Demand/Supply 154
Maturity model 202
Methodological flexibility 89, 110

M-GRACH. *See* Multi-GARCH
Mindset 191
   definition 191
   fixed 191, 192
   growth 191, 192
Mobile computing 10, 15
Model
   ethics 132
   explainability 129
   self-calibration 133
   topology 152
Modeling
   ethics 132
   non-linear 131
Modeling problem
   two-step 127
Model initialization 149
Model parameters 74
Model Result unit 109
Modularization 90
Monte Carlo simulations 130
Monzo 20
Mortgage bank 153
Motor insurance 127
Multi-GARCH 97
Multiple GAAPS 48
Multivariate GARCH Model 141

N

National Health Care Anti-Fraud Association 124
Natural language processing 10, 16
Negative effects 169
Net promoter score 37
Network dynamics 148
New data sources 119
NFT. *See* Non-fungible tokens
NHCAA. *See* National Health Care Anti-Fraud Association
Nibelungenlied 170
Non-financial risk 161
   big data 180
   framework 164

approach 164
impact graphs 167
impact graphs, events 168
impact graphs, risk domain 168
impact graphs, risk events 168
impact graphs, vulnerabilities 170
impact graphs. preconditions and vulnerabilities 168
risk categories 165
taxonomy 166
machine learning 181
profile 182
reporting approach 179
technical infrastructure 179
vulnerabilities 170
Non-financial risk management 181
integrated models 172
reporting 177
risk category 174
risk-category-specific models 172, 173
threat level 174
Non-fungible tokens xii
Non-life insurance 127
pricing 127
Non-linear modeling 131

O

Offshoring. *See* Remote, project
Open source 111
Open source software 111
Operant conditioning 194
Operational effectiveness 44
Optimization
internal x
Orchestrator 23, 308
Organizational behavior 186
Organizational structures
fundamental 201
Orientation 189
Outside digitalization xiv

Overall bank management 85

P

P&C.
insurance 124
P&L. *See* Profit & Loss
Pandemics. *See* Remote, work
Pattern recognition
general process 88
Pay-as-you-drive xii
Pay-how-you-drive xii
Payment liabilities 127
PayPal vii
PD. *See* Probability-of-Default
PDD. *See* Process, design document
Perception and behavior
individual 202
Permissioned distributed ledgers ix
Person's mindset 191
Planning 53
quality 54
Planning poker 231
Planning process 53
Planning quality 54
Portfolio
concentration and composition 139
Posting hub 48
transaction-level 48
Precision 77
Predictive analytics 55, 59
definition 60
Predictive power 127
Private blockchain ix
Probability-of-Default 94, 98, 155
Process
design document 293
identification 299
Process automation 123
Process mining xi, 10
Product
Backlog 220
Qwner 218

Index

Profit & Loss 53
Project fatigue 258
Proof of concept 68
Property and casualty insurance 124
Property value 95, 104
Psychological safety 200
Public blockchain ix
Python 111

Q

Quality improvement 76
Quantum computing 10, 16

R

Random forest 74, 99, 141
Real estate 95
Real-time calculations 141
Real-time capability 88, 109
Recall 77
Record-to-report 46
Recurrent neural network 141
Regression analysis 63
Regtech 32
Regulatory capital 121
   insurance 121
Remote
   managing 274
   onboarding 275
   project 264
   reasons for 265
   scaling 279
   tech 270
   tools 277
   work 263
Reporting approach 179
Research on fraud 124
Residential real estate 153
Resilient 200
   teams 200
Responsible 195
Retail bank 153
Retrospective 199, 223, 231

Revolut 20
RI. *See* Risk indicators
Risk analysis 157
Risk-category-specific models 172, 173
Risk connection graph 165
Risk control 38
Risk controlling 85
Risk events
   classification 168
Risk indicators 174
Risk management 137
Risk reporting 95, 106
Risk weight assets 54
RNN. *See* Recurrent neural network
Robo-advisors 23
Robotic Process Automation 9, 13, 289
   center of excellence 293
   change management 300
   conformity 291
   expectation management 298
   go-live 296
   hypercare phase 297
   implementation 295
   long-term integration 302
   process identification 299
   suitability 291
ROE 58
RPA. *See* Robotic Process Automation
R Package 63, 111
   dplyr 73
RPA Project
   four phases 290
RWA
   calculation 142

S

SAP HANA 111
   database 111
SAP HANA database 111
Scenario Information unit 108

Scenarios 92
Scrum 184, 195, 213, 214
   board 229
   Burndown Chart 228
   development team 219
   events 220
   Master 218
   planning 221
   planning poker 231
   Product Owner 218
   retrospective 199, 223, 231
   sprint 220
   timeboxing 233
   values 215
   velocity 228
Seamless connectivity 44
Self-calibration 133
Simudyne 157
Single source of truth 274
SORC model 199
Spark 141
Sprint 220
   Backlog 220
   review 223
SQL 74, 112
Stacey matrix 224
Standard risk costs 155
Standard unit costs 155
Story points 226
Stress test 137, 138
   EBA 81, 138
   tranditional 137
   US 138
Stress testing 81
Subtech 32
Successful digitalization 187
Suitability 291
Supervised learning 75, 124
Sustainability 286

T

Target culture 204
Target vision 203

Team spirit 276
Teamwork 202
Technology-driven transformation 36
Temporal structure 93
Thinking in scenarios 92
Threat level 174
Threshold
   definition 175
Threshold values 175
Timeboxing 227, 233
Time zones 272
Tokenization xii
Topology of the model 152
Traditional risk models 172
Transparency and consistency 200
Two-step modeling problem 127

U

Unemployment rate 94
Unexpected credit default risk 155
Unexpected loss 95
Universal bank 153
Universal journal 47
Unpermissioned distributed ledgers ix
Unscheduled repayment 61
   challenge 62
   definition 61
Unsupervised learning 75
Usage-based insurance xii

V

Value based management 56
   definition 56
Value chain 121
Value driver 122
Value driver map 56, 57
   framework 57
Value driver planning for insurance 56
Value driver-oriented framework 58

Value driver-oriented planning 55, 140
 insurance company 58
 value driver map 56
VAR. *See* Vector auto regression model
VBM. *See* Value-based management
VDM. *See* Value driver map
VDoP. *See* Value driver-oriented planning
Vector autoregression 97
Vector auto regression model 141
Velocity 228
Virtual
 communication 272
 culture 282
 planning 271

Virtual culture 184
VUCA 41, 137, 162

W

Water-scrumban-fall 257
Wearables 125
 Apple 126
 Fitbit 126
 Garmin 126
 Xiaomi 126
Work Design Questionnaire 207

X

XaaS xi
Xiaomi 126

Printed by Printforce, the Netherlands